STUDIES IN IMPERIALISM

General editor: Andrew S. Thompson

Founding editor: John M. MacKenzie

When the 'Studies in Imperialism' series was founded by Professor John M. MacKenzie more than thirty years ago, emphasis was laid upon the conviction that 'imperialism as a cultural phenomenon had as significant an effect on the dominant as on the subordinate societies'. With well over a hundred titles now published, this remains the prime concern of the series. Cross-disciplinary work has indeed appeared covering the full spectrum of cultural phenomena, as well as examining aspects of gender and sex, frontiers and law, science and the environment, language and literature, migration and patriotic societies, and much else. Moreover, the series has always wished to present comparative work on European and American imperialism, and particularly welcomes the submission of books in these areas. The fascination with imperialism, in all its aspects, shows no sign of abating, and this series will continue to lead the way in encouraging the widest possible range of studies in the field. 'Studies in Imperialism' is fully organic in its development, always seeking to be at the cutting edge, responding to the latest interests of scholars and the needs of this ever-expanding area of scholarship.

Egypt

Manchester University Press

SELECTED TITLES AVAILABLE IN THE SERIES

WRITING IMPERIAL HISTORIES
ed. Andrew S. Thompson

EMPIRE OF SCHOLARS
Tamson Pietsch

HISTORY, HERITAGE AND COLONIALISM
Kynan Gentry

COUNTRY HOUSES AND THE BRITISH EMPIRE
Stephanie Barczewski

THE RELIC STATE
Pamila Gupta

WE ARE NO LONGER IN FRANCE
Allison Drew

THE SUPPRESSION OF THE ATLANTIC SLAVE TRADE
ed. Robert Burroughs and Richard Huzzey

HEROIC IMPERIALISTS IN AFRICA
Berny Sèbe

Egypt

BRITISH COLONY, IMPERIAL CAPITAL

James Whidden

MANCHESTER UNIVERSITY PRESS

Copyright © James Whidden 2017

The right of James Whidden to be identified as the author of this work has been asserted by him in accordance with the Copyright, Designs and Patents Act 1988.

Published by Manchester University Press
Altrincham Street, Manchester M1 7JA, UK
www.manchesteruniversitypress.co.uk

British Library Cataloguing-in-Publication Data is available

ISBN 978 0 7190 7954 2 *hardback*
ISBN 978 1 5261 3934 4 *paperback*

First published by Manchester University Press in hardback 2017

This edition first published 2019

The publisher has no responsibility for the persistence or accuracy of URLs for any external or third-party internet websites referred to in this book, and does not guarantee that any content on such websites is, or will remain, accurate or appropriate.

Typeset
by Toppan Best-set Premedia Limited

CONTENTS

Founding editor's introduction—vii
Acknowledgements—ix

	Introduction	*page* 1
1	Capitulations	25
2	Civilising mission	52
3	Projects	83
4	Colonial life	140
5	Imperialists and colonials	175
	Conclusion	215

Select bibliography—221
Index—226

FOUNDING EDITOR'S INTRODUCTION

Egypt was always highly anomalous within the structures of nineteenth-century European imperialism. While it had become effectively independent from the Ottoman Empire, European states often continued to treat it as continuing to lie within the orbit of Ottoman imperial power. As it was progressively drawn into the mesh of trading relationships in the eastern Mediterranean, it was also sucked into highly expensive modernist ambitions in the provision of infrastructure, aspects of urban and rural change, as well as civil, military and economic institutions that would enhance the opportunities of its ruling elites to match European models. These developments, as well as longer-term trading relationships, served to pull in a striking range of settlers and sojourners of a variety of ethnicities, creating complex social and cultural patterns, particularly in its major cities. Although the British expatriate community was never numerically dominant among these immigrants, British trading and financial power, initially in league with the French, came to predominate. This constituted the background to Egypt's inevitable centrality in British strategic and economic concerns after the opening of the French-built Suez Canal in 1869. Financial destabilisation and nationalist revolt triggered the British invasion of 1882, after which it became effectively a British colony, backed by a considerable British garrison.

Despite all this, Egypt was never a colony in any formal or constitutional sense. While it was regarded as the key to the Middle East and the vital staging post to the British Indian, Australasian, Indian Ocean, and (progressively) East African empires, it was never formally engrossed into imperial structures, except for the period from 1914 to 1922, when the exigencies of war led its being declared a Protectorate. Apart from those years, it was often described as the 'veiled Protectorate', operating by a series of fictions, including attempts at a form of internationalisation, but more significantly through the activities of British 'advisers' who in reality exercised a good deal of executive authority through the Egyptian structures of theoretical royal authority and ministers. As it had been throughout history, it remained the pivotal point between Europe, Africa and Asia. It also became a vital test case in the interplay of foreign influences, indigenous nationalism, and in the survival and transformation of a traditional regime and the elites associated with it. All of this set up the stresses and strains that were exacerbated by twentieth-century world wars, by the decline of British power, and by

FOUNDING EDITOR'S INTRODUCTION

the emergence of modern Middle Eastern conflicts, culminating in the Suez crisis of 1956. All of this has ensured the prominence of Egypt within a political, diplomatic, and military historiography.

The fascination of modern historians follows some of the obsessions of nineteenth- and early twentieth-century travellers, intellectuals, and writers. A combination of characteristics ensured the prominence of Egypt in the tourism of European elites, in the work of travel writers, novelists, and others. Egypt's cultural centrality was of course closely bound up with its geographical significance. The relative proximity of Egypt to Europe ensured easy access for Europeans. They shared an enduring fascination with its antiquities as one of the cradles of ancient civilisation, as well as its notable connections with the Greco-Roman world. Napoleon's expedition, the work of his savants, and the entry of Egyptian styles into European aesthetics – not to mention the eagerness of European museums to acquire Egyptian artefacts of all sorts – helped to stimulate all of this.

This book by James Whidden sets out to bring these related phenomena together. In his innovative approach, he has undertaken to consider the wide-ranging historical controversies about Egypt and imperialism in the light of the modern Orientalist debate. More significantly, he surveys the imperial and indigenous conflicts over the status and political formations of Egypt against the background of the social and cultural life of the expatriate communities, particularly the British. To do this, he brings together a range of sources, including memoirs, novels, diaries, letters, and a striking range of archival material, some of it hitherto unused, to build up a remarkably vivid account of the ways in which the lives and predilections of resident expatriates and observers in Egypt, commercial, professional, scholarly, and political, influenced the struggles over its status and future. The result is a richly textured work which sheds fresh light on imperial Egypt. The relationship between the British and Egypt was by no means a monolithic one. As well as being fractured into a variety of approaches, it was also a matter of multiple voices reflecting multiple identities, all participating in a considerable debate. He concludes that expatriate communities in Egypt – and the politics which they influenced – possibly exhibited a degree of cultural porousness and exchange that may have mirrored some of the characteristics of the older khans (or protected trading posts) of the Levant writ large. The arrogance and apparently social and cultural exclusiveness of the British may have been a defence mechanism against a much more profound set of cultural interchanges than some expatriates would have recognised.

John M. MacKenzie

ACKNOWLEDGEMENTS

Research in England was made possible by the Acadia Research Fund. Some of the material in this book previously appeared in Robert Bickers (ed.), *Settlers and Expatriates: Britons over the Seas* (Oxford: Oxford University Press, 2010).

INTRODUCTION

In the spring of 1882 the Egyptian crisis was coming to the boil just as there was an attempt on Queen Victoria's life in London. But these events paled in the public imagination against the plan by London's Regent's Park Zoo to sell Jumbo the elephant to P.T. Barnum of the famed Barnum & Bailey Circus. Jumbo's story embodies elements of Britain's relations with Egypt during the era of high imperialism. Captured in the French Sudan, a mere calf at his dying mother's side, Jumbo was sold, shipped to Paris, then London. During his training, his handlers chained, beat, and tortured him. Later, the British public adored him, were bereaved by his exile in 1882, and mourned his death in 1885, his back broken in a collision with a railroad steam engine during a circus tour in Ontario. Meanwhile, the events in Egypt boiled over, the British bombed Alexandria, mowed down thousands of Egyptian troops on the march to Cairo, captured and tried the leader of the Egyptian resistance, Ahmad 'Urabi, who was branded a rebel by the British ruling classes (including Queen Victoria) and very narrowly escaped public execution. He was exiled to Ceylon. After the military defeat of Egypt, its colonial status was slowly formalised by a doctrine of British–Egyptian relations that made the British guardians and protectors of the fellahin, or Egyptian peasantry, against the imagined (and real) tyranny and brutality of Egypt's hereditary ruling classes, commonly described by the British political elites and press as 'Turks' or 'pashas'. Throughout all these events, the excavation of Egyptian antiquities and the development of the tourist industry made Egypt one of the premier objects of fascination in the British public's imagination.

The juxtaposition of cruel mastery and loving adoration in Jumbo's story signifies some of the extremes of British relations with Egypt. The contradictory tendencies are missing in many accounts that direct all the evidence along the iron rails of British military domination after Egypt had become an issue in mainstream British politics. The Suez

Canal made Egypt central to British international relations and imperial security calculations. After the military occupation, there was a debate in London and Cairo on how to define the British imperial mission in Egypt: Was it merely a short-term strategic move? Were the British 'civilisers' engaged in a long-term remaking of Egypt? Were there essential differences between British and Egyptians? Was it a necessity to construct clear boundaries between Britain and Egypt based on concepts like the advanced and primitive? Much colonial policy thinking was spent defining Egyptian 'status hierarchies' and the 'conservative order' of Egyptian society. These characterisations inevitably prompted plans for constitutional reforms that were premised on the idea of exporting liberty and democracy, but on a lower scale of 'evolutionary' advancement suitable to Egypt.[1]

Like Edmund Burke's critique of the East India Company a century earlier, the military occupation of Egypt exposed the British government to charges of self-interest and the betrayal of Britain's liberal political principles. For Egyptians, the question prompted by the colonial occupation was also how to define Egyptian identity and restructure its society and economy: Was Egypt to be remade in the image of European modernity (British or French versions)? To what degree could modernisers depart from the limitations imposed by colonial descriptions of Muslims, Orientals, or Arabs?[2] Or was the modern project to restore cultural roots, whether Arab, Muslim, or uniquely Egyptian?[3] Was political society and citizenship to be defined universally or in terms of class, national, or religious categories? Critical studies on these questions of identity have concluded that the colonised nation was fragmented, not homogenous, countering claims of a cultural identity essentially Arab, Muslim, or Egyptian.[4] By this logic, British colonial identities might also be more complicated than sometimes represented. The tendency in recent scholarship has been to dispense with the rigid duality of the labels 'coloniser' and 'colonised' and investigate how these categories overlap. That is not to say that new scholarship on imperialism defuses nationalist or imperial narratives based on themes of cultural difference, racism, or social exclusivity. It does, however, re-evaluate some very influential accounts of imperialism where there was no room for the colonial who 'says no' or the nationalist who adopted the colonial point of view.[5] The referent point for all such debates is Edward Said's *Orientalism*, wherein he said that imperialism was a cultural, as well as political, system that projected power through ideas and practices that negated non-European, particularly Arab and Muslim, people.[6] By moving away from cultural representations towards actual individuals and groups, professional or other associational networks, recent studies suggest that imperial 'projects' were various, often contradictory, and distributed across British and colonial societies in competing organisations and interest groups. Also, the social composition of the colony was diverse, with the categorisation of the 'British' never fixed.[7]

Method

This study takes Edward Said's theory of colonial culture as a first reference and follows his method of analysing various cultural products, mostly produced by the British, that involved some sort of cultural exchange.[8] As Said demonstrated, this exchange placed more value on some cultural ideas, some types of activities, over others. Something less investigated by Said was that one cultural strain, or voice, could be muted by a more dominant one.[9] The imperial narrative involved major themes like civilisation, progress, race, and exoticism, and muted themes, like coexistence, acculturation, or cultural relativism. The dominant themes represented difference between East and West, black and white, civilised and not, as the foundation of power. Said's method involved identifying the formulaic ingredients of a dominant discourse. For example, he asserted that it is correct to say that 'every European, in what he could say about the Orient, was consequently a racist, an imperialist, and almost always ethnocentric'. Or, more specifically, 'Orientalism was the distillation of essentialist ideas about the Orient – its sensuality, its tendency to despotism, its aberrant mentality, its habit of inaccuracy, its backwardness – into a separate and unchallenged coherence.'[10] The dominant discourse of imperialism achieved a coherent structure with identifiable reference points, usually presented in a dualistic logic – ideas of progress/backwardness, democracy/despotism, industry/sensuality, and so on. Such doctrines were propagated by the publicists of empire and had an impact on cultural attitudes generally, although it is questionable if these ideas achieved the status of an irrevocable 'truth', as Said argued. Yet, the way the colonised was represented in these negative terms is central to any understanding of imperialism or the imperial mentality. Ironically, the Orientalists were those who were probably least likely to voice racist views as compared to others whose opinions were formed by popular media.[11]

Even as Said was penning his indictment of Western social scientific analysis, there were some dissenting voices. One of the most prominent experts on modern Arab culture, Albert Hourani, argued that Jacques Berque's characterisation of the colonial British in *Egypt: Imperialism and Revolution* did not accurately represent British attitudes, suggesting that under the veneer of social exclusivity and racial supremacy British identity was more complex. In his turn, Jacques Berque questioned Said's straightforward identification of 'Orientalists' with imperial power.[12] Alongside these voices, there were the protests of former British residents of Egypt after the publication of Peter Mansfield's *The British in Egypt* and Berque's text in the early 1970s.[13] It would be easy to accuse British colonials as apologists for empire; less easy to make that charge stick in the case of Hourani and Berque, whose reputations as sympathetic observers of Arab and Muslim cultures and societies are well known.[14] The implication was that just as colonial individuals might respond to their colonial location by asserting, perhaps exaggerating, their Britishness, that did not capture the entirety of the colonial experience. Social mixing might defuse the tendency to represent essential differences between the colonial and the colonised. Paul Fussell argued that tolerance and openness to other cultures occur through travel, migration, or temporary relocation, evident in a travel literature genre that celebrated the breaking down of British cultural conventions in foreign locales. His study focused on the period between 1918 and 1939 and included British writing on Egypt. More recently, Nicholas Thomas came to similar conclusions based on his study of colonial projects in the Pacific in the late imperial era.[15]

These methods can be applied to colonial time periods and locations more generally. Anthony Sattin's study of Florence Nightingale implicitly questioned some of the conclusions of another writer on colonial Egypt, John Barrell.[16] Sattin's sympathetic treatment of a young woman's impressions of Egypt while on a tour contrasts with Barrell's description of her genocidal urges in 'Death on the Nile', which appeared in a volume on the cultures of empire.[17] The former indicates the popular appetite for the exotic – harnessing a cultural icon like Florence Nightingale to illustrations or letters on Egypt is irresistible – whereas the latter represents academic interest in the way a cultural product, such as travel literature, served imperial power. Each is valuable: firstly, the humanisation of the British in Egypt and, secondly, research on the 'system of European or Western knowledge about the Orient'.[18] The latter phrase was Said's, who said that culture could only be understood in terms of hegemony and power and that literature, art, and travel were a kind of performance or set of practices that demonstrated that fact. Said's discussion of this phenomenon suggested that there was a combination of fear and desire in the European exploration of the exotic; the 'exotic' was largely an invented thing, saying more about Victorian conventions and taboos than it did about Middle Eastern realities. Cultural interaction was more illusion than reality. In Said's analysis some of the most renowned British Orientalists and travellers were represented as cold and distanced colonisers. Edward William Lane repressed his desire whilst feigning an Oriental identity to establish the objective authority of the imperial narrative.[19] On Richard Francis

INTRODUCTION

Burton, Said noted that in spite of his individualism and desire to escape the conventions of England through travel, his cultural work radiates a 'sense of assertion and domination over all the complexities of Oriental life'.[20] As a result, in Burton's literature two voices merge: the idiosyncratic individual, renowned expert and adept on the Arabs, and the 'voice of Empire' or the European ambition to rule over the Orient. In 'Death on the Nile', Barrell came to similar conclusions.[21]

One way to pull apart the convergence of voices is to identify dominant and muted discourses. Depending on the historical circumstances, the individual's voice could be muted by the official imperial voice, or vice versa. It is therefore possible to identify references that diverge from the formula identified by Said. An obvious conclusion is that separated from homeland or locality, customary identities altered, as did perceptions of the colonial setting and the 'home' country. British colonials far from the United Kingdom acculturated to Egyptian society in spite of best efforts to replicate 'home' in the colony. Memoir and travel writing can represent a 'transcultural' experience, prompting diverse responses, inventions, fantasies, including reaction and racism, as well as the questioning of conventional interpretations of the colonial relationship – even the entertaining of novel ideas on race, gender, and class associations.[22] Reading colonial texts with an eye to the permutations in the dominant imperial theme identifies certain common observations or characteristics: relations between British and Egyptians were often good socially, but strained politically; colonials had a better understanding of local cultures than metropolitans, which parried their political opinions; colonials held views often contrary to British government policy; there was also a shared sense among many colonials that 'home' was not Britain, and not quite Egypt; the colonial identity was never reified, in spite of very determined efforts to draw a clearly defined boundary between coloniser and colonised.

The official line attempted to delineate clearly the 'British' colony by asserting British cultural supremacy and racial difference. Works in this vein had considerable impact upon social relations, thus the famed exclusivity and insularity of the severe British. In *Modern Egypt* Lord Cromer created a coherent narrative on the British occupation and colonial administration of Egypt which codified ideas on race, civilisation, and religion.[23] Colonial society was hierarchical, based on racial differences, with Arab, Muslim Egyptians at the bottom of the social pyramid. This official narrative was worked out in many other texts on engineering, industry and finance, politics, education, health reform, and scientific enquiry, solidifying the view of an unambiguous imperial voice.[24] Lord Cromer, Lord Milner, Lord Lloyd, and others of lesser note, composed a public narrative and a public memory of Britain in

Egypt.[25] That memory was guarded by many in British public life, most notably by Winston Churchill. Yet, it is useful to distinguish between this public narrative and private memories. Public memory is enshrined in texts that continually point to the 'higher' cultural order of religion, nation, empire, wherein individuals live only in so far as they serve or interact with that higher narrative. Private memory is less likely always to fit into the norms of thought or codes of behaviour laid out in a collective memory, yet is not less valid for revealing this plurality within society.[26]

Take, for example, two important figures in British colonial culture, Gertrude Bell and E.M. Forster. Bell was an accomplished writer, administrator, traveller, and expert on ancient sites and peoples of Syria, Iraq, and Arabia. During the First World War she worked briefly with the Red Cross and then travelled to Cairo to connect with British intelligence networks preparing for the Arab Revolt. Afterwards, she assisted in establishing the colonial administration of Iraq. E.M. Forster was a successful author who had recently travelled to India and had thus transited through Egypt. He was a pacifist objector to the war. In 1915 Forster was interviewed by Bell for a position with the Red Cross in Egypt. Forster recalled of Bell that she was 'hard and severe' and unsympathetic towards Egyptians. During the interview Forster asked Bell what the Egyptians were like. Bell responded that he would be far too occupied with his wartime service ever to meet or get to know any Egyptians.[27] That was the official line, which Forster ultimately rejected, but only after experiencing various forms of attraction and revulsion towards his fellow Britons and Egyptians. Forster's subsequent, and controversial, intimacy with an Egyptian flew in the face of colonial conformity. Yet, he was not unique. His experience underlined the fact that official colonial narratives were theoretical, indeed mythical, and colonial lives often diverged from them.

In part, the differing attitudes of Bell and Forster can be credited to vocation. Each profession or imperial project carried its own 'genres of representation' that did not easily fit into the binaries of a singular imperial project.[28] Or, more broadly speaking, official colonials (Bell) differed from unofficial (Forster); the former promoted a civilising mission, the latter might never adopt it or abandon it in mid-step as a result of its contradictions and ambiguities. Colonial lives were conditioned by circumstances and thus require historical context attuned to sequences (phases, turning points), various historical contingencies (war, revolution), or social settings (professional, regional, class, family). To highlight these factors, this study focuses on individual narratives or biographical treatments to avoid generalisations and categorisations. The method involves capturing dominant and muted discourses, as

INTRODUCTION

described above, with the object being to broaden the way the British colony can be viewed over periods of time, across various localities (class, faith, professional, geographic), or, as has been said, the 'changes in subjectivity wrought by dwelling in, and actively experiencing multiple colonial places'.[29] Given that a study of the entire colony involves a fairly wide scope, this study will introduce multiple characters as a way of following the colony across time and place. In certain cases, the study is able to capture a full biographical treatment, in others the documents reveal only a 'moment' in a colonial life. The result is not simply a collection of capsuled biographical treatments in lieu of a historical narrative, but a selection that illustrates the complexity of the colonial experience by charting the dominant themes of race and civilisation, as well as shifts, ruptures, and long-term changes in these themes.

There is a problem of historical accuracy in the method because public and private memory is subjective, with a propensity to self-mythologise through aggrandising colonial achievements in official narratives, but also of nostalgia and thus of distortion, particularly in private recollections. However, certain characteristics are common. One is the idea that there was a golden age of British rule and that this period, which saw its twilight in the interwar period, was notable for the 'cosmopolitan' character of colonial Egypt that preceded the full flowering of nationalism and Islamism from the 1920s. Academic histories have made similar observations, most renowned being Albert Hourani's *Arabic Thought in the Liberal Age*.[30] A golden, liberal age under British patronage is not entirely accurate: the Egyptians were quick to resist British rule from the outset and colonial society was never free of national or communal tensions. Yet, the myth served specific purposes. For colonials in the period after the 1919 Egyptian national revolt there was a desire to resurrect the era of Lord Cromer (1883–1907) and the sureties that his imperial texts exemplified. Also, once nationalism was on the march and the two 'nations' seemingly irrevocably estranged, British residents grieved a lost colonial world, only part fantasy. In the interwar period there was some chance of retrieving that world, after the Second World War none. Yet myth or nostalgia can carry a valid historical memory, reflecting a previous state or lifestyle. It was accurate to say that British and Egyptians of a similar class and cultural background shared common interests and ideals in the 'liberal age'. Colonialism was defined by the Enlightenment project: science and progress, liberalism, humanitarianism, and social justice were its objectives, even if not realised in practice and rejected by the nationalists when the dead end was reached. Still, imperialism found no terminal point, its ideals were adapted by, and shifted to,

Americans and Soviets. And so, because of these shared ideals within some social sectors, there was a degree of social permissiveness between Egyptians and British of a certain class or within specific colonial enclaves in the 'liberal age'.[31]

The colony

Egypt was, with the exception of Algeria, the most heavily colonised region in the Arab and Muslim Near and Middle East. As the military occupiers after 1882, the British were the symbol of that colonisation in spite of the fact that the largest foreign colony was Greek, followed by Italian and French.[32] Before the First World War there were attempts to incorporate Egypt formally into the British Empire; however, international complications and nationalist resistance militated against it. In 1882 there were maybe six thousand British residents in Egypt, within a European population of perhaps sixty thousand. The British population quadrupled over the next thirty-five years, while the overall European population doubled. In 1897 the British population was 19,557 in a foreign population of 112,000.[33] In 1907 there were 20,653 British; in 1917, 24,354.[34] The majority of these 'British' were Maltese, with the Maltese version of Arabic the mother tongue for most British subjects.[35] The British colony therefore dovetailed with the majority Egyptian population, which by 1917 was 13 million in number, with the total foreigner population therefore amounting to approximately 1 per cent, according to the census. It has been observed that, on close inspection, the census figures are inconsistent. The Egyptian state census was an attempt at self-identification for the Egyptian locals (later, 'nationals') against the foreigners of that period. The census categories and quantities were more representational of the Egyptian state project than social reality. So, while the British Foreign Office accepted at face value the figures and social categories for reproduction in British parliamentary reports, there is no certainty to these figures.[36]

What is certain is that the British colony included British diplomatic corps, officials in Egyptian state services, and the 'Army of Occupation', alongside non-official classes of various types, including business people, professionals, and labourers, with the non-official classes inclusive of diverse groups defined as 'British', mostly Maltese and 'Levantine' (the latter term representing those of eastern Mediterranean origin with British legal status, including Syrian Christians and Jews). There were also British Indians, South Africans, Australians, and Canadians. According to 1917 census figures, most British lived in Alexandria, followed by Cairo, with perhaps something less than a fifth in Isma'iliyya, Suez, and Port Said.[37] Many British colonials did not seem to engage in any

INTRODUCTION

way with the official establishment in Cairo. These were the 'marginal' majority, groups particularly sensitive to the mixed messages of their situation because of their cultural marginality in a British colony defined to a large degree by 'race' origin. Take, for example, the following portraits by Henry Montfreid, whose memoir of ventures in the Red Sea contained the vignette, 'Two Types of Englishman'. The first portrait runs according to stereotype, readily identifiable to anyone familiar with the literature on colonial racism. Montfreid and his crew were tacking up the Red Sea en route to Suez, harried by the usual crosswinds, and dangerously short of water. Coming upon an oil-drilling site, complete with workshops, temporary residences, and great stores of machinery, Montfreid put to shore and sought out the directors of the operation to ask for assistance. As he said, no one would deny water to a traveller in need. The British engineers did, calculating in machine-like fashion the limits and requirements of their duties; they gave Montfreid a cold, disdainful reception. Only momentarily distracted, they seemed utterly indifferent as they pored over the engineering blueprints spread across the back of a prostrate African serving as a writing desk. The next portrait was of a British subject of Maltese origin, but, as Montfreid said, more 'English than any Englishman': he spoke to his servants with cold formality, cluttered his house with golf clubs and tennis rackets, and prominently displayed pipe, whisky and soda alongside *The Times*. His final portrait of the 'Englishman' was a lighthouse keeper employed by the Ports and Lighthouse Administration of Egypt, who, observing that Montfreid's ship was in distress on a dark sea notorious for its shoals, swung a light from the end of his dock. When at last Montfreid cast his line to his anonymous saviour, the keeper, having done his duty to a fellow mariner, simply secured the line and, with a crisp 'Good night', went off to his bed. While each of these types is very 'British' – recognisably so – they are not all the same.[38]

The lighthouse keeper was a servant of the Egyptian state. During the colonial period Egypt employed many Europeans with technical expertise, including British, French, Greek, Italian, and others. Many of these were motivated purely by career ambitions or professionalism and were not obviously members of the official colony or the 'ruling caste', a concept normally reserved for those British with status as members of the British diplomatic staff, officers in the Egyptian or British armies, or as high-level advisers and inspectors in the Egyptian administration. Consciously representative of the British imperial state, the official classes were normally insular and exclusive groups, and that fact very much contributed to the image of the colony as a 'ruling caste' in the Raj tradition of empire. Horse racing, polo, cricket, football, golf, tennis, and hunting were the officials' main pursuits, with the bequest by the Egyptian state of lands in Cairo and Alexandria for sporting clubs and free range of the marshes and desert tracks. Yet, horse racing and polo were known to the Egyptian elites; tennis and football were readily adopted. Therefore, the sporting grounds were arenas where British and other elites (European and Egyptian) met socially. Segregation was not institutionalised; however, there was an informal tendency towards social segregation (snobbery combined with classism/racism) aimed at certain cultural or 'racial' types, particularly in the period before the First World War.[39] The rules of decorum for the British official classes in Egypt were, like those of the Egyptian elites, based as much on class difference as on race. Rapid development of the British and other European colonies meant that towns like Isma'iliyya, Suez, and Port Said, and to a lesser degree Cairo and Alexandria, had distinct Egyptian and European quarters, with the social composition of these cities divided between European elites and Egyptian working classes, although there were significant numbers of European workers in the poorer quarters and Egyptian elites in the affluent. The distinctions between coloniser and colonised were blurred, even within the colony. Marginal British included non-British 'races', sometimes referred to as 'out-land' British, as well as those who had 'lost caste' as a result of long-term residence or involvement in the unofficial side of colonial life; 'marginality' was not simply a distinction between the white British and the Levantine or Maltese British.[40] On the other hand, even those 'marginal' British that had gained professional or financial status were subject to 'colonial fault lines' and were sometimes accepted and at others excluded from British colonial society; for instance, the example of the prominent Maltese lawyer, Henri Curmi, who was harassed and excluded by his 'in-land' British associates.[41]

It is possible to imagine the practices of the Indian Civil Service transplanted from India to Egypt. However, the Egyptian flag flew over government buildings, English was not an official language, and, in spite of the construction of modern suburbs on the European model, there was no ethnic segregation in neighbourhoods. The British colony was diverse in its composition, therefore lifestyles and places of residence were also. Alongside soldiers and officials in the consulates and Egyptian administration, there were the shipping staffs at Alexandria, merchants, bankers, professionals (teachers, governesses, doctors, nurses, engineers, chemists, and so on), and clerical staff, all important components of the colony. Then there were the common soldiers and sailors, domestics, trades people, many employed in projects like the railways, the canals, and industry, who composed a colonial underclass.[42] The less affluent British lived in older neighbourhoods that were largely Egyptian, French,

INTRODUCTION

Greek, and Italian in composition. It is difficult to fix these lower strata into a demographic map of colonial Egypt because many were transient or melted into the other social categories through intermarriage. Quarters catering to the upper classes were easily identifiable, constructed in the Italianate architectural style and popular with affluent British comforted by the proximity of imperial institutions like the consular residency, barracks, and sporting clubs.[43] Zamalek and Garden City in Cairo or Manshiyya and Attarin in Alexandria were built according to this model in the mid- to late nineteenth century, with the suburbs of Ma'adi on the perimeter of Cairo or Ramla on Alexandria's eastern extension conforming more to Anglo-American suburban standards.

Social segregation was relative to historical phase. The British official establishment, including the military, was in a dominant position after 1882, magnified by the influx of service people during the First World War. The colony achieved its greatest solidarity in this era. The interwar period and the rise of nationalism changed the character of the colony. According to the British Foreign Office, by 1939 there were seven thousand 'in-land' or United Kingdom Britons in Egypt, whereas the British Maltese and Cypriot population was thirty thousand, and there were approximately thirteen thousand soldiers.[44] The number of British was thus around fifty thousand in a total foreign population of approximately two hundred thousand, of which there were eighteen thousand French, forty-seven thousand Italians, and sixty-eight thousand Greeks. The interwar era, sometimes referred to as the 'long weekend' in the history of modern Britain, also saw many British visiting Egypt for business and pleasure.[45] The official British no longer predominated. The nationalist project after 1922 meant that the British colony was more civilian, with the officials mostly teachers in government schools. Edward Said, a resident of Zamalek through the 1930s and 1940s, observed that British residents were corporate executives, their families, and teachers.[46] The leaders of the British colony in this period were business people; other prominent categories of that era included nurses, domestics, doctors, professors, technicians, and clerks.[47] Far from nurtured in British imperial institutions, the colony was characterised by a 'laissez-faire' attitude. British residents turned to non-British institutions for basic services, such as schools and hospitals, and attempts to build British institutions before and after the First World War were met with indifference.[48] Social mixing was required in neighbourhoods, clubs, schools, churches, at work and leisure, although often according to class barriers. Many individuals refused even to enter into the perceived norms of colonial society and adopted Egyptian lifestyles, dress, and food. Because most British children attended non-British schools, they were brought up with little knowledge of British history or culture. In short, there were endless social and cultural variables. Whereas the British imperial identity formulated by Lord Cromer before the First World War was exclusivist and supremacist, dividing the world between civilised British and the uncivilised, the British colony in Egypt was an imperial society of mixed regional origins, multiple languages, and diverse confessions of faith, with the obvious result that British imperial identities were also somewhat multifaceted, belying the dualistic thinking of the imperial narrative.

Imperial capital

Sir Miles Lampson, British high commissioner in 1934, said, 'The plain fact is that nothing can ever be done here quite right in the eyes of the [British] community – not that it matters a hoot.'[49] The commentary reflected the position of the British government: the occupation of Egypt was driven primarily by strategic interests. Indeed, Egypt occupied the British cabinet more than any other imperial issue, with the exception of India.[50] The British military occupation was sustained for the defence of imperial communications, not for settlement, commerce, or cultural work, all of which operated with little supervision under the eyes of the consuls before 1882. Egypt fell under the authority of the Foreign Office, not the Colonial Office, before and after 1882. It was not a formal colony, but an area of informal political influence and military occupation after 1882. As a result, the resident British colony or 'community' was not very influential. Nor were the interests of the British government and the colony necessarily in agreement. The colonial business community was interested in an Egyptian government favourable to trade and investment, which implied the ability of the British government to intervene if the Egyptian government failed to protect European property, as well as taxation and legal privileges. Uncertainty over those issues was one of the causes of the military occupation, if not the most important. Likewise, the Anglican Church and the various Christian missions needed protection for religious minorities to ensure a field for missionary activity. After 1882 the British officials in the diplomatic service and the Egyptian administration formed another lobby group, with an interest in the British government supporting 'reform' as an imperial duty or 'civilising mission' in Egypt. The imperial mission to 'civilise' involved the British curbing corruption, 'tyranny', or 'despotism' (normally characterised as the self-interest of the Egyptian ruler and a narrow clique of Egyptian 'notables' or 'pashas') to ensure the welfare of the Egyptian fellahin. That justified the continued employment of British staff in the Egyptian administration, embassy, and consulates. In short, geo-political strategy was somewhat checked

INTRODUCTION

by a set of colonial interests, including business, cultural, and official.

British rule in Egypt after 1882 followed the pattern of indirect rule. Ideas like divide and rule capture some of the methods, but were less easily exploited in a situation where the British were limited in their power to define the political system through ethnic constructions or a powerful settler lobby. British rule in Egypt relied upon negotiation, co-opting or political pacts with the Egyptian elites or notables.[51] Elizabeth Monroe said that the tradition of British rule in Egypt was founded on intimate relations between the British and these elites.[52] The point was to exert influence and safeguard interests, but also to enable the Egyptians to direct their own domestic politics and redirect energies away from anti-British nationalism. The durability of these methods was built on the shared values and lifestyles of the British and Egyptians through administrative, financial, and commercial development, and thus the shared faith in the mission to 'civilise' Egyptian society and 'modernise' the Egyptian political system. For British and Egyptian administrators, the fellahin were the object of a 'civilising mission' and the ruling dynasty of Muhammad 'Ali the object of liberal 'reform'. These ideas cemented the colonial pact and only fractured when sacrificed to the purely geo-political requirements of the British Empire, such as the military occupation of 1882, the proclamation of a protectorate in 1914, and the perception that the terms of the Anglo-Egyptian Treaty of 1936 were betrayed by British policies during the Second World War. Nevertheless, the constitutional arrangements throughout this period were not unlike those of other self-governing parts of the British Empire – Ireland, Canada, Australia, New Zealand, and South Africa – the British government had 'reserves' over foreign policy, defence, and finance.[53]

British colonial rule in Egypt cannot be summed up as a clear line of policy because it involved differing and sometimes conflicting objectives. William Gladstone was a reluctant imperialist, prodded by the bondholders in London and Paris after the French and British financial controllers failed to resolve the debt crisis. Whereas the political storm in France created by the crisis in Egypt between 1879 and 1882 resulted in the French military withdrawing, the strategic importance of the Suez Canal meant that Gladstone's government gave the nod to a well-laid military plan. Once in Cairo, the military mind found it difficult to imagine withdrawal, identifying threats in domestic nationalists and foreign imperialists, Ottoman, French, Russian, Italian, or German. Strategic interests required political interference because, it was said, the Egyptian administration lacked the necessary expertise in finance, engineering, and education – in short, all the facets of a modern state. The modernising rationale was worked out in many texts composed by Egyptians, many of them students of British policies in education, health, engineering, and administration. Therefore, the period between 1882 and 1914 saw a degree of consent among these Egyptians, partly the result of the trauma of defeat and occupation, but also that British reforms opened opportunities for Egyptian notables and met the ideological orientation of Egyptian liberal nationalists, as represented by the careers of Ahmad Lutfi al-Sayyid or Sa'd Zaghlul. However, the First World War undermined this pre-war status quo.

After the war, Churchill led the campaign to recreate the pre-war order through a British-backed Egyptian monarch, not unlike the experiments with the Hashemites in Transjordan and Iraq. This policy coexisted uncomfortably with the simultaneous policy of concession to nationalists and the drawing down of British military personnel after the war, as pursued by Lord Milner, Edmund Allenby, as well as Churchill, in the sort of typically schizophrenic moves of an imperial administration divided between Foreign Office, Colonial Office, War Office, and a cabinet of multiple stripes. For five years after the war, Allenby sought a meaningful partnership between the British and Egyptian states, which implied cooperation with the nationalists and treaty negotiations. The British business community mostly opposed the policy and acted as an effective lobby group among like-minded groups in Britain, which served the strategic interests of some members of the cabinet and the military chiefs of staff. Nor was there consensus among the colonial administrators in Cairo. The implications of imperial duty meant that many could not accept Egyptian self-government; others took the contrary view that strategic interests could only be secured by meaningful political consent among the Egyptians. These battles over the course of British rule were not only bureaucratic or governmental, but involved diverse groups and sites, including the metropolitan press and business pressure groups, which, when the situation worsened, were sometimes more willing than the British government to make concessions to nationalists.[54]

Nevertheless, the interventions of the British government at critical junctures indicated that the geo-political was paramount. As Lampson said, the British colony in Egypt was not a major consideration for the British government. The colony did not determine policy, as might have been the case in British South Africa or French North Africa. However, the colony did represent a lobby group. There was some muted dissent in the period before the First World War, more so after the war. Diplomatic histories have noted the high turnover of consul generals and high commissioners.[55] British agents were compromised

INTRODUCTION

by the contradictions of a policy that combined persuasion and coercion. Cromer's resignation was the result of a perception that his disciplinary hand fell too hard and provoked the national demonstrations of 1906 and 1907. Eldon Gorst was criticised for his liberal 'Egypt for the Egyptians' policy, Reginald Wingate for poor judgement in entertaining a national delegation in 1918, Allenby for 'weakness' in the face of nationalist violence, and Lord Lloyd for his failure to follow the non-interventionist policy devised in 1922 at Allenby's bidding. When treaty negotiations after 1922 threatened to remove the privileges of the British financial elite in Egypt, the colony rallied against Allenby's policy of concessions.[56] The colonial lobby was probably a factor in Allenby's decision to restore British 'prestige' through the forced resignation of the Egyptian government and a punitive indemnity after the assassination of a top-ranking British officer in November 1924. The shift from conciliation to domination had the almost 'unanimous support of the British and foreign communities in Egypt'.[57] Thus, colonial voices had an impact on politics, imposing upon the decisions of high commissioners in Cairo and opinion in London.[58] But there was no such thing as consensus. Allenby's delivery of British demands with an escort of Bengal Lancers in 1924 was not unlike Sir Miles Lampson surrounding the royal palace with tanks in 1942. Applauded by some members of the colony, others interpreted these acts as spoiling any chance of reconciliation. Even the government ministers were unable to agree on policy, as Churchill said in a conversation with one of the Cairo officials on a cabinet proposal to revoke Allenby's ultimatum:

> But I told them all that if Allenby had stopped being a cow and had become a bull again it was thanks to you fellows in Cairo. And do you know what they wanted to tell you to do? To ask for your ultimatum back and to give Zaghloul [the Egyptian prime minister] theirs instead. 'Good God!!' I said, 'You can't have Allenby going to Zaghloul with an ultimatum and an escort of a British regiment of lancers on Saturday and on Sunday send him to ask for it back with an escort of Egyptian Camel Corps.'[59]

The commentary suggests that Churchill approved of Allenby's decision to switch from concessions to a demonstration of force. It was also Churchill's policy during the Second World War not to tolerate any sign of dissension among the Egyptians; therefore Lampson had an escort of armoured cars and tanks when he imposed a change of government in 1942. Churchill's attitudes reflect the ambiguity of colonial identities more generally. His adherence to liberal ideas of self-government was checked by his strategic thinking: for instance, in 1919 he could

[15]

at one and the same time assert his belief in Indian and Egyptian national autonomy and that Egypt must not be allowed independence because of the Communist threat.[60]

The resort to force, as represented by the notorious (to some) Allenby and Lampson ultimatums, have reified an image of a British regime resolute and relentless. Certainly, the primacy of imperial 'prestige' applied at specific moments in history. Official cultural products underpinned the idea, serving as manuals of conduct for British officials in Egypt and as guides to 'native' ways. The most notable of these was Lord Cromer's *Modern Egypt*, a master discourse on cultural difference. Indeed, many officials produced variations on Cromer's work, normally published as memoirs of imperial service or accounts of colonial lives, with each version joined by a common cultural purpose to construct an ideological and social wall that set the 'Englishman' apart as uniquely endowed to rule the 'Asiatic and African races'.[61] But even these political memoirs and histories can be subjected to the kind of analysis outlined above. Churchill, Lampson, and Allenby were capable of coercion *and* conciliation, whereas some of the historical literature has delineated only the racist or supremacist fundamentals of imperial policy.[62] Examining historical memoirs more widely might find that the British colony did not represent an impermeable caste; muted themes found voice.

Sources and plan

It is difficult to identify an authentic voice, in the sense of some special claim to represent Britain or Egypt. A good example of this is Edward Said. Born in Jerusalem, he grew up in Egypt in an Anglophone milieu: he attended the Anglican Church and Victoria College. Yet, he identified with the Egyptian locale against the British colony, an identity that deepened with his first-hand experience of colonial racism. Eventually, he transferred to the United States and reacquired a Palestinian identity that led to his book *Orientalism* (prompted by the 1967 war), which took the Egyptian colonial scene as its primary site of analysis. The presence of multiple strands in his personality was typical of colonial settings, as was the trend to narrow down the points of identification under the impact of racism, war, nationalism, or other factors.[63] This study seeks to illuminate these multiple strands as an ordinary feature of colonial society, a bricolage that was not anomalous, not a sign of degeneracy, but typical of social identification at different settings: work, leisure, family, nationality, religion, locality. These characteristics are revealed in the mundane and everyday, mostly in British memoirs designed to record ordinary colonial life. Egyptian sources were not consciously excluded, but the balance remains British because of the

INTRODUCTION

difficulty of acquiring Egyptian memoirs that deal with these mundane concerns, as opposed to political memoirs, such as those of Ahmad Lutfi al-Sayyid and Muhammad Husayn Haykal. In some cases, Egyptians consciously avoided social contact with the British, and therefore memoirs do not always convey the sort of evidence required.[64] Although memoirs reflective of colonial relationships do exist, few were available to the author, with some exceptions, such as Said's *Out of Place: A Memoir* and Chafika Hamamsy's *Zamalek: The Changing Life of a Cairo Elite, 1850–1945*.[65] Although this book is not consciously a study of colonial elites, the difficulty of capturing lower-class or subaltern voices is also well known. Consular and police reports have served as sources to reconstruct lower-class lives, yet the innuendo, allegations, and conscious advocacy that characterise the content of these types of reports do not necessarily provide a more authentic reflection of social 'reality', but only glimpses of lower-class life in extremis. Moreover, lower-class voices in official reports are mediated by the elites – another level of distortion.[66] While many of the sources investigated in this study were produced by upper- and middle-class persons, British and other nationalities, the intent has been to uncover ordinary colonial lives, neither elite nor marginal.

There are two bookends that hold together the multiple topics and characters discussed. These are the papers and letters of Michael Barker (d. 1999) and Gerald Delany (d. 1974). Roughly contemporaneous, their lives intersected as witnesses to the twilight years of the British colony in Egypt, with each articulating a critique of the imperial state from a uniquely colonial perspective. Delany left after the violent street confrontations and assassinations that rocked the renegotiation of treaty stipulations in 1946. Barker left after the Suez War of 1956. Each had served the imperial state in war and peace, Barker as a soldier during the Second World War and shipping agent in Alexandria, Delany as political intelligence adviser to military headquarters during the war and reporter at Reuters beforehand. The war and the years leading up to it saw heated debates on empire and its future. The issue of Egypt's place in the imperial system remained a subject of dispute until 1956, when British forces failed to bring about regime change. That affair pointed to the issue that remained unresolved at the conclusion of the First World War: Could the British government trust its imperial defences to an independent Egyptian administration? Would the colony have a life after British troop withdrawal?[67] Delany and Barker offer ordinary, colonial points of view on these issues of high politics. Their opinions were shaped by location, lifestyle, and professional or family networks. The point of following their narratives is to capture colonial sentiment, as opposed to the 'imperial sentiment' experienced more broadly by the British public through identification with a global empire.[68] Delany's and Barker's critiques of policy were founded on attachment to colonial place and suggest that the interests of metropolitan Britain and colonial Egypt diverged. The recollections of these colonials offer a poignant account of the breaking of those links that held the web of empire together.[69] Delany's and Barker's stories, as told in the first and final chapters of this book, cover a large portion of history: Michael Barker recounts the events of three generations of Barkers in Egypt; Delany's career straddles the high point of empire before the First World War, the revolt in 1919, through the crisis of 1942 and the disappointments that followed as the British, of all types, were estranged from their Egyptian hosts, and finally alienated by the war of 1956. As pillars of the British colony, Barker and Delany were servants of empire, imperialists by habit and choice. Yet, the trauma occasioned by what to them were the reckless and careless acts of their own government – neither blamed the Egyptians – meant that they were capable of identification with Egypt against the imperial state at critical moments, and later from exile.

Each was non-official British. Their social networks revolved around family business or profession. Yet, for each, contacts in British and Egyptian political circles were essential. Attachment to the British colony was obvious in each case: the Barker family had been involved in political efforts to secure citizenship rights for all British – 'out-land' and 'in-land' British – before the Second World War and in securing compensation for lost property after 1956. Delany was more closely linked to the official classes; he mixed with diplomats, administrators, and soldiers, yet never part of the colonial administration. Barker's disillusion with British imperialism had to wait to the post-1956 period, whereas Delany was deeply disappointed by the policies of the British imperial state from the 1925 appointment of Lord Lloyd, a conservative 'die-hard' who took hold of a sector of metropolitan and colonial opinion by underlining the nationalist threat to the empire. Unwavering service to empire was a hallmark of the imperial age, and Barker's and Delany's letters memorialise that ethos, yet without negating the Egyptians in the process. In this regard, their memories contradict the imperialistic doctrine that the British nation had a duty to lead lesser peoples of the world and that colonial nationalism was nothing less than revolt against a natural order of things. It should be underlined that in 1946, the Labour Party held to this view as surely as the Conservatives, as a sign of the prevalence of such views in metropolitan Britain.[70] While Delany's opinions (Barker was less outspoken) are not startling from the post-colonial perspective, such views were very much muted by more conventional opinion in the mid-twentieth century; indeed, for some

INTRODUCTION

the conventional view that the British government's actions in 1942 or 1946 or during and after 1956 were a justified response to real security threats, prevails. For Delany, these threats were the imaginings of minds incapable of meeting Egyptians on equal terms.

In between these bookends, chapters on the British invasion, imperial projects, and colonial life entertain multiple perspectives: those of travellers, artists, business people, engineers, nurses, teachers, children, chaplains, soldiers, and more. The chapters extend the colonial history of Egypt to the early nineteenth century and demonstrate that British of diverse types were animated by an imperial doctrine that represented the British as carriers and disseminators of British liberty. These first-generation colonials were concerned with the question of how a region described as 'despotic' could be brought securely within the sphere of liberal self-governing nations. In the meantime, these colonials were often employed by the Egyptian state, not the British, contributing not only to knowledge on Egypt in Britain, but to the body of Egyptian expertise as well. In this sense, the British were contributors to Egyptian power; the eventual application of this knowledge to British conquest and rule was less self-evident.[71] The British in this period found it necessary to collaborate with the Egyptian ruling class as technical experts; also, the British in Egypt had to collaborate with Egyptian officials to gain access to cultural sites, resources, and markets. This meant considerable compromises with the discourse on British liberty and, in many cases, the British adopted the demeanour, if not the identity of the Egyptian lord or pasha. On this contradiction, much of the subsequent colonial lifestyle and politics were built. Wilfrid Scawen Blunt is one such example, a Conservative with essentially liberal imperialist views, he defended the Egyptian right to self-government, but only after the British helped bring down the 'tyrant', Isma'il Pasha. Although the events that began the march towards British military occupation in 1882 created a crisis in Blunt's perception of himself and his country, nevertheless Blunt's doctrine of British intervention on liberal principle was a defining feature of the period before 1882. The doctrine, however, did not sit comfortably with practice, leading to contradiction. When Blunt realised that intervention meant crushing the nascent liberalism of Egyptian reformers, he put on Arab dress and retired to a desert tent. After the military occupation, he took an obstructionist position vis-à-vis the British administration while adopting the lifestyle and pursuits of an Egyptian country squire (horses and horticulture).

The third chapter, 'Projects', adopts a more communal approach to the colony, investigating some of its most important institutions: military, administration, church, schools, and the municipality of

Alexandria. The point in each case is to show the diversity of opinion within these institutions on the orientation or mission of each, as well as the way the stated mission of one institution might counter or check another. Exemplary in this regard is the history of schools, where the apparently sacrosanct mission to safeguard the purity of the 'ruling race' through strictures on education met with apathy and obstruction, so that in the interwar period the British government intervened to terminate funding for schools that would have adopted exclusive rules of admission barring Egyptians from attendance. This of course did not kill informal types of racial segregation in clubs or schools, as discussion of these is worked out in Chapter 4 on 'Colonial life'. Here we find the colony in a domestic realm, at leisure and at work. Where colonial women accepted or rejected the model of decorum, restraint, and social propriety, set as much by the norms of Egyptian society as by those of Edwardian England. Where soldiers slipped from barracks to marry locally, or at least momentarily succumbed to the temptation to adapt lifestyles to the colonial setting. The fifth chapter traces the subject of racism, which was barely disguised in some of the practices, if not policies, of high commissioners and diplomats in the interwar period and afterwards. This tendency was bemoaned by many at the time, including Reuters correspondent Gerald Delany and literary light E.M. Forster, alongside all those who gathered at mixed cultural settings in a conscious effort to confound the blaring marching bands that regularly paraded from embassy gate and barracks. These nationalistic strains multiplied during the wars, as did church-going and the size of crowds at sporting and social clubs – all to the ruin of a colonial society built from its inception on accommodation and integration, not confrontation and exclusion.

The point in this compendium of stories is to chart divergences in the imperial discourse, as outlined by Edward Said, and plurality in colonial society. The research does not seek to refute Said's thesis that culture was an arm of imperial power, but suggests that categorical statements such as his based on theoretical principles are not always in conformity with the facts. It is important to trace how discourses and practices changed across historical periods, with some bracing juxtapositions and contradictions taking shape: that the British government was able to put itself ahead of conservative opinion on issues of racial exclusion; that colonials defended the inclusiveness of the colony against attempts by the British government to exclude 'out-land' British; that attachment to the colonial setting could trump the financial interests and security of the cotton magnates; that some were willing to risk existential threats in the pursuit of a more equitable balance of international relations. While it might be argued that these moves and

INTRODUCTION

turns were not representative of the colony because the norm of colonial society was to define the British colony against the others, or, in other words, racism and exclusivity. That is not necessarily supported by the evidence: the process was more like a game of Chinese chequers, wherein those of a similar type seek proximity based on similarity, not difference. Of course, given the ordering of the world on the basis of wealth, that fact was obscured by the weight of the Egyptian Muslim population in the lower classes. Nevertheless, in the race to get to the other side of the board – a destination defined normally in opportunistic terms (wealth or status or a living) – the pieces mixed together and formed some remarkable patterns and contiguities, even if only momentarily.

Notes

1 Frederick Cooper, *Colonialism in Question: Theory, Knowledge, History* (Berkeley & Los Angeles: University of California Press, 2005), p. 11.
2 Yoav Di-Capua, *Gatekeepers of the Arab Past: Historians and History Writing in Twentieth Century Egypt* (Berkeley & Los Angeles: University of California Press, 2009) & Michael Ezekiel Gasper, *The Power of Representation: Publics, Peasants, and Islam in Egypt* (Stanford: Stanford University Press, 2009).
3 Israel Gershoni and James P. Jankowski, *Egypt, Islam and the Arabs: The Search for Egyptian Nationhood 1900–1930* (New York: Oxford University Press, 1986).
4 Partha Chatterjee, *The Nation and its Fragments: Colonial and Post-Colonial Histories* (Princeton: Princeton University Press, 1993).
5 Albert Memmi, *The Colonizer and the Colonized* (Boston: Beacon, 1967), pp. 19–44. Memmi rejects the idea of the colonial liberal for this very reason: for viewing colonised culture through the coloniser's lens. On critiques of liberalism as a universal concept, see Catherine Hall, Keith McClelland and Jane Rendall, *Defining the Victorian Nation: Class, Race, Gender and the Reform Act of 1867* (Cambridge: Cambridge University Press, 2000).
6 Edward W. Said, *Orientalism* (London: Routledge & Kegan Paul, 1978).
7 Tim Harper joins the 'new' imperial history focus on associational networks with the complications of colonial identity in diverse social settings; see his 'The British "Malayans"', in Robert Bickers (ed.), *Settlers and Expatriates: Britons over the Seas* (Oxford: Oxford University Press, 2010), pp. 233–6.
8 Catherine Hall, 'Culture and Identity in Imperial Britain', in Sarah Stockwell (ed.), *The British Empire: Themes and Perspectives* (Oxford: Blackwell, 2008), p. 202.
9 Edwin Ardener, 'Belief and the Problem of Women: The Problem revisited', in Shirley Ardener (ed.), *Perceiving Women* (London: Malaby, 1975) & Nicholas Thomas, *Colonialism's Culture: Anthropology, Travel and Governmentality* (Princeton: Princeton University Press, 1994), p. 3.
10 Said, *Orientalism*, pp. 204–5.
11 Robert Irwin, *For Lust of Knowing: The Orientalists and their Enemies* (London: Penguin, 2006).
12 Jacques Berque, *Mémoires des deux rives* (Paris: Éditions du Seuil, 1989), p. 42.
13 Peter Mansfield, *The British in Egypt* (London: Weidenfeld and Nicolson, 1971) & Jacques Berque, *Egypt: Imperialism and Revolution* (London: Faber & Faber, 1972).
14 Albert Hourani, *Islam in European Thought and Other Essays* (Cambridge: Cambridge University Press, 1991), pp. 129–35.
15 Paul Fussell, *Abroad: British Literary Travelling between the Wars* (Oxford: Oxford University Press, 1980) & Thomas, *Colonialism's Culture*, pp. 5–6.

16 Anthony Sattin, *A Winter on the Nile: Florence Nightingale, Gustave Flaubert and the Temptations of Egypt* (London: Hutchinson, 2010).
17 Florence Nightingale, *Letters from Egypt: A Journey on the Nile 1849–50*, ed. Anthony Sattin (London: Parkway Publishing, 2002) & John Barrell, 'Death on the Nile: Fantasy and the Literature of Tourism, 1840–60', in Catherine Hall (ed.), *Cultures of Empire: Colonizers in Britain and the Empire in the Nineteenth and Twentieth Centuries* (Manchester: Manchester University Press, 2000).
18 Said, *Orientalism*, p. 197.
19 Ibid., p. 163.
20 Ibid., p. 196.
21 Barrell, 'Death on the Nile', p. 203.
22 Mary Louise Pratt, *Imperial Eyes: Travel Writing and Transculturation* (New York: Routledge, 1992) & Sami Zubaida, 'Cosmopolitanism in the Middle East', *Amsterdam Middle East Papers* 12 (Dec. 1997): 1–21.
23 Roger Owen, *Lord Cromer: Victorian Imperialist, Edwardian Proconsul* (Oxford: Oxford University Press, 2004), pp. 247–9.
24 Timothy Mitchell, *Colonising Egypt* (Berkeley: University of California Press, 1988).
25 Alfred Milner, *England in Egypt* (London: Edward Arnold, 3rd edn, 1893) & Earl of Cromer, *Modern Egypt* (London: Macmillan, 1908), 2 vols & George Ambrose Lloyd, *Egypt since Cromer* (London: Macmillan, 1933).
26 Susan Slyomovics, 'Memory Studies: Lebanon and Israel/Palestine', *International Journal of Middle East Studies* 45/3 (2013): 589–601.
27 E.M. Forster, 'The Lost Guide', in E.M. Forster, *Alexandria: A History and a Guide and Pharos and Pharillon*, ed. Miriam Allott (London: André Deutsch, 2004), p. 354.
28 Nicholas Thomas, 'Colonial Conversions: Difference, Hierarchy, and History in Early Twentieth-Century Evangelical Propaganda', in Hall, *Cultures of Empire*, p. 299.
29 David Lambert and Alan Lester (eds), *Colonial Lives across the British Empire: Imperial Careering in the Long Nineteenth Century* (Cambridge: Cambridge University Press, 2006).
30 Albert Hourani, *Arabic Thought in the Liberal Age 1798–1939* (London: Oxford University Press, 1966).
31 Sami Zubaida, 'Iraq: History, Memory, Culture', *International Journal of Middle East Studies* 44/2 (2012): 333–45.
32 Cromer, *Modern Egypt*, vol. 2, p. 245: 38,000 Greeks, 24,000 Italians, 14,000 French 7,000 Austrians, 10,000 other nationalities.
33 British Parliamentary Papers, Accounts and Papers, vol. cvii, Egypt, no. 1 (1898): *Reports on the Finances, Administration, and Condition of Egypt and the Progress of Reforms* (London, 1898).
34 Egyptian Government, Ministry of Finance-Statistical Department, *The Census of Egypt Taken in 1917* (Cairo: Government Press, 1917), vol. 2.
35 Will Hanley, 'Foreignness and Localness in Alexandria, 1880–1914' (PhD dissertation, Princeton University, 2007), p. 9.
36 Ibid., pp. 278–82.
37 Egyptian Government, Ministry of Finance-Statistical Department, *Census 1917*. There were 7,524 British in Cairo, 10,656 in Alexandria, and 2,539 in Port Said and Isma'iliyya, and 933 in Suez.
38 Henry de Montfreid, *Hashish: True Adventures of a Red Sea Smuggler in the Twenties* (London: Penguin, 1946), pp. 100–7.
39 Robert Tignor, *Modernization and British Colonial Rule in Egypt* (Princeton: Princeton University Press, 1966), p. 196.
40 Anne Laura Stoler, *Race and the Education of Desire: Foucault's 'History of Sexuality' and the Colonial Order of Things* (Durham, NC: Duke University Press, 1995).
41 Hanley, 'Foreignness', pp. 194–7, discusses the case of Henry Curmi, a prominent British Maltese lawyer in the consular courts subject to exclusions by metropolitan British.
42 The problem of a colonial underclass was discussed in The National Archives (TNA) Foreign Office (FO) file (hereafter, TNA FO) 141/463/1411, British Consulate, 10 June

INTRODUCTION

1924. See also Lanver Mak, *The British in Egypt: Community, Crime, and Crisis 1882–1922* (London: I.B. Tauris, 2012), which offers a social history of this underclass based on consular reports.

43 Magda Baraka, *The Egyptian Upper Class between Revolutions 1919–1952* (Reading: Ithaca, 1998), p. 236.
44 Frances Donaldson, *The British Council: The First Fifty Years* (London: Jonathan Cape, 1984), p. 93 & TNA FO371/20125 Lampson, 14 Aug. 1936, 'Strength of the British Garrison in Egypt', which noted that after the 1936 treaty troop numbers were reduced to 13,000. The total allowed by the treaty was 10,400.
45 Robert Graves and Allan Hodge, *The Long Weekend: A Social History of Britain 1918–1939* (New York: W.W. Norton, 1940).
46 Edward W. Said, *Out of Place: A Memoir* (New York: Vintage, 2000), p. 47.
47 TNA FO369/3866, 1948, Consular, 4 Mar. 1948, 'Future Position of Maltese British Subjects in Egypt'.
48 TNA FO141/680/4069, McMahon to Balfour, 22 Dec. 1916.
49 Sir Miles Lampson, *Politics and Diplomacy in Egypt: The Diaries of Sir Miles Lampson 1935–1937*, ed. Malcolm Yapp (Oxford: Oxford University Press, 1997), p. 192.
50 Observation based on examination of British Cabinet records.
51 John Darwin, 'Decolonization and End of Empire', in Robin W. Winks (ed.), *Historiography: Oxford History of the British Empire* (Oxford: Oxford University Press, 1999), p. 550.
52 Elizabeth Monroe, *Britain's Moment in the Middle East 1914–1956* (London: Chatto & Windus, 1964), pp. 71 & 82.
53 The primacy of the geo-political in British imperial thinking as it related to Egypt is captured in Richard Toye, *Churchill's Empire: The World that Made him and the World he Made* (London: Pan Books, 2011) & Wm. Roger Louis, *In the Name of God Go! Leo Amery and the British Empire in the Age of Churchill* (New York: Norton, 1992).
54 The diverse interest groups in Britain are covered by Andrew S. Thompson, *Imperial Britain: The Empire in British Politics, c. 1880–1932* (Harlow: Longman, 2000). The example of business interests in opposition to geo-political priorities can be followed in Robert L. Tignor, *Capitalism and Nationalism at the End of Empire: State and Business in Egypt, Nigeria, and Kenya, 1945–1963* (Princeton: Princeton University Press, 1997).
55 C.W.R. Long, *British Pro-Consuls in Egypt, 1914–1929: The Challenge of Nationalism* (London: Routledge Curzon, 2004).
56 Field Marshall Viscount Wavell, *Allenby in Egypt* (London: George G. Harrap & Co., 1943), p. 110.
57 Ibid., p. 115.
58 Ibid., pp. 121–2.
59 Middle East Centre Archives, St Antony's College, Oxford (hereafter MECA), GB165-0115, Sir Robert Allason Furness, Box 3, File 1, Kerr to Furness, 8 Dec. 1925.
60 Lawrence James, *Churchill and Empire: Portrait of an Imperialist* (London: Phoenix, 2014), pp. 123 & 128.
61 Cromer, *Modern Egypt*, vol. 2, p. 570.
62 Anouar Abdel-Malek, *Ideologie et renaissance nationale, l'Égypte moderne* (Paris: Editions Anthropos, 1969) & Said, *Orientalism*.
63 In 1954 on meeting the Palestinian Ibrahim Abu Lughod, Edward Said answered a question on his place of identification: 'I am *from* Egypt now.' His identity would change over time and place. Edward Said, 'My Guru', *London Review of Books* 23/24 (2001).
64 Huda Shaarawi, *Harem Years: The Memoirs of an Egyptian Feminist*, trans. Margot Badran, (New York: The Feminist Press at The City University of New York Press, 1987), p. 94.
65 Chafika Soliman Hamamsy, *Zamalek: The Changing Life of a Cairo Elite, 1850–1945* (Cairo: American University in Cairo Press, 2005). For a list of Egyptian memoirs in Arabic, see Baraka, *Upper Class*, pp. 306–10.

66 Khaled Fahmy, 'Towards a Social History of Modern Alexandria', in Anthony Hirst and Michael Silk (eds), *Alexandria, Real and Imagined* (Aldershot: Ashgate, 2004), pp. 263–80.
67 Wm. Roger Louis, *Ends of British Imperialism: The Scramble for Empire, Suez and Decolonization* (London: I.B. Tauris, 2006).
68 Thompson, *Imperial Britain*, p. 50, where he distinguishes between 'the sentimental as opposed to the strategic appeal of the imperial system'.
69 The web paradigm of empire seems to begin with John Darwin's 'Imperialism and the Victorians: The Dynamics of Territorial Expansion', *English Historical Review* 112/447 (1997): 614–42.
70 Labour Foreign Secretary Ernest Bevin was critical of collaboration with the Egyptian elites and called for an imperial policy directed towards the 'fellahin', a version of the civilising mission, *The Times* (26 May 1946). Bevin was criticised by Sir Ronald Campbell, the British ambassador to Egypt, for introducing a new form of political interference: TNA FO141/1216, 1947.
71 Said, *Orientalism*, & Cooper, *Colonialism in Question* & Frederick Cooper and Ann Laura Stoler (eds), *Tensions of Empire: Colonial Cultures in a Bourgeois World* (Berkeley: University of California Press, 1997).

CHAPTER ONE

Capitulations

It would be incorrect to identify the origin of the British colony with the military occupation of 1882. Nor is there an origin in the sense of a founding script of the colony, like the Boer Treks. But there is an origin in the sense of the conditions that enabled Britons to travel to Egypt and establish residency. From that perspective, it is difficult to determine when the British acquired enough gravity to be considered a colony, except to say it was certainly before 1882. The characteristics of the colony before the invasion differed from it afterwards, involved different interests and enterprises, more economic and cultural than strategic or militaristic; these characteristics did not disappear with the military occupation, but continued to make up some of the various strands of the colonial experience.

British residence in Egypt was facilitated by commercial treaties, known as the 'Capitulations'. The term capitulation came from the Latin *caput* or *capitulum* and literally referred to headings or articles in a legal contract. The origins of the idea of capitulations can be traced to the Crusades when the Italian city-states were granted legal privileges to trade in Fatimid Egypt in 1154, with Salah al-Din making similar grants in 1173. The Mamluk sultans continued the practice, for instance with the commercial agreements between the Italians and Sultan Qala'un (reigned 1279–90).[1] Like the subsequent Ottoman 'Capitulations', these legal agreements allowed Christians to reside within a khan or *funduk*, a fortified warehouse and hostel, situated in the marketplace or *suq*. The British first entered into such agreements with the Ottoman Empire in 1580, when 200 Capitulations were granted to the English Crown to enable trade. In the following year the royal charter of the Company of Merchants of the Levant gave it a monopoly of trade in the region. Shortly afterwards, British diplomatic representatives were sent out to the Ottoman capital, Istanbul, and consuls were appointed to the entrepôts of the Levant, including Alexandria and Cairo, with Aleppo the most important British commercial centre until the nineteenth century. Throughout the following two and a half centuries, the Company covered the expenses of the diplomatic appointments. Only in 1825 did the British state take responsibility for selecting and appointing consuls.[2]

A history of the Levant Company by James Mather has shown that there was a high degree of cultural tolerance exhibited by the British merchants towards the Ottoman inhabitants of the Levant, something that contrasted with the modern colonial period.[3] The Levant merchants mixed with their Ottoman counterparts in business, integrating some Ottoman cultural norms, such as language, dress, and diet. Also, certain categories of the Ottoman subject population were absorbed into the British colony, notably Christian and Jewish residents of the Levant ports, who were attracted to the protection provided by the Capitulations. Incredible wealth was produced: 300 to 400 per cent profits in the early period, with most cargos consisting of silk products. In a development that would transform Egypt in the nineteenth century, the Levant merchants found that cotton fibre was readily adapted to British markets by the weavers of Lancashire.[4] Commercial and manufacturing profits in cotton, as well as the traditional luxury items of the Orient, had social consequences in the growth of an urban 'Levantine' social sector, part European and part Asian, in a 'process' that continued well into the twentieth century. Lord Cromer recognised the social category in 1908:

> The process of manufacturing Levantines is at least as old as the Crusades. Thus, Mr. Stanley Lane-Poole says ... 'The early Crusaders, after thirty years residence in Syria, had become very much assimilated in character and habits to the people whom they had partly conquered, among whom they lived, and whose daughters they did not disdain to marry; they were growing into Levantines; they were known as *Pullani* or Creoles.'[5]

It is this 'process' that Mather highlights in his study, demonstrating that, in the pre-1800 era, consul and merchant colony had to obey the rules and customs of local institutions; as a result, British merchants of the Levant Company adapted to local norms. As he observed, the most important factor driving this process was that the market was a great leveller of national and religious difference. Individuals adapted their lifestyles to the requirements of trade.[6] Whereas in the later period the European consuls held the balance of power, in the earlier period local Ottoman governors had the capacity to put the foreigners in their place at any perceived slight or transgression. If a 'freeman' of the Company lost the legal protection afforded by the Capitulations, the Ottoman officials could strip him of fortunes and stockpiles; for instance, marriage to Ottoman subjects was regarded as dangerous because it could be interpreted as removing the legal status of a British subject. Nevertheless, intermarriage occurred, there were also concubines and 'harems', but because of the relative power of the Ottoman state fewer than among their counterparts in the East India Company. The merchants of the Levant Company were wary of the Ottomans and therefore mostly pursued their own interests and leisure activities – notably drinking, feasting, and the hunt – somewhat aloof from the locals.

The relationships between Ottomans and British were defined more by ambiguity than cross-cultural harmony, but far from the animosity between foreigners and locals that, apparently, characterised relations of the post-1800 period. Mather's narrative is thus hopeful, suggesting that cultural ruptures are not inevitable; however, that characterisation of the Levant merchant colonies is not conventional. Other accounts have described the Company 'factories' as tight-knit organisations where British merchants had very little contact with the local population, did not speak Arabic, Turkish or other local languages, and lived in constant fear of the plague and the hostility of the local population. Therefore what contact the British had was through local intermediaries, normally Christian or Jewish, also under the protection of the Capitulations by a mechanism known as the *berat*.[7] From these accounts the Capitulations were easily corrupted to favour Europeans, with British and French consuls winning more and more concessions and privileges so that the legal status of British merchants and their clients came to resemble something like 'diplomatic immunity'.[8] The contradictions inherent in these divergent narratives of the Levant Company can at least partly be explained by historical method. Mather describes individuals and their everyday lives within a Levantine milieu, drawing a contrast between the Levant merchants and those of the East India Company or modern colonialism. On the other hand, economic historians analyse larger structures over the long term and, with hindsight, the process afoot amounted to the eventual domination of the Europeans. Thus, Robert Ilbert has shown that in the nineteenth century Europeans in Egypt were increasingly assertive, and the consuls, particularly the British and French, insinuated themselves within the Egyptian system.[9] After the Levant Company monopoly on the export trade was terminated in 1825, competition increased among foreign and local merchants. British consuls and merchants campaigned to limit or abolish Egyptian internal tariffs on the movement of goods or state monopolies over valuable export commodities.[10] By re-orienting the economy towards Britain's export and import requirements, the consuls and the merchant colony served as a 'bridgehead' for imperialism in Egypt well before the British occupation of 1882. Capitulations were the primary instrument to assert power, so that rather than a grant from the Ottoman ruler, the Capitulations were interpreted, at least from the nineteenth century, as a guarantee of European 'rights' that extended into all areas of Egypt's economy and administration.[11] The British resisted Egyptian efforts to revise the commercial agreements imposed upon them from the 1820s. As a result, the Egyptians had to wait until the 1930s to reform the basic rules of international trade and finance with the abolition of the Capitulations in the Anglo-Egyptian Treaty of 1936. The 'bridgehead' was finally dismantled, the British and other colonies retreated, and the Egyptians occupied the Levantine quarters of Alexandria and Cairo.[12]

Philip Mansell's study of the Levant offers a synthesis of these differing interpretations of colonial relationships. While recognising that the imperial states of Europe shaped unequal social relations between Europeans and Ottoman subjects, Mansell has also said that it is important to investigate the Levantine milieu in specific locales. As Mansell said, the 'cities of the Levant were protagonists in the dialogues between cities and states, ports and hinterlands, as well as between East and West'. Note the different levels of interaction: regional, state, and global. From this perspective, the 'Levant' represented a culture that negotiated at several intersections or 'bridgeheads', as well as historical periods. Mansell refers to a Levantine 'mentality' that survived the Byzantine Empire into the period of the Ottoman Empire and, one assumes his inclusion of nineteenth- and twentieth-century Alexandria in his category of the Levant, survived the British Empire also. In the Levantine urban space the hard boundaries of nation-state, ethnicity, or religion were not fully formed and might, in certain historical locales or periods, reveal a 'third way', to which Mansell applies terms such as 'cosmopolitan', 'global cities', and 'coexistence'.[13] Mansell is thus attentive to trends submerged by the emergence of the nation-state. This in effect brings Mather's observations on the pre-nineteenth-century Levant into the colonial period, albeit adopting a more multifaceted approach whereby imperialism has to be understood as a contradictory phenomenon. Take, for example, the term 'bridgehead' as applied by Michael Reimer to capture the way social and spatial change in Alexandria in the nineteenth century prefigured the military occupation that forced Egypt into the British Empire. According to Reimer, foreign control over Egypt's people and territory existed before 1882 and thus the term 'bridgehead' has the sense of foreign intrusion. Reimer's argument is essentially that the foreign colony originated in the economic transformation of Alexandria, its integration into the imperial networks of trade, migration, and European financial investments after 1850. The Capitulations enabled this organisation of the foreign communities and their control over the economy and the Egyptian government, which created the 'bridgehead' for colonisation.[14] But the concept 'bridgehead' has also been used to describe a multifaceted phenomenon involving the multiple interests of the British colony, including trade and investment, as well as others, like scientific, missionary, the professional networks of engineers, doctors, and lawyers, and travellers, many of them very critical of the transformations underway in other sectors of the 'bridgehead'. David Lambert and Alan Lester built upon this concept by investigating the connections holding the strands together through biographical treatments of colonial persons, not unlike Mather's method.[15]

The method can be applied to the case of the Barker family of Alexandria, a pre-eminent British commercial family in the Levant from the eighteenth to twentieth century. In many ways, the family narrative that was constructed by Henry 'Michael' Barker (1923–99) corresponds in references and content to the official texts of Cromer and Milner. However, there are some dissonant notes that reflect a Levantine orientation or colonial sentiment, most notably that the family's cultural and social connections to Egypt, specifically Alexandria, outlasted the family's financial and commercial connections and, at decisive moments in the family's centuries-long residence, social identity or cultural sentiment trumped economic interest. The family portrait that emerges from reading the memoirs (a series of files of notes taken from diaries, letters, and memorabilia, and thus not a cohesive narrative) supports a highly localised identity of that merchant family. In the following pages the particular history of the Barker family is recounted, based on the archive, while placing that history in the larger and long-term economic structures, as described by the economic historians.

Commercial and financial origins

The Barker family was unabashedly wealthy; it required a caravan to transport the family's possessions when the Barkers departed Aleppo for Alexandria in 1825. John Barker (1771–1849) was appointed consul to Alexandria in 1826. This was a dynamic period when European commerce was rapidly expanding and the British consul general, Henry Salt (serving 1809–27), established a partnership with the Egyptian ruler, Muhammad 'Ali. The latter was primarily concerned with increasing revenues through exports of grain and cotton to Europe to build up a territorial military state. Salt was mostly interested in winning concessions to profit from the export of Egyptian antiquities and acquire gentlemanly status in Britain.[16] Each assisted the other in opening access to resources and markets; hence the partnership. The shift in British economic interests from Izmir and Aleppo to Alexandria in this period was the result of the development of Egyptian export commodities and Alexandria as a transit port, mostly on the initiative of Muhammad 'Ali. John Barker was very involved in the cotton export end of the relationship – the origin of the family as 'cotton magnates'.

The British population in 1827 was approximately two hundred; in 1830, one thousand, mostly Maltese and Ionians (from the British colony of Malta and the British Protectorate over the Ionian Islands). The majority worked in the transit trade at the port in Alexandria as semi-skilled labourers. The number of British trebled over the next couple of decades. There was one British commercial house in 1821, Briggs & Thurburn, which had been founded after the Napoleonic Wars by Samuel Briggs and Robert Thurburn. Briggs had served as British consul between 1803 and 1807. Cotton exports began in the 1820s and by 1839 there were nine commercial houses in Alexandria. In the same interval, Thomas Waghorn convinced the governor of the Bank of England and the directors of the Peninsular Shipping Lines of the advantages of the short route to India through Egypt. Waghorn, with the assistance of the British consul Patrick Campbell, persuaded Muhammad 'Ali to sign the 'General Agreement on the Overland Route' in 1840. The transit agreement through Egypt was held by Robert Thurburn. Briggs & Company was the agent for the Peninsular & Orient (P&O) Line.[17] These developments brought tourists and migrants, transforming Alexandria's cultural face. An equally revolutionary event was the migration of Egyptians from the rural hinterland to Alexandria and the resultant formation of a local working class.[18] The working class was European and Egyptian, as were the commercial and administrative elites. The Egyptian elite was more administrative and professional, their wealth and status also founded on rural estates producing for local consumption and the export markets. The European elite was primarily involved in the transport of these goods and investment in the necessary infrastructure, but less so in landholdings. The relationship between these elites was therefore mutually beneficial, involving an economic and political pact.

Edward Barker's (1784–1844) papers from his consulship in Cairo in 1830 and 1831 show that in the early nineteenth century the lingua franca of the British consulate was Italian, which had been the case for centuries.[19] Edward's son Frederick (1825–99) founded the Barker & Company shipping firm in 1845 and was joined by his brother, Henry Barker (1829–1907), who founded the Alexandria line of the family. In this period the family acted as merchants and shipping agents for Burns McIver & Company (Cunard's), in addition to other lines carrying commodities such as cotton, cottonseed, grain, coal, as well as passengers on transit to India or on tour. Henry Barker married Alice Joyce in Notting Hill, London. Alice was of Italian descent and had grown up in Trieste, but went to school in London; her grandfather (family name, Tibaldi) had served as Muhammad 'Ali's personal doctor. Alice was also a stepdaughter of Robert Thurburn, whom her mother married after her first husband's death. These patterns of intermarriage indicate a Levantine cultural orientation among the British merchant colony. Henry's sister married into the Remana family, its origins in Venice; a nephew married an 'Ionian' (a maid turned out into the street) to the 'great sorrow of his mother'. First- and second-generation Barkers often employed Italian domestics. The Levantine connections of the family were diverse and enduring. The preference seemed to be to make connections through marriage within a Levantine milieu, without sacrificing British identity. When Henry Barker's mother, Anna (Mavrogouni) Barker, died, she was buried in the Greek cemetery in Alexandria, with inscriptions in English and Greek.[20] This Levantine orientation extended to consular staffs, which continued to be the case into the twentieth century.[21]

In the nineteenth century, the Barker family's formal relationship with the Egyptian ruler fitted a patron-and-client type. The bond was durable, so that while the national movement of Jamal al-Din al-Afghani and Muhammad 'Abduh began in the early 1870s, Henry Barker demonstrated his loyalty to Khedive Isma'il by accepting from him the honorific title of the Order of 'Uthmaniyya in 1874. A year later the Disraeli government purchased the khedive's 44 per cent shares in the Suez Canal, followed shortly by the European Debt Commission of 1876, by which France and Britain appointed financial controllers to oversee the Egyptian debt to European lenders. There is nothing in the archives to suggest Henry Barker's opinions on the relative decline of the Egyptian ruler's powers in relation to nationalists and imperialists.[22]

Henry Barker rose to prominence during the second phase of Egypt's economic transformation: the era of high finance. The indigenous industries developed by Muhammad 'Ali to equip his army and navy collapsed in the 1840s after the Europeans terminated his state monopolies and imposed 'free trade'. Afterwards most commercial and financial activity was undertaken by Europeans; British businesspeople did not dominate the Egyptian economy in this period. If the primary cause of the British military occupation of 1882 was the indebtedness of the Egyptian state, then there was nothing specifically British about it. In his history of the great European financial houses in nineteenth-century Egypt, the economic historian David S. Landes described a transnational web of financial families of diverse ethnic backgrounds. One of the most powerful of the financial houses, Oppenheim, was German, seeking the support of the Prussian consulate in Alexandria when needed, but with headquarters in Paris. A leading member of the Oppenheim firm, Henry Oppenheim, was the family agent in London. He married into aristocratic English society, settled in London, and took British citizenship. Ultimately, Henry Oppenheim helped set in motion the fateful events that led to the British military occupation by using his contacts in finance and the British press to alert the British government to the sale on the public market of Egypt's shares in the Suez Canal Company.[23] The purchase by the Conservative government of Benjamin Disraeli in 1875 merged the financial with the strategic interest of the British in Egypt. Oppenheim might have discerned this and been motivated to secure his own investments by aligning his family's financial interests with those of the British government. According to Landes, 'cosmopolitan' identity was the chief characteristic of the business elite and its motivations were profit and career advancement, not national interest. This was partly the result of the dispersion of the merchant community across Europe and the Levant, necessitated by the movement of money and commodities, and thus business depended upon an ability to work in various localities, languages, and cultural settings. Paradoxically, although the financial community was necessarily fluid, the commercial houses were tight-knit units. The best insurance for trustworthiness in business dealings was that the firms were bound by familial, religious, or national ties. In part, this was because one needed to have confidence in agents holding capital in far-flung locations with clients or patrons governed by foreign cultural norms, different law codes and systems of government. Under these conditions, the family bond, or those of religion or nationality, created unity in dispersion.[24]

The greatest financial houses in Egypt were those held by the Suares, Cattaoui, and Menasce families. These families were also known as the most 'cosmopolitan' and were celebrated as such in Lawrence Durrell's *The Alexandria Quartet*. London and Paris were their capitals. Egypt became a field for investment in the mid-nineteenth century. The oldest public bank in Egypt, the Bank of Egypt, was established as a British chartered corporation in 1856. Other banks followed, such as the Ottoman Imperial Bank, which opened in 1863 with British and French capital, and the Anglo-Egyptian Bank in 1864. Buoyed by the immense profits with the quadrupling of the price of cotton during the American Civil War, the London and Paris financial houses and their Egyptian outlets floated loans to Egyptian rulers on the money markets of Europe, mobilising the enormous resources necessary to finance the state projects carried out during the reigns of Sa'id (1854–63) and Isma'il (1863–79), including railways, telegraphs, irrigation canals, barrages, quays, palaces, urban renewal, and the Suez Canal. The Capitulations enabled Europeans to operate outside the controls of Egyptian law. Legal cases involving European financiers were tried in consular courts, which invariably ruled in favour of their own nationals. Harsh and unfair indemnities were imposed by these courts upon the Egyptian government, shielding European nationals from the usual risks of venture capital. The first major case involved Prince al-Hami, a dissolute member of the royal family who borrowed from the Oppenheim financial house in the 1850s. Over-extended, the Oppenheim firm borrowed from the Bank of Egypt. When the prince prematurely died and the loans had to be settled, the Prussian consulate shielded the Oppenheims; the British consul protected the Bank of Egypt; and in the end the Egyptian ruler, Sa'id, was forced to settle, by not only liquidating the prince's estates, but also resorting to the Egyptian state treasury to satisfy the demands of the creditors. The resultant state debts led, in 1862, to the first major public loan taken out by the Egyptian government (60 million French francs at 11 per cent), with the payment of annuities secured by land tax revenues.[25] The Egyptian public paid for the profligacy of the prince and the risky ventures funded by European financial houses at enormously high interest rates (from 10 to 30 per cent). Another instance was the huge indemnity imposed upon Egypt (84 million French francs) in a case arbitrated by the French ruler, Napoleon III, after Isma'il attempted to renegotiate the terms of the 'concessions' awarded to the Suez Canal Company in 1864, which involved huge amounts of unpaid Egyptian labour in the Canal's construction.[26]

That year, the second of Isma'il's rule, saw a downturn in the price of cotton. Alongside Paris and London, the private commercial houses of Alexandria had been very much involved in speculative finance. Henry Barker managed the Imperial and Mercantile Credit Association, described by Landes as a 'typical product of boom finance': its profits were illusory, its funds tied up in risky ventures, and its prosperity (20 per cent dividends) would last only as long as the cotton boom.[27] One of the oldest private British commercial houses in Egypt, Briggs, was swallowed by one of the joint-stock firms, Commercial and Trading Company, in 1864. Like others, the collapse of cotton prices caught Briggs over-extended: half of Briggs's capital was frozen in cotton and the other half in loans to the Egyptian royal family, neither of which could be liquidated. When Commercial and Trading Company folded in 1866 at the peak of the financial crisis, the Barkers purchased Briggs's assets.[28]

Some survived the crisis, others did not. The Egyptian government resorted to the unlimited sale of short-term government bonds, promoted by the financial houses of Paris and London, and thus racked up state debt to such a degree that even payment of the interest on the debt was suspended in 1876. Bankruptcy brought increasing degrees of European financial intervention and control so that the British regarded the 'Law of Liquidation' of 1880 as an international treaty. When the Egyptian government was unable to find a means to meet its obligations under that law, the perceived breach of the 'treaty' served as the primary justification for British military invasion.[29]

Imperial zenith

With the treasury bankrupt, the army in mutiny over pay, and the Egyptian landholding class threatening revolution to avoid increased taxes, the British military invasion of 1882 had the appearance of being driven, as Wilfrid Scawen Blunt said, by the bondholders.[30] Obviously, cotton magnates like the Barkers were interested parties; the family was one of those that had profited from the cotton boom and bust. The Barker memoirs record the coming of the European Debt Commission and the formation of the Nubar Pasha ministry in 1878, with the latter viewed by the nationalists as a proxy for the financiers. Cleopatra's Needle was finally transported to the Embankment in London that year (the ancient obelisk had been a gift to the British government by Muhammad 'Ali in 1819) in a cylindrical-hulled ship built by John Dixon. There is in this combination of political infiltration and cultural appropriation the sense of an inexorable imperialist encroachment. The memoirs also record that Colonel Ahmad 'Urabi controlled the Egyptian government from early 1882 and that his government was described as a 'threat' to the Europeans and Isma'il's successor, Khedive Taufiq. The British and French fleets arrived. On 11 June 1882, the Barker papers record that 'Urabi's 'rebel army' occupied Alexandria while also subduing the 'massacre' that left around two hundred Europeans dead (including a British naval officer and two seamen). The British evacuated approximately seven thousand subjects, mostly Maltese. The French fleet withdrew. The British fleet remained. Reflecting the press reports of the day, the Barker account in the archives claimed that the British government negotiated an agreement with the European powers and the Ottoman sultan to intervene. On the contrary, the British avoided diplomacy.[31] The British fleet bombarded the harbour forts of Alexandria on 11 July. During the bombing, Henry Barker spent the night on a ship in Alexandria's harbour. After the bombardment, 'Urabi's forces withdrew, looting ensued, and the city was set aflame.

British forces landed to hold Alexandria, with the main force sailing to Port Said. In a curious but revealing note, the diaries record that the British government paid fully the Suez Canal tolls in the passage of the army through the Canal. The observance of international protocol was followed by the orderly disembarking of troops at Isma'iliyya, the canal port within striking distance of Cairo. After the defeat of 'Urabi's forces beyond Isma'iliyya at Tal al-Kabir, the Egyptian leader was captured and subsequently tried in an Egyptian court. He was defended by the British lawyer Alexander Meyrick Broadley, who was able to argue that there was no proof of 'Urabi's complicity in the massacre of Europeans or the torching of Alexandria. 'Urabi was exiled to the British colony of Ceylon.[32]

The memoirs record but offer no opinion on the course of events, although elements in the narrative reconstructed by Michael Barker reflect common aspects of imperial sentiment: terms like 'rebel' and 'massacre' negate the legitimacy of the national resistance; also a specifically imperialistic mentality is evident in the idea that European investments, such as the Canal, had international or supra-national status. It is hard to imagine Henry Barker opposing the British invasion, except perhaps during those nervous moments when the 'threat' of exile or annihilation hung in the air in June of 1882.

Foreign control over Egyptian state revenue was one result of the occupation, and the key economic restructuring was to disengage the banks from the business of financing the Egyptian government. In the future they concentrated instead on commerce.[33] Under British financial and administrative controls, European investors and the Egyptian landholding class profited with the liquidation of the royal estates – most of the new lands on the markets fell into the hands of the big rather than small Egyptian cultivators. Mortgage laws introduced through the 'mixed courts' (courts created in the 1870s to try cases involving Europeans and Egyptians) were only advantageous to those with property to use as security – that is to say, the Egyptian elites and the foreign investors. Underlining the larger political and strategic importance of Egypt to the British Empire, the new consul general, Lord Cromer, was well versed in the advantages of compliant, collaborating elites; also, and unique to the Egyptian locale, Cromer was unwilling to take on the vested interests of the various European communities protected by the Capitulations, particularly the French. The European colonies continued to use the Capitulations as a means to circumvent laws regulating business transactions, keep tariffs at a low 8 per cent, and block the introduction of even a rudimentary form of income tax. In 1901, the British in Egypt upheld the low tariffs in spite of the demands of a nascent Egyptian industrial lobby.[34] However, the British-led administration created economic growth that brought benefits to elite Egyptians in the years before the First World War, in spite of unanticipated problems, such as shortage of land to population and degradation of soil as a result of biennial and triennial cultivation. The links forged between the British and Egyptian economies through trade and finance were such that by the First World War Egypt was as much a part of the 'British area' as were Australia and Canada.[35] In short, the Capitulations enabled the institution of the defining features of a colonial economy: an 'open' or 'free' economy based on export commodities, dominated by foreigners, directed from the capitals of high finance, London and Paris, with minimal government restrictions on trade and commodity prices.[36]

The British colony entered its golden era. The Barker papers record the building of a new house in the Greek quarter at rue Abbasides where three generations of Barkers and their domestic staff were to live, including an Italian nanny and Cypriot cook. The latter lived with the family until 1956.[37] Henry Barker's eldest son, Henry (Harry) Barker (1872–1942), went to school in England and took over the family business in 1905. Henry's other son, Oswald, went to the Royal Naval College, Dartmouth, joined the Lancashire Fusiliers and died in the South African War of wounds sustained at the siege of Ladysmith; another son, Percy, died in Johannesburg in 1898.

As a sign of colonial permanence, the British Union Club was established shortly after a khedival decree of 1904 recognised Britain's special position in Egypt, which, according to the Barker papers, meant that Egypt fell just short of 'Protectorate' status. The period was also one of increasing national resistance to the British military occupation: a decree in 1906 reaffirmed Ottoman formal sovereignty over Egypt during negotiations between the British-run administration in Egypt and the Ottomans over the border in the Sinai (on the present line of the Egypt–Israel border, it meant territorial expansion, whilst negotiations with the Italians on the western frontier meant contraction). Nationalist support for the Ottoman cause in that dispute preceded the national protests of 1907. The memoirs refer to newspaper clippings that pointed to the 'failure' of the British to carry out their promise to establish a representative system of government in Egypt, as declared in the Dufferin Report of 1883. The nationalists described the employment of British officials as administrators, rather than strictly advisers, as 'illegal'. In the same year Henry Barker was honoured with a state funeral that included a representative of the khedive, the governor of Alexandria, the commandant of police, officers of the Egyptian police force (twelve mounted police and fifty on foot), and representatives of the banks, consular corps, and other notables from Alexandria. The family narrative thus underlined the quasi-official status and imperial pedigree of Henry Barker and sons.[38]

Henry Barker oversaw the founding of the British Chamber of Commerce in 1896; its membership included Percy Carver, Robert Moss, W. Peel, G.B. Alderson, and A.A. Ralli, collectively representing the British commercial elite of Alexandria. The chamber connected manufacturers in Britain with reliable commercial houses in Egypt through confidential credit ratings. In its meetings the chamber discussed municipal supervision of transport facilities, weights and measures, international mail, government tenders, and bankruptcy laws. One of the chamber's first concerns in 1897 was a discussion of the 'exclusion of English language from the Mixed Courts'.[39] The judges in the mixed courts were from any of the European nations under the Capitulations, but the language of the courts was French. Egypt's modern culture was heavily influenced by France. Although elements in the French colony and in metropolitan France supported Egyptian nationalists in the period before the First World War, they did so largely to check British influence. The French, however, clung to the Capitulations as the basis of their 'rights' in Egypt and thus blocked any attempt at their reform. That principle was enshrined in the 1904 Anglo-French *entente* by which France finally acknowledged the British military base in Egypt, but the *entente* also involved an undertaking by Britain not to undermine French customary powers and practices as enabled by the Capitulations. In his Annual Report of 1904, Lord Cromer reported that the mixed courts and the Capitulations were problematic because they imposed an effective veto on any legislation proposed by the Egyptian government with British advice.[40] Cromer proposed a reform that would appease the French and other Europeans, without limiting the powers of the Egyptian government: the creation of a legislature that had representation in it of the foreign European powers and thus instituting an international political community. According to Cromer, Egyptians could not be trusted to safeguard foreign interests, nor conduct responsible self-government without British supervision. That doctrine did not dissipate with nationalist protests or Cromer's resignation, nor the establishment of the Protectorate in 1914; thus, a Commission of Reform established during the war (March 1917) and led by the British judicial adviser, William Brunyate, considered a new administrative system modelled on Cromer's 1904 proposals, which had the support of the new high commissioner of the Protectorate, Sir Arthur Henry McMahon. Given the revolutionary outburst in 1919 and the subsequent unilateral declaration of Egyptian independence in 1922, these proposals suggest an illusion of colonial permanence characteristic of the pre-war era.

The impact of nationalism

After 1922 the British official community – that is, the profile of British personnel employed in the diplomatic service and the Egyptian government – was significantly reduced to placate the nationalists. The British colony reverted to something nearer its pre-1882 state. The commercial community and its representative institutions, the Chamber of Commerce and the British Union, were forced to rely on the power of wealth and influence, without the ready ear of British advisers directing the Egyptian government. A critical issue in this period was the future status of the foreign colonies, as defined by the Capitulations. These continued to sustain an autonomous colonial lobby that effectively divided legislative authority between the Egyptian parliament, representing 14 million Egyptians, and the assembly of judges on the mixed courts, who represented two hundred thousand Europeans. As the press clippings in the family archives document, the assembly of European judges invariably construed Egyptian legislation as somehow affecting its jurisdiction.[41] The Capitulations also enabled a colonial economy built on the export of agricultural commodities, mostly cotton, to British markets and therefore symbolised the ruin of Egyptian manufacturing by keeping tariffs down until the 1930s.[42] The manufacturing sector of the Egyptian economy suffered, as did the majority of impoverished Egyptians who served as agricultural labourers on the great estates. Therefore, in treaty negotiations after the First World War, foreign privileges and the concessions afforded by the Capitulations were chips on the bargaining table in negotiations with nationalists. The British government was mostly interested in Egypt as a strategic asset, thus British government policy and the interests of the British business colony in Alexandria diverged after 1918.

High commissioner between 1919 and 1925, Field Marshal Edmund Allenby, discussed the abolition of the Capitulations with leaders of the commercial community. According to Mabel Caillard, 'One leading merchant, who had been called in consultation on the subject with the High Commissioner, informed me that he had unhesitatingly given his vote in favour of their abolition.'[43] Opinion was divided. Harry Barker argued that abolition had to be attenuated with provisions that safeguarded the residency rights of the British colony in Egypt. In speeches given throughout the 1920s and 1930s, many of them at the Chamber of Commerce, Harry Barker argued that the Capitulations had created a British colony that included not only officials, soldiers, and a merchant elite, but also, as he said, grocers, butchers, bakers, cabinet makers, builders, plumbers, and clerks.[44]

As national lines hardened, Barker made the case that the colonial was not a privileged sector, but an integral part of Egyptian society. In a 1929 speech attended by High Commissioner Lord Lloyd, Harry Barker argued that the British colony was beneficial to the Egyptians. As he said, among 200 million Egyptian pounds worth of stocks quoted on the Egyptian Bourse, 90 per cent was owned by foreigners; however, property in towns and cities was evenly divided between Egyptian nationals and foreigners. In a key point, Barker said that rural property, valued at 600 million Egyptian pounds, was 90 per cent held by Egyptians.[45] The figures thus countered the popular idea of a gross monopoly of wealth by the colonial communities. Moreover, he said that the tax burden on foreigners was comparable to direct taxation on Egyptians because direct taxation was lower per capita than indirect taxation (almost half that of indirect). Indirect taxes on business activity were mostly absorbed by foreigners. He also said that foreign colonies did not enjoy the same state benefits as did Egyptian nationals, having to sustain private schools and hospitals for the respective foreign communities.[46] The archives also contain nationalist critiques of Barker's speeches, which argued that elites monopolised most of the wealth to the exclusion of the majority. It was this inequity that nationalists protested. Supporting the nationalist argument, indicators showed child mortality in an elite Alexandria suburb like Muharram Bey was low; whereas in a working-class neighbourhood like Labban, predominantly Egyptian, the figures were nearly ten times higher. However, academic studies have shown that in some lower- to middle-class neighbourhoods the population was more or less evenly divided between locals and foreigners, 'indigènes' and 'étrangers', as in the districts of Karmus, Manshiyya, or Attarin, where the child mortality indicators were not skewed along colonial or national fissures, but only those of wealth.[47] Barker's arguments were not simply an apology for colonialism, but spoke of the complications of the Levantine category to which many British belonged.

As the British government moved closer to a treaty that would abrogate the Capitulations, Barker's arguments were less economic, more social, and concerned the category of 'British' inclusive of the lower-class British, mostly Maltese.[48] As it turned out, the appointment of Sir Miles Lampson in 1934 ended the stalemate in treaty negotiations and spelt the end of the de facto constitutional 'rights' or privileges of the European colonies. The Anglo-Egyptian Treaty of 1936, negotiated by Lampson and Anthony Eden with the Egyptian government of Mustafa al-Nahhas Pasha, bargained away the Capitulations in exchange for

Britain's continued strategic control of the eastern Mediterranean from military bases in Egypt. The treaty gave the Egyptian government full autonomy on internal matters and therefore free to define the terms of Egyptian nationality, foreign residence, and business regulations.[49] The treaty set guidelines for a subsequent convention on the Capitulations, completed in 1937 at Montreux, with the effect that after 1937 the British colonial community was stripped of its special status: consular courts and mixed courts were shut in 1946 and 1948 respectively.[50] The treaty opened up complex questions on nationality and colonial legal status, something apparent from the first discussions on the termination of the Capitulations by Lord Cromer. The issue was made more pressing during the First World War when a regulation of 1915 required all British nationals travelling outside the United Kingdom to be in possession of a valid passport. At that time, Victor Naggiar, president of the British Chamber of Commerce in Egypt, acted to preserve the British status of the colony in Egypt by initiating an amendment to the British Nationality and Status of Aliens Act of 1914. The amendment was designed to ensure British citizenship to those born to British fathers 'out of His Majesty's Dominions'.[51]

The crystallising of British national identification mirrored the Egyptian. Therefore, when extra-territorial status offered by the Capitulations was erased in 1937, prominent members of the British merchant community campaigned for official recognition of the British citizenship status of residents in Egypt previously defined as such only by recognition under the Capitulations. One interpretation of this campaign is that it was another example of British exclusivity or fear of immersion in the Egyptian nation.[52] Yet, the primary objective was not to assert 'Britishness' against the 'natives', but to establish the rights of long-term residents in Egypt, who otherwise would be rendered stateless. In 1939 a test case was initiated by Harry Barker. He sought a judgement on whether the application of the British Nationality and Status of Aliens Act of 1914 negated citizenship rights for those born in an extra-territorial jurisdiction as defined by the Capitulations. He took his own genealogy as a test case. The evidence showed that Henry (Harry) Barker was born in Egypt in 1872, his father born in Santa Maura, Ionian Islands, 1829, his grandfather in 1784, at Smyrna (Izmir), and great-grandfather in Derbyshire, England, 1738. All of the Barkers born out of Britain had regularly registered as British subjects at consulates across the Mediterranean. The case resulted in a ruling of the consular court in 1940 that recognised expatriate Britons like Harry Barker as British citizens because such births had taken place in countries subject to the Capitulations and therefore the parents had been subject to British sovereignty. The ruling was an important act of inclusion: the sizeable

Maltese population, as well as Jewish and Christian Levantine British subjects, had their British citizenship status affirmed.[53]

As an example, members of the Harari family had identified themselves as British subjects in Egypt and Syria for generations; a consular investigation into their status after the First World War cited a report from 1893 that had concluded that many Jewish residents of Damascus had gained British status illegally. Therefore, that report had argued for the rejection of the claims of the Hararis. Records showed that Abdou Soliman Harari was of Indian origin, born in Aleppo, and registered as a British subject in Damascus in 1855; his son Yusuf was born in Venice and had registered as a British subject in Cairo and Damascus. When the 1893 ruling was made the Hararis ignored it and registered at the British consulate in Izmir before embarking for Egypt. Their citizenship claims were recognised in 1929 after British consular officials argued that the family had for generations lived under the protection of the British Crown and therefore should continue to be regarded as such. The Hariri case had the support of the Council of the British Community in Alexandria, its leadership practically synonymous with the British Chamber of Commerce. The position of the Council between 1924 and 1929 was that the 'character, status, and interests of the British community of Alexandria' should be preserved.[54] Given the implications of rulings during the First World War, the 1920s, and the Barker case of 1939–40, it is safe to say that the self-perception of the British merchant community was 'Levantine', one inclusive of diverse groups, not exclusively 'British' in any racial, ethnic, or cultural sense of the word. Indeed, many British colonials were practically invisible to occasional visitors, tourists, and those in transit through Egypt, who were the source of many of the conventional descriptions of the British colony. This marginal majority was sometimes described in Foreign Office reports as 'out-land' British, a category inclusive of Jewish and Christian Levantines, Cypriots, and Maltese. These out-lander British were integral to the British colony. Their formal inclusion was the work of community leaders like Harry Barker. The history of the British community in Egypt after the abolition of the Capitulations involved a kind of rearguard action to protect what remained of the colony in a diminished colonial space.

Take, for example, the Smouha family. During and after the First World War Joseph Smouha was the managing director of the Mashal Brothers Company of Manchester. Exporting cotton piece goods across the Middle East, the firm had agents in Basra and Baghdad, which connected to Bedouin as well as Persian representatives further afield. The company's regional headquarters were in Alexandria and Cairo. Alongside the export of Manchester fabrics, Smouha's agents were involved in money trading and the resale of Middle Eastern luxury commodities such as Persian carpets, as well as the export of cotton, onions, and other agricultural goods to Europe.[55] After the 1956 Suez War and the forced expulsion of British nationals, the British government negotiated the 1959 Anglo-Egyptian Agreement for compensation of lost property. The Smouha family made the largest single claim, amounting to 12.5 million Great Britain (GB) pounds within a final total claim of the collective British community of 94 million GB pounds. Most of the actual payments made by the British government were scaled down to about 20 per cent of compensation value, as determined by the compensation commission. Thus, although officially valued at 3.1 million GB pounds, the Smouha family received only 1 million pounds in compensation payments.[56] The figures suggest that the Smouhas were one of the leading British commercial families in Egypt, although otherwise invisible in standard accounts.

One of the last, but not the only, service the Barkers made to the British colony of Egypt was to lead the lobbying efforts for the compensation package after 1956, acting as representatives for the entirety of the British colony in Egypt to the British government, but particularly for those without fluency in English. Again, the campaign was a combination of self-interest or colonial solidarity, but also one that required a broad and inclusive definition of the 'British'. Indeed, this process of return and repatriation was a largely untold part of the making of a multicultural Britain. The post-colony narrative is poignant in its sense of abandonment and exile – exile in the homeland – and the search for compensation, consolation, and recognition. And it is on this note that the memoirs diverge from the dominant imperial narrative, although the wounded tone of these last pages was one probably shared by many more 'British' than ever before.

After empire

Harry Barker was the only Barker to have been born and died in Egypt. He was a leader of the British business community and appeared to have managed a critical period of change until the Second World War broke out. Whereas the rhetoric of economic nationalism spoke of breaking the links with British finance and markets, Egypt remained dependent upon both in the 1930s and into the 1940s. Bank Misr was founded as a specifically Egyptian (*misr* means Egypt) bank and created subsidiary textile factories to compete with British and Japanese imports; however, one of the more important of these subsidiaries allied with a British textile firm.[57] British businesses adapted even after Egyptian cotton manufacturers succeeded in raising tariff barriers and nationalist governments imposed restrictions on foreign capital investment, as well as new rules on hiring practices. Textile factories and other concerns like construction that primarily involved manual labour had to employ a 90 per cent Egyptian workforce. The personnel of British firms, large and small, had to be 75 per cent Egyptian.[58] Yet, British businesspeople were on the boards of Egyptian companies through the 1940s.[59] British business leaders collaborated with Tal'at Harb, renowned as the founder of Egyptian economic nationalism, in the formation of the Misr Insurance Company. Likewise, Tal'at Harb collaborated with British partners in the founding of Misr Airways, Misr Shipping, and Bank Misr.

The 1936 Anglo-Egyptian Treaty certainly reduced the scope of British business.[60] But the Second World War was the major rupture. Egyptian industry was redirected towards domestic production during the war, with the British army the major consumer of Egyptian goods.[61] The result was to give an economic impetus towards nationalisation of industry, invigorating economic nationalism. Wartime industry sped up rural to urban migration, a factor that increased the size of the Egyptian working class and led to political unrest. The war also exhausted the British community in multiple ways. It certainly took a toll on the Barkers. Harry Barker was the Egyptian representative to the British minister of war transport and took charge of commandeering ships for the Allied war effort. The Barker business warehouses and offices at Shouna Briggs were destroyed in the first German air raid. Overall, trade was disrupted, and investments threatened by market uncertainty. Run down by the worry and strain, Harry Barker died in July 1942.

However, the Barkers, as well as other British colonials, not only held out during the war, but refused to budge until forced out in 1956. All the indicators suggested deteriorating conditions for trade and finance: the price of cotton and land depreciated from the early twentieth century, precipitously from 1929; the 'open' economy that had enabled business dealings from the era of Muhammad 'Ali was dismantled after 1936; trade and infrastructure development was disrupted or destroyed in the war. Yet, the Barkers seemed to be adapting to post-war conditions, as evident in the stories of the last patriarchs of the Barker dynasty in Egypt, Harry Barker's son Alwyn (1898–1966) and grandson Michael (1923–99). Alwyn's career felt the full impact of nationalism: the revolt of 1919 and British gradual political disengagement after 1922; the 1936 Anglo-Egyptian Treaty; the Second World War and its crises; the violent nationalist outbursts from 1946; and the military coup of 1952 that brought down the monarchy. Throughout, Alwyn showed a marked reluctance to be unnerved. His attachment to Egypt was apparently more cultural or social than economic: he had a very strong sense of being 'deeply rooted'.[62]

Henry Alwyn Barker was brought up by an Italian nanny until sent to boarding school in England at eight years of age. He attended Sandhurst Royal Military College and was injured at Ypres during the First World War. He married Ida Sybil, daughter of Henry Alfred Cumberbatch (another Levantine dynasty), in 1921. Ida was born in Angora, Turkey, 1895, her father the British consul general at that time, which suggests that the custom of interlocking Levantine families persisted. After his marriage, Alwyn joined the family firm. Leisure and social pursuits documented in the archive of family photos are of golfing, tennis, sailing, riding, races, polo, days at the beach, charity work, theatrical and musical entertainments, with a social circle including familiar names: Carver, Haselden, Peel, and Finney. One photograph is of an engagement at the British Benevolent Fund in 1939, attended by the ambassador, Sir Miles Lampson, and the Admiral of the British Fleet, Sir Dudley Pound, as well as the leading lights of the colony, such as the Sir Edward Peel and Mrs Oswald Finney.[63] Like Sir Henry Barker previously, Alwyn's generation had sterling political and commercial connections. During the Second World War, Alwyn was in uniform at the rank of first lieutenant; he and Harold Finney temporarily took up command at the Mustafa Barracks in Alexandria; he was also responsible for prisoners of war. After the war, he re-entered the familiar round of engagements, while the size of the British colony shrank as British troops were withdrawn from Cairo and Alexandria to the Canal Zone. But most telling was Alwyn's attitude towards investment and divestment in Egypt.

During the war the British paid for Egyptian resources and services with promissory notes, in effect IOUs to the Egyptian treasury. The debts to Egypt, known after the war as 'sterling balances', amounted to 425 million GB pounds. In 1947, Egypt left the sterling area. However, the British government blocked the Egyptian government from any wholesale conversion of their balances, allowing only limited annual withdrawals. The sense of a rupture in British–Egyptian financial relations led to a flight of capital from Egypt: the value of the Barker family's holdings on the Egyptian stock market was reduced to a quarter of their previous value between 1947 and 1956.[64] Yet Alwyn had moved much of his UK financial holdings to Egypt and delayed the decision to repatriate his capital as the situation worsened. Egyptian currency holdings could still be transferred to the UK before the Egyptian balances were exhausted (estimated 1957). Alwyn made the decision in 1956, but too late to avoid the 'disaster'. That delay, inexplicable in hindsight, meant penury for the Barkers after 1956. All property held by Britons in Egypt was sequestered by the Egyptian government as a consequence of the Suez War of 1956. Only the compensation funds drawn from the sterling balances provided some redress for former British property owners when these began to be paid out between 1960 and 1966. Also, the British and Egyptian governments worked out agreements for the de-sequestration of property in Egypt belonging to British nationals by the early 1970s. Most of these properties, like the family residences at rue Abbasides and rue Fendrel, were sold to the Egyptian government at a huge discount.

A glimpse of the final years of the Barker family in Egypt can be had in the Michael Barker file of the Barker family archives. Born in 1923, Michael was sent to boarding school in England at age eight, including Eton, and was commissioned in the Rifle Brigade in 1942, trained in Egypt and served with the 8th Army in Italy and Austria. As family legend recounts, he carried silk pyjamas and umbrella throughout the gruelling campaign from Cassino to the Gothic Line in northern Italy. Michael married Shelagh Moore in 1946, the same year he joined the family firm. At that time, the family business was mostly shipping for Ellerman's Shipping Line and Rotterdam & Lloyd's Line, carrying cargos of cotton, onion, grapes, rice, and rags. He cooperated closely with ship's captains, senior officers, port authorities, stevedores and ship's chandlers. Michael and Shelagh resided in the Alexandria suburb of Rushdi in a pillared villa with a large garden at rue Fendrel. The shift to the suburb suggests changing circumstances. As was customary, a beach house was rented in the summers at Sidi Bishr, but within a couple of years Sidi Bishir was abandoned for a gated resort at Muntaza. The house at rue Fendrel had two acres of property with the servant quarters at the bottom of the garden; there were five indoor servants, three gardeners, a Bedouin ghaffir (watchman), a chauffeur, and two nannies. There were two floors, with the ground floor designed for entertaining, upstairs a master suite with a walk-in closet that served as the gun room. Evenings included cocktail parties, cinema, dinners, visits to nightclubs ('Romance' to hear Edith Piaf sing 'La Vie en Rose'), opera, charity balls, and a regular Sunday gramophone soirée after the duck shoot, usually held at the villa of Comte Patrice de Zogheb.[65]

In spite of the comforts, life in Alexandria in the decade before the 'disaster' of 1956 was uneasy. The memoirs show that in March 1948, during a police strike that marked national protests against the British, Alwyn and Michael were shot at while leaving their offices. They ran for their cars. On that day a foreign consular official was shot dead on his porch. The leader of the Muslim Brotherhood, Hasan al-Banna, was killed, 'probably by the political police', on 13 February 1949. Like a signal of imperial decay, Donald Maclean was head of the Chancery at the Cairo Embassy, prone to drunkenness and violence; he later absconded to the Soviet Union with Guy Burgess. In August of 1951 treaty negotiations between the British government and the government of Mustafa al-Nahhas, leader of the Wafd Party, broke down. At the same time dinner parties brought the Barkers and other members of Alexandria's commercial elite together with Egyptian landholding notables, Egyptian political figures, and diplomatic staff from the foreign embassies, including the Americans. While the burning of colonial Cairo on 26 January 1952 took the British colony by surprise (on that day Michael had a drinks party for twenty at his residence at rue Fendrel), rumours of the coming coup were rife in the weeks before 23 July 1952. Still, the government and the monarchy were immobile. After the coup, Michael's residence served as headquarters for the American ambassador, Jefferson Caffery, and was the scene of much international activity. Michael was in Britain by early August, but returned to Cairo by BOAC Comet from Heathrow via Rome. His grandmother, Lena, died in her residence at rue Abbasides in January 1953. The house was emptied but not sold because the market for real estate was flat. In June 1953, the leaders of the 1952 coup, the 'Free Officers', held a luncheon at Antoniades Gardens in Alexandria for leading members of the foreign communities. Attending were Jamal 'Abd al-Nasir, Anwar al-Sadat, Husni Mubarak, and Saleh Salem; Michael spoke to several, indicating a willingness to work with the new government. Meanwhile, Michael organised a dance at his residence at Fendrel and went to the Cairo sale of King Faruq's collection – he bought a gold snuff box (lost in a burglary in London years later). These anecdotes suggest that the Barkers were confident that their place in Egypt was secure, and were adapting to the new republican regime and the ascendancy of the Americans.

At the same time the memoir indicates a dwindling of British life in Alexandria. The character of the colony changed. It was composed of expatriates with short-term contracts in the various public/private services or professions. Many long-term British residents began to divest and depart. An Old Etonian dinner at the British Union in 1955 could only muster some thirty officers. There were few civilians because most families had already taken up residence in the Canal Zone. In January 1956 British troops evacuated the Canal Zone.[66]

The tripartite (British-French-Israeli) invasion of October 1956 was left to pass in silence in the memoir files collated by Michael. Only its consequences were discussed, and his terms of reference were decidedly critical of the British government, not the Egyptian. As the memoirs record, as a war measure British residents of Egypt were confined to house arrest and some few were immediately expelled, all property sequestered. Alwyn and Michael Barker were treated well by Egyptian authorities, as each had a long history of good relations with Egyptian officials and friends. There was a sentimental concern for their Egyptian staff. Charles de Zogheb helped Michael and Alwyn raise money to pay off their domestic staff, many of whom had served the family for generations, by the sale of personal property, such as jewellery and alcohol. Finally the family received a letter from the Ministry of the Interior, addressed to Henry Alwyn Barker, advising members of the family 'to leave the country as soon as possible'. Michael and Alwyn waited for the final notice, delivered as a note to appear at the offices of the Governorate of Alexandria, where a policeman said, 'I am sorry but you have to go to the Passport Office to get your exit visa.' The visa read, 'Never to Return'. They purchased first-class tickets but were allowed to take only 5 Egyptian pounds out of the country.[67]

After resettlement in London, where he lived for a while at his club, Michael began to lobby the British government to award immediate funds for those exiles without any resources. The British government paid out loans in 1957 and 1958 against possible future compensation, but only up to a maximum of 10,000 GB pounds per person. In October 1956 the Egyptian sterling balances were at 77.5 million and the memoirs suggest that the British government netted a profit after its compensation scheme to British colonials and repayment to the Egyptians.[68] The 1959 Anglo-Egyptian Agreement covered the financial claims of both countries, a compensation order, and also involved resumption of diplomatic relations. This meant that Alwyn Barker could return to Egypt, as he did in 1959. However, Barker & Company was liquidated in 1962 after another round of state nationalisation of businesses, foreign and domestic. One of the two family residences, the house at Fendrel, was desequestered, but it had been a turned into a state-controlled rental property at 50 Egyptian pounds per month. The leaseholder was a supply department of the army. The property was valueless on the market. In 1959 the dockyard properties, Shounah Briggs, were purchased compulsorily by the Egyptian government and later turned into a school. Alwyn died in 1966.[69]

Michael found work with a shipping company in London and took out a mortgage on a house. His social life revolved around 'Old Egyptians' – expatriates like himself.[70] Final compensation payments were made in 1971. This coincided with a change in Egyptian economic policy, from Nasir's nationalisation to Sadat's 'opening up' or *infitah*. An

Egyptian law in 1971 created 'free zones' where commerce was not subject to state regulations and there were tax exemptions for foreign companies, as well as protections under international law from arbitrary expropriation or nationalisation. In other words, there was something like a restoration of the sort of provisions originally found in the Capitulations.[71] There was also official encouragement to the Egyptian courts to enable, with favourable rulings, the restoration of properties sequestered in the 1950s and 1960s.[72] The Barker residence at rue Abbasides, built by Henry Barker for his wife, Alice, who then gave the property to her daughter-in-law, Lena, had been sequestered in 1956 and used as a police headquarters. Michael Barker sold the property to the Alexandria Governorate in 1974 for 20,000 Egyptian pounds. The Union Club closed in 1968; the boat club in 1970. All that was left was the family tomb in the Protestant Cemetery at Chatby, Alexandria, maintained by the British consulate.[73]

The colony had an afterlife. One of its manifestations is the Alexandria Schools or Victoria Trust, created with the compensation settlement. True to its Levantine roots, the Barker family promoted the idea to enable English instruction in schools across the eastern Mediterranean. The schools also evoked the memory of the family's part in founding Victoria College, Alexandria, which had been expropriated and turned into an Egyptian state school after 1956. The family legacy lives also in the memoirs, a series of files under the headings of prominent members of the family, deposited at the archives of Exeter University; and there is a visual shrine at the website levantineheritage.com. The memoirs, particularly Michael's reflections on the ending of the colony, suggest that members of the family were protagonists in the dialogue between the local and the imperial state, East and West, in so far as the family suggested a level of cultural and social engagement with the Egyptian locale lacking in the British government at critical junctures. Alwyn and Michael's insistence on remaining in Egypt against the odds suggests that sentiment, rather than status, wealth, and power, was the primary motivation. All was invested in Egypt, all was lost. The last remnant of the Barker family in Egypt is the tomb in Alexandria, where Michael Barker's remains were 'repatriated' and put to rest after his death in 1999. The family ensured the up-keep and preservation of the family tomb by regular correspondence with the British consulate in Alexandria, necessary because it was a target for tomb raiders dealing in marble. Overall, the family's insistence on remembering, not forgetting its Levantine roots, acts as a claim to the past, which would have been erased except for those who remember – like a claim to a right of ownership, otherwise withheld.

CAPITULATIONS

Notes

1 James Harry Scott, 'The Capitulations', in Arnold Wright and H.A. Cartwright (eds), *Twentieth Century Impressions of Egypt: Its History, People, Commerce, Industries, and Resources* (London: Lloyd's Greater Britain Publishing Company, 1909), p. 110.
2 Alfred C. Wood, *A History of the Levant Company* (Oxford: Oxford University Press, 1935).
3 James Mather, *Pashas: Traders and Travellers in the Islamic World* (New Haven: Yale University Press, 2009).
4 Barbara W. Tuchman, *Bible and Sword: England and Palestine from the Bronze Age to Balfour* (New York: Random House, 1984), pp. 97–8.
5 Earl of Cromer, *Modern Egypt* (London: Macmillan, 1908), vol. 2, pp. 246–7, fn. 1.
6 Mather, *Pashas*, p. 95.
7 Donald Quartaret, 'The Age of Reforms', in Halil Inalcik (ed.), *An Economic History of the Ottoman Empire* (Cambridge: Cambridge University Press, 1994), vol. 2, p. 838.
8 Robert Irwin, *For Lust of Knowing: The Orientalists and their Enemies* (London: Penguin, 2007), p. 112.
9 Robert Ilbert, *Alexandrie 1830–1930: Histoire d'une communauté citadine* (Cairo: Institut Français d'Archéologie Orientale, 1996), 2 vols, vol. 1, pp. 75–81.
10 Roger Owen, *The Middle East in the World Economy* (London: Methuen, 1981), pp. 89–91.
11 Ibid., p. 61.
12 The Ottoman government attempted to raise duties paid by British merchants in the negotiations over the Anglo-Turkish Commercial Convention of 1820; the British strongly objected. Only tariffs on imports were raised from 3 to 5 per cent ad valorem in 1837.
13 Philip Mansel, *Levant: Splendour and Catastrophe on the Mediterranean* (London: John Murray, 2010), pp. 2–3.
14 Michael Reimer, *Colonial Bridgehead: Government and Society in Alexandria 1807–1882* (Cairo: American University in Cairo Press, 1997), p. 87.
15 David Lambert and Alan Lester, *Colonial Lives across the British Empire: Imperial Careering in the Long Nineteenth Century* (Cambridge: Cambridge University Press, 2006), pp. 5–13.
16 Maya Jasanoff, *Edge of Empire: Conquest and Collecting in the East 1750–1850* (London: Harper Perennial, 2006), pp. 234–43.
17 Exeter University Special Collections (EUSC), Barker Family Collection, MS 238 Box 1, Folder 1 (hereafter, EUSC MS 238 1/1), File F, 'Henry Barker'.
18 Ilbert, *Alexandrie 1830–1930*.
19 EUSC MS 238 1/1/E, 'Edward Barker'; as consul in Cairo, Edward's official correspondence was in Italian.
20 EUSC MS 238 1/1/F, 'Henry Barker'; the Sydney Barker line of the family moved to Corfu, but one member returned to Alexandria and worked in the Egyptian Customs Administration.
21 Will Hanley, 'Foreignness and Localness in Alexandria, 1880–1914' (PhD dissertation, Princeton University Press, 2007), p. 137.
22 EUSC MS 238 1/1/F, 'Henry Barker', document '1882 Britain and Egypt, The Reluctant Occupation'.
23 David F. Landes, *Bankers and Pashas: International Finance and Economic Imperialism in Egypt* (Cambridge, MA: Harvard University Press, 1958), p. 309.
24 Ibid., pp. 16–28.
25 Ibid., p. 117.
26 Ibid., pp. 160 & 255–6.
27 Ibid., p. 285, n. 1.
28 EUSC MS 238 1/1/A.
29 Owen, *World Economy*, p. 134.

EGYPT

30 Wilfrid Scawen Blunt, *Secret History of the English Occupation of Egypt: Being a Personal Narrative of Events* (New York: Alfred Knopf, 1922, originally published 1907), pp. 224 & 244.
31 A.P. Thornton, *The Imperial Idea and its Enemies: A Study in British Power* (London: Macmillan, 2nd edn, 1985), p. 57 & Michael D. Berdine, *The Accidental Tourist, Wilfrid Scawen Blunt, and the British Invasion of Egypt in 1882* (London: Routledge, 2005), pp. 192–3 & Elizabeth Longford, *A Pilgrimage of Passion: The Life of Wilfrid Scawen Blunt* (London: I.B. Tauris, 2007), p. 184.
32 EUSC MS 238 1/1/F, 'Henry Barker'.
33 Landes, *Bankers and Pashas*, pp. 305–6 & Owen, *World Economy*, p. 235.
34 Owen, *World Economy*, pp. 225 & 239.
35 Roger Owen and Şevket Pamuk, *A History of Middle East Economics in the Twentieth Century* (Cambridge, MA: Harvard University Press, 1999), p. 4.
36 Ibid., p. 33.
37 EUSC MS 238 1/1/G, 'Henry (Harry) Barker'.
38 EUSC MS 238 1/1/F.
39 Wright and Cartwright, *Twentieth Century*, pp. 324–5.
40 Cromer, *Modern Egypt*, vol. 2, pp. 316–20.
41 TNA FO371/18011, Egypt Annual Report, 1933, Yencken to Simon, 12 Feb. 1934.
42 Owen, *World Economy*, p. 239.
43 Mabel Caillard, *A Lifetime in Egypt, 1876–1935* (London: G. Richards, 1935), p. 254.
44 EUSC MS238, 1/1/G.
45 EUSC MS238, 1/1/G & Owen, *World Economy*, pp. 237–8.
46 EUSC MS238, 1/1/G.
47 Ilbert, *Alexandrie*, vol. 2, pp. 790 & 799. The figures are from government surveys from the year 1920.
48 EUSC MS 238 1/1/G.
49 TNA FO141/660/349/17, 3 Feb. 1937.
50 TNA FO141/753/8940.
51 TNA FO141/7838, Curzon, 28 July 1921 & Wright and Cartwright, *Twentieth Century*, p. 327 & Hanley, 'Foreignness', pp. 233–6 & 249–53, discusses the transformation of identification as a foreigner or local from social status towards various forms of legal registration as Egyptian or foreign nationals, in the period from the 1890s to the First World War. The British process was similar and simultaneous with the Egyptian and French registrations of legal status.
52 Mansel, *Levant*, pp. 254–5.
53 EUSC MS 238 1/1/G & EU MS 238 1/3 *Egyptian Gazette* (4 May 1940).
54 TNA FO141/813/10, 'Council of the British Community in Egypt'.
55 TNA FO841/172, dossier 81, 1918.
56 EUSC MS 238 1/2/J, p. 41.
57 Owen and Pamuk, *Middle East Economics*, p. 44.
58 TNA FO141/660/349/17, 3 Feb. 1937.
59 Obituary, Gerald Delany, *The Times* (15 June 1974), shows the persistence of British business personnel. The Barker archives show that alongside directing Barkers & Co., Harry Barker worked with partners to negotiate ventures in wireless telegraph, telephone, and radio broadcasting. He was on the board of Marconi Radio and Telegraph Company, the National Bank of Egypt, Alexandria Water Company, National Insurance Company, and Filature Nationale d'Egypte, which owned three textile factories. Barker also sat on the board of the Bourse Minet el Bassal (the cotton exchange) and those of the Egyptian Engineering Stores and the Alexandria Engineering Company: EUSC MS 238 1/1/G, 'Henry (Harry) Barker'.
60 TNA FO141/1398.
61 Owen and Pamuk, *Middle East Economics*, p. 44 & Robert Vitalis, *When Capitalists Collide: Business Conflict and the End of Empire in Egypt* (Los Angeles: University of California Press, 1995).
62 EUSC MS238 1/2/H, 'Alwyn Barker', p. 17.
63 'Barker Family Picture Archive', at http://levantineheritage.com/barker.htm.

CAPITULATIONS

64 EUSC MS 238 1/2/H. The figures are supported in approximate value by those quoted in Lawrence James, *Churchill and Empire: Portrait of an Imperialist* (London: Phoenix, 2014), p. 332.
65 EUSC MS 238 1/2/J, 'Michael Barker', the file is based on Michael's diary entries, as well as other material. See also Mansell, *Levant*, p. 287.
66 EUSC MS 238 1/2/J.
67 EUSC MS 238 1/2/H.
68 EUSC MS 238 1/2/H, p. 24.
69 EUSC MS 238 1/2/H.
70 EUSC MS 238 1/2/J.
71 Andrew Metcalf, 'Reshaping Egypt's Legal Landscape: The Growing Role of Arbitration in Egypt', Middle East Studies Association Annual Meeting, Rhode Island, 1996.
72 Owen and Pamuk, *Middle East Economics*, pp. 134–5.
73 EUSC MS 238 1/2/J & EUSC MS 238 1/3.

CHAPTER TWO

Civilising mission

The Egyptian expedition of 1882 was the last time that the British army marched to battle in redcoats. It was also, so it was said, the first time the British army demonstrated the kind of unblinking calculation to annihilate the enemy later recorded at Omdurman. Although not genocidal, the large-scale slaughter, including the killing of those in flight and the injured, was regarded as unprecedented, as was the cruelty and avenging manner in which the punishing blows were delivered.[1] Tactically, Major General Garnet Wolseley's strategy was to give the Egyptian army a decisive knock-out punch. The plan drawn up in London during the winter of 1882 was to make a rapid march on Cairo from the Suez Canal. The army consisted of thirty thousand British troops against thirteen thousand Egyptian troops (numbers given of fifty to sixty thousand indicate Egyptian levies or volunteer forces, which were untrained and fit only as a labour corps).[2] Ideologically and politically, the campaign involved a restoration of khedival authority. Egyptian governors, police, and officers in the military were in some cases supportive, or at least calculated the odds in favour of the khedive, and therefore abetted British forces. The British specifically declared their invasion to be in the name of the Egyptian ruler, Khedive Taufiq. Press reports described the Egyptian national leader, Ahmad 'Urabi, and his followers as 'rebels', whereas those supporting the Egyptian ruler were 'loyalists'.

In the winter of 1882 the British confronted the undying dilemma of Western governments interested in the region: whether to collaborate with despotic rule or its liberal opponents. Like many since, William Gladstone's Liberal government chose despotism. Official reports even celebrated that fact by representing the British Empire as trustee of an Arab and Islamic civilisation conceived of in a highly archaic form. This enraged sectors of liberal opinion in Britain, not to mention in Egypt. In 1883 Wilfrid Scawen Blunt described the events of the 'bloody year'

(1882) as 'a comedy to those who think, a tragedy to those who feel'.[3] The comedy was that the idea of Britain's 'civilising mission' had become justification for the repression of Egypt's liberty. The tragedy was that in 1882 Britain made a 'mockery of self-government' by using military force to restore an Egyptian regime that had been the object of liberal critiques over the previous half-century.[4] Blunt had spearheaded the opposition to the planned invasion of Egypt through his professional connections with Foreign Office personnel (he was trained in the diplomatic service) and leaders of British political society, including Prime Minister Gladstone. In papers, journals, and books he argued for an interventionist foreign policy on the side of the Egyptian nationalists, described by Blunt as liberals or constitutionalists, not the hereditary monarch. Support for the latter was, according to Blunt, no more than an unambiguous expression of British 'selfish interests', and thus the civilising rhetoric offered by Gladstone or Lord Dufferin was an absurd comedy.[5]

That a British Conservative like Blunt could represent himself as a defender of British liberalism and Egyptian liberty whilst calling for some form of British political intervention in Egypt tends to support the view of Edward Said that Western discourses of all types were manifestations of imperial power.[6] It does not support the view that all were racists or supremacists. Rather than racist, the civilising mission discourse in Bunt's hands identified the positive features of Egyptian culture against the negative: identifying with the fellahin and Islamic reformers against the tyranny of the khedivate. Other British commentators made similar cultural turns, defending women against patriarchy or Islam against its Christian critics. These themes appeared both in critical and sympathetic treatments of Egypt. An overtly negative representation of Egypt was penned by Harriet Martineau in 1848.[7] Martineau's narrative reflected the influence of racist ideas and a well-formed supremacist mentality: 'We do not agree with travellers who declare it necessary to treat these people with coldness and severity, – to repel and beat them. We treated them as children; and this answered perfectly well.'[8] On the adoption of Egyptian customs, Martineau advised 'any English woman' against any alteration of 'dress or ways'. She argued that it was impossible for an Englishwoman to resemble the 'Eastern woman' and that 'an unsupported assumption of any native custom will obtain her no respect'.[9] Florence Nightingale's *Letters from Egypt* (1854) reflected similar influences. She commented upon the 'animal' nature of Egyptians, who, she implied, had only marginally emerged from 'mud and clay'.[10] John Barrell has suggested the probable influence on her of Samuel Morton's *Crania Aegyptica*, published in 1844.[11] Upon arrival in Egypt on 19 November 1849 Nightingale described a 'crowd of Arabs' as 'an intermediate race, they appeared to me, between the monkey and the man, the ugliest, most slavish countenances'.[12] A more common sentiment expressed in her letters, however, is her critique of the government of Muhammad 'Ali, 'Civiliser of the East', whom she described as the despoiler of the fellahin. In a passage that likened Muhammad 'Ali to Percy Bysshe Shelley's 'Ozymandias' (Muhammad 'Ali had died six months before her visit), Nightingale asked: 'what is *human* greatness, when you look at this desolation of the finest country in the world?'[13] Nightingale's *Letters* situated her between the ruler and the Egyptian people and thereby marked out a colonial space that was highly political. This is a typical characteristic of memoir and letter writing from the 1820s through the 1870s (Blunt's *Secret History of the English Occupation of Egypt* was based in part upon journal entries from the 1870s).

In these works, the idea of British liberty is the essential signifier of difference between Britain and Egypt. To this degree the civilising discourse was designed to establish the superior qualities, the authority, of the British over the Egyptians. Eliga H. Gould has used the term 'legal geography' to refer to the complicated boundaries of British liberty, and to what degree its principles extended to the colonial world beyond British shores. Even British subjects in colonial locations were suspected of transgressions of British concepts of justice or norms of behaviour.[14] Indeed, for British travellers in Egypt the idea of the unique liberties of the British sat uncomfortably with other characteristics of the British in Egypt. Permanent or semi-permanent residence in Egypt meant that many British had to acquire status on local cultural grounds, had to adopt local habits, which created a paradox, not resolved, based on the compromises made by colonials on their principles (British liberty) to ensure power and status according to the customs of the pashas or the other hereditary lords of Egypt. In other words, the colonial had to wrestle with the old dilemma of the Levantine. These themes are evident in the writings of the first generation of British dwellers in Egypt, including John Gardner Wilkinson, Edward William Lane, Robert Hay, Henry Westcar, and James Burton, a relatively elite group of British travellers in a European colony composed mostly of French, Italians, and Maltese.[15] A generation later the colony had been transformed by large-scale tourism, the financial boom of the 1860s, and the fiscal bust of the 1870s; however, the complications of the colonial location persisted.

The first colonial generation

An exemplary colonial tale in 1827 told of a bandit in Upper Egypt by the name of Eissa (Jesus) recently captured by Muhammad 'Ali Pasha and subsequently executed and his head displayed on the city gates of Cairo. Eissa had for several years made a practice of robbing tax officials. In one case he and his band had taken on a whole troop of Egyptian soldiers carrying the tax payments of an entire district. The story was recorded by Robert Hay during an excursion in Upper Egypt undertaken with Edward William Lane.[16] Eissa's tale clearly struck a chord in Robert Hay's imagination as a metaphor for the condition of the common Egyptian in relation to the state – in this case Eissa as a kind of everyman's Robin Hood in relation to Muhammad 'Ali's rapacious state. The story was also emblematic of the relationship between Muslim and Christian and thus indicative of the precarious position of a Christian minority in Muslim society. Given the tenor of Hay's writing, it is probable that each of these narratives appealed to an imagination wherein the British in Egypt represented modern ideas of liberty infused with Christian thought (saviours of an oppressed people), while also holding up the enduring belief that the Egyptian landscape was a great ruin, social as well as material, under which there was a repressed, ancient civilisation linked to Christianity and the West through the Coptic faith.

This might well have been the case, yet the diaries record more pragmatic engagements with the Egyptian setting. Before setting out from Cairo, Hay and Lane were delayed for several days when a British fleet appeared at Alexandria harbour in response to Muhammad 'Ali's launching of Egyptian warships against the Greeks. The travellers retired to their boats on the Nile, lying low, clearly fearful of reprisals against Europeans as a consequence of the British blockade. It was not the last time an action of the imperial state threatened the security of the colony. Members of the colony were in a delicate situation, given that most of them were indebted to the good will of the pasha, Muhammad 'Ali, who was the source of travel permits and excavation rights arranged through the consul, Henry Salt. But Muhammad 'Ali's military expedition to Greece was regarded by the British government as dangerous. Moreover, public opinion in England, led by Lord Byron, championed Greek liberty against the 'Turk'. This complex relationship of British colony to the pasha and his servants was evident in the ensuing events when Hay and Lane advanced towards the ancient tomb at 'Toona el-Jebel' (or Tuna al-Jabal) in Mallawi province.[17] Their intention was to gather provisions, including horses, and make their way to the village where a work party of fellahin could be arranged. Hay noted in his diary that while donkeys were more comfortable and practical, they desired horses 'for the honour of the thing'.[18] Hay wrote at some length on 'Turkish' horsemanship, praising a kind of training that meant that horses responded to the slightest movement of rein or spur. The 'Turks' were admired and British travellers, like Lane and Hay, sought status on elite terms and so borrowed obvious symbols of 'Turkish' status, hence the desire to ride horses. The horses and provisions were collected at the riverside and the two proceeded to the village where they hoped to collect workers for excavations at the site. However, the Turkish sub-governor or 'cachief' (*kashif*) was in 'occupation' of the village in reprisal for a recent revolt against tax payments. As Robert Hay said, this involved exacting as much grain as could be 'squeezed out of this oppressed and enslaved race, the Fellaheen'.[19] As a result of these exactions, the travellers were unable to gather a work crew. They rode unaccompanied to the site, a tomb door in the mountainside marked with inscriptions but, as Burton had already informed them, empty of grave goods. The two cleared dirt away from the door to record the ancient writings. Hay was engaged in making drawings to record the site when the *kashif* and his retainers rode up on horseback. Addressing Lane, who knew Arabic, the *kashif* accused Hay of having just shut and covered up the door and asked why he had done this. Hay denied the accusation. The *kashif* accused Hay of being a liar. Hay recorded in his diary that he had missed this insult because he was distracted with his drawing, but that Lane had responded that such language was unacceptable. It contravened the respect due to 'Franks' (Europeans). The sense that the balance of power belonged to the *kashif* is apparent in the exchange, as was the competitive market for treasure. Running throughout is the implicit critique of a government that exploited its citizens and whose agents were little better than robber barons.

That appraisal of the Turkish elite was a constant theme in Hay's diaries, but, like other members of the colony, he was both client and ideological opponent to the Egyptian ruler. To resolve the dilemma, the cause of liberty was somewhat muted by the necessity to compromise and accommodate. On an excursion to Abu Simbel he arrived at Wadi Halfa and was met by the local *kashif*, who asked for baksheesh (a customary gratuity) in exchange for his organising a work party of as many as fifty Egyptians. Once assembled, the workers almost immediately staged a protest for higher pay and so Hay resorted to the *kashif*, who said that there was only one way to ensure obedience and respect, and with drawn sword threatened to have the head of the local shaykh or village head. Hay intervened and recorded that these were 'somewhat different proceedings' from what he was used to in his own country.[20]

While Hay had to accommodate himself to the manners of the Egyptian elite, his sense of cultural difference meant that he devoted considerable attention to documenting the conditions and cultural habits of the lower classes. He noted, for instance, that workers would at intervals drop their tools and, forming a circle, begin a song accompanied by the

'Gulla drum'. Some would attain a trance-like state and finally drop to the ground in a heap.[21] Hay also noted that a local saint inhabiting a shrine at Wadi Halfa sometimes went into recluse to live among the crocodiles. He observed domestic relations, such as the case of a woman complaining bitterly about the injustices of her husband, who had divorced her. She easily found a marriage partner with one of his crew.[22] On the river he sketched bathers – noting women's attractive faces and figures – and that exposing arms and legs whilst bathing carried none of the social impropriety it would have done in the street. Men watering horses nearby paid no attention to the women's nakedness – only he, as Hay observed, made a spectacle of himself by his desire to sketch.[23] These comments contrast with observations made at the outset of his journeys when travelling up the Mahmudiyya Canal from Alexandria towards Cairo, when he said that each and every village had the same 'miserable' aspect, hardly distinguishable from the heaps of delta 'mud' except for the minaret raising its head above all the rest.[24] In other words, Hay's voyage involved a working out of cultural difference, from repulsion to attraction.

Critical observers of travel literature have made much of the oft-repeated comparison of Egyptian villages with 'mud'.[25] Robert Hay's attitudes towards Egyptians were, however, not simply negation through broad cultural or racial categorisations, as indicated by his reflections on Egyptian social life. These characteristics were equally apparent in the narrative of one of Hay's contemporaries, Henry Westcar, who took a tour through the same country during 1823 and 1824. Like Hay, he observed that the 'Arabs' in relation to 'Turks' were 'little better than slaves'.[26] Westcar initially made the rounds of Alexandria, meeting the merchant and banker Samuel Briggs as well as Henry Salt. Alexandria was unremarkable, a typical Mediterranean Levantine port. The 'Frank' quarter consisted mostly of French, Italian, and Greeks, some dressed in Turkish costume. Indicating the fuzzy cultural boundaries, there was no appreciable difference between the Turkish and Frankish quarters of the town. There were slight cultural variations: Greek women wore black coverings, their faces exposed. Egyptian women's faces were mostly covered. Turkish women were unseen. The obligatory sites of the tour were already established: the obelisks or 'Cleopatra's Needles', 'Pompey's Pillar', ancient tombs and catacombs, 'Caesar's Camp' along the eastern shore, and the monument to Nelson's victory at Abu Qir (or Aboukir). From Alexandria, Westcar set out with an Egyptian crew and one British travelling companion, the artist Frederick Catherwood, whose illustrations of Karnak and Luxor would be exhibited in London in 1833. Entering the delta region by the Mahmudiyya Canal, Westcar recorded that the northern or left bank of the canal was littered with the ruins of ancient Alexandria, as if marking the limits of civilisation. His first impression of the ordinary Egyptians ('Arabs') evoked something like a Columbian encounter with the Amerindians. While walking along the bank of the canal, which ran from Alexandria to the Nile, the British men unexpectedly came upon an Egyptian woman. She screamed and ran. The startled village men came down to the river. After wary greetings, they asked for tobacco and offered sugar cane. Out of bread, the villagers 'offered us all they had'. Westcar reflected that it was a shame that 'Mohammedans' should 'go to the devil' because their prayers were conducted in the 'greatest fervour and the true spirit of religion'.[27] However, at one riverside stop he witnessed what he called an 'obscene dance'.[28] He likened it to a dance of the ancients, describing a male dancer throwing himself into distorted postures to the sound of the pipe, while all the rest of the company kept time with their hands. A circle of men tightened around the contorted dancer until another man threw himself into the ring. Westcar described their conduct in indecipherable cryptography. He concluded in the vernacular that such rituals seemed to give cause to the bad name the 'nations of the East' had attained in the West.[29] Here was an example of a clash of 'profoundly different ideas about the meaning and nature of sexual relations', with the foreigner consigning the culturally different to the category of the perverse.[30] Relations between crew and Westcar degraded thereafter, with conflicts over the butchering of a sheep (Westcar insisted upon butchering the animal contrary to Muslim regulations) and his keeping of a dog on board (flouting Muslim taboos). He described Egyptians dining as being like 'pigs at a trough'.[31] The Egyptian *rais* or captain of the boat was apparently equally disgusted, abandoning ship just outside Cairo. So Westcar approached the new man at the helm and 'clapped a brace of pistols to his head'. A Greek passenger assured the helmsman that 'the English always kept their words' and so the crew made way for Cairo. In this way Westcar's diary resembled a fantastic travel account with the 'English' holding a firm grip throughout. His astonishing experiences culminated at a Turkish bath in Cairo where, with only a towel to cover his nakedness, he was laid on a slab and cracked, scrubbed, put in a hot bath, removed to another chamber where he was shaved and soaped, and then splashed down in yet another marble chamber. Finally, he was restored to the first vestibule where he had been stripped. A boy appeared and pummelled him all over, rubbed down his feet with a pumice stone, and gave him a coffee and pipe. In a state of shock Westcar observed, 'The boy I believe thought me mad.' In a final note of bemused cultural exploration he wrote, 'I have never felt more pleasant or was better shaved in my life, but the operation did not much suit my taste.'[32]

There is a strong sense of the distinctive qualities of the 'Englishman' in Westcar's account. Indicative of his pugnacious attitude, he recorded that the firman (official writ) of the pasha established his right of passage whereas his firearms were the principal means throughout.[33] Indeed, violence was characteristic at many levels of Egyptian society. Shortly after setting off from Cairo for Upper Egypt, one of the crew on his boat was kidnapped by villagers, with, he said, the intention of selling the man to the 'pasha' for military service. In another instance, he witnessed 'Turks' on a government river boat beating the 'Arabs' on board. One jumped overboard and, upon reaching the shore, fled. He recorded many signs of the rapid development of the state economy, including sugar, indigo, tobacco, and cotton plantations, as well as sugar processing factories and professional merchants servicing the boats plying up and down the river. During the voyage Westcar made a habit of walking along the banks hunting pigeon. Terrified Egyptians picked up their robes and their tools and ran away at the sight of him: 'They are all wonderfully afraid of firearms.'[34] At first suspecting that fear was associated with the foreigner, Westcar soon came to understand it was terror of the Egyptian ruler and his men. 'At the time the Pasha was collecting men for the army throughout the country and every man they see with a gun they suspect came to press them.'[35]

Like Robert Hay reflecting on the symbolic value of the horse, Westcar observed that the British had secured the right to be accepted as the social equals of the Egyptian elite. He accepted invitations to dine with Egyptian officers, but refused an appearance at a review of troops because he could not hire a horse: 'Would not be seen at a review without appearing as Englishmen might. It would not do to go otherwise than as gentleman and Englishman.'[36] Westcar's commentary indicated that the British had established a 'right' to stand as equals to the elite and thus integration into Egyptian political culture. In some cases, this process had resulted in cultural immersion. Westcar's first Christmas in a 'pagan country' was spent in the company of a Frenchman, known as Suliman Aga after his conversion to Islam. He was a captain (aga) in the Egyptian army, which, as Westcar said, afforded immense power and prestige. But Westcar marvelled at his conversion because it meant throwing off all connection with his home country – losing French protection, 'its rights and laws, to put himself under the power of an Infidel, a Tyrant, a Turk'.[37]

The legal geography was thus imagined as European, with the primary threat the lawless tyranny of the pasha. In this case Westcar's reflections distinguished himself, as a British subject, from the Egyptians and the 'Frank' turned 'Turk'. Yet, Suliman Aga was not alone among Europeans in his preference for the culture of the 'Turk'. In Cairo, Westcar met one of the most renowned of the naturalised Britons of the era, Donald Thomson, who took the name 'Uthman ('Osman') Effendi after his conversion.[38] A 'Scotchman', he had come out to Egypt in the medical department of the 'fatal' British expedition; his was among those companies 'taken and cut to pieces' by the Mamluks above Rosetta in 1807. He was sold to a Turkish aga; 'The man made him turn Turk to save his life.'[39] When the aga joined Muhammad 'Ali's expedition to Arabia, 'Uthman, as he was afterwards known, accompanied him as surgeon. On his return to Cairo, he found that all the British prisoners had been released, but he was bound to the aga. A British military officer referred him to Henry Salt. It was only after 'Uthman entered the service of John Lewis Burkhardt, whom he accompanied to Arabia, that the British consul was persuaded to overlook his conversion and obtain his release from bondage. Salt's reluctance to intercede indicated the limitations of British power; it might also suggest a cultural pale, which 'Uthman had transgressed. However, 'Uthman was restored to the colony in the service of Salt as a kind of British consular agent, guide or dragoman. Westcar described him as the friend of all 'Englishmen', whom he faithfully served. He was known to all the Turks of Cairo and as a result there was no fear of 'insult or injury' when in 'Uthman's company. All saluted him by the title 'Hajj Osman', a sign that he was regarded by Cairenes as a true Muslim. In any dispute, all submitted to his advice. 'He is, with all this, a gentleman in his manners and behaviour and of the greatest use at the Consulate, especially to officers to and from India and travellers.'[40] Before long, Westcar had also adopted a shaven head (imagine another trip to the baths), a 'Mamluke turban and a proud look'. As he said, whereas previously he had been pressed upon by 'ragged Arab' and elbowed by the soldiers in the streets, 'as a Turk, and with my pipe bearer before me, all got out of my way, and the Arabs that were sitting down got up as I passed and saluted me. – Then I was a great man.' The colonial location took Westcar to a state he had never intended upon assuming: 'turning Turk' had become a symbol of British power and its privileges.[41]

In Cairo, Westcar joined company with Hay, James Burton, and Edward William Lane: 'They lived in real Turkish fashion and we passed the time very merrily.'[42] One school of thought on these 'Oriental British' is to view their lifestyles as something feigned, as a means to facilitate observation and collect data. Consequently, there was a great degree of sublimation of normal social life to enable objectivity.[43] Indeed, colonials had ambivalent attitudes towards 'turning Turk'. Burton kept a harem of women. Hay did not censure him. Likewise, when Edward William Lane offered Hay rooms in his Cairo residence, Hay accepted. He thought it strange, however, that Lane wore Turkish costume not only in public, but also in his residence, and that he dined according to Turkish custom, as did James Gardner Wilkinson. Hay observed, 'I must confess that I think it a proper thing for all Eastern travellers to learn to do like the natives to avoid being thought awkward when they are obliged to dine or eat in their company, but to do so when there is no necessity seems to me little short of ridiculous.'[44] The commentary suggests that some colonials turned 'Turk' only as a public performance, a means to an end, whereas others internalised it, which contradicts Edward Said's line of analysis in *Orientalism* where he claimed that Lane repressed desire or social engagement to enable the dissection, description, and the analysis of the Egyptian social body; and that therefore Lane cultivated a dispassionate distance from the Egyptians characteristic of the colonial point of view.[45] This is debatable. It is difficult to reconcile that analysis with Lane's immersion in local customs. Nor did the ideology of civilising mission or British liberty intervene between Lane's observation and description of the Egyptian government. Lane's *Manners and Customs of the Modern Egyptians* was bereft of the type of moral judgement evident in other narratives. On Egyptian government, Lane acknowledged that the power of Muhammad 'Ali was arbitrary, his power unlimited. Hence, Lane's image of Muhammad 'Ali condemning a subject to death with no more than a wave of his hand might evoke scenes from 'The Arabian Nights' (*Alf layla wa layla*), translated by Lane. However, Lane said that, rather than 'wanton cruelty', Muhammad 'Ali was motivated by political 'ambition'.[46] Moreover, the Egyptian ruler's actions were limited by the precepts of Islamic law.[47] Lane did not condemn the government for its tyranny but concluded that the oppressive character of the state was the consequence of the necessity to build up and maintain a powerful army and navy. He put these observations in historical context, noting the oppression of the fellahin during the 1820s and 1830s had subsided by the 1840s, when the state had directed its energies to the amelioration of the harsh conditions of the subject population.[48] Rather than enthralled to Britain's liberal discourse, Lane's identification with Egypt meant that he was able to imagine a world outside that discourse and yet logically coherent.

Lane's cultural works were not necessarily designed to produce knowledge about Egypt to establish colonial authority over Egyptians. His Arabic–English *Lexicon* exhibited a high degree of engagement with Egyptian scholars. The lexicon was produced with the assistance of an Egyptian collaborator. It corrected errors in earlier Orientalist renditions of Arabic texts.[49] 'Ali Mubarak described the lexicon as valuable to Muslims as well as Europeans, and Lane as a kind of cultural ambassador because he corrected false descriptions in Orientalist literature. This commentary echoed Stanley Lane-Poole's assertion that Lane viewed his work as a corrective to Orientalist distortions.[50]

James Burton, like Lane, also distanced himself from earlier Orientalist imaginings by offering objective, scientific observation. Burton was a scientist, employed by the Egyptians to survey Egypt's natural resources. During his first expedition in 1822 he crossed the Eastern Desert to Suez. Burton relied on Egyptian officials, Arab guides, and a British military map. However, he found that being 'English' counted for little, with only the local merchants having had dealings with the 'English' through the tea trade.[51] In the geological survey Burton recorded geographical features, minerals, plant and animal life, archaeological sites, and aspects of social life. He noted that the fellahin used the 'Persian wheel' (sakia) and produced silk. He described the fisheries, the canals, as well as ancient monuments and mosques. He collected local legends. His project was scientific, not 'Orientalist'. For instance, Thomas Shaw's travel accounts had attempted to make the Egyptian landscape fit Biblical references, claiming that the wadi named after the Beni Israel was proof of the Biblical 'Exodus'. Relying on the testimony of local residents, Burton found more mundane explanations, contrary to Shaw's interpretation.[52] After several long sojourns among the residents of the wadi he concluded that the 'hyperbole of Orientalist descriptions' disfigured the natural causes that explain historical events.[53] The commentary suggests that scientific method foreshortened attempts to construct a distinctive colonial claim to the landscape.[54]

But these attempts to remove Orientalist fantasies from British representations of Egypt do not capture the entire complexity of the colonial experience. Descriptions of colonial social life in *The Manners and Customs of the Modern Egyptians* suggest that Lane wavered between objective distance and immersion in Egyptian life. He mixed with crowds and participants at 'periodical public festivals' and 'succumbed' to the impulse to participate in customary modes of social interaction, dance, and ritual communion. Lane attended the festival of Ashura at the shrine to Husayn in the Hassanein mosque in 1834. He observed that it was common knowledge that no man in Cairo attended except 'for the sake of the women – that is to be jostled among them'.[55] Cheek to cheek with an Egyptian woman in the crowd, Lane detected an amused smile through her veil. During the procession of the 'Mahmal', a royal litter that accompanied the pilgrimage to Mecca, Lane was so caught up in the festivities that he ran alongside the 'sacred object' and touched its hem three times, kissing his hand afterwards. An Egyptian instructed him to utter a prayer. The event was interpreted by his Egyptian friends as a sign that 'the Prophet had certainly taken a love for me'.[56] The festival of the Prophet's birth, *mulid al-nabi*, which took place in 1834 in the great open field known as Azbakiyya ('Ezbekiya'), involved reciters, conjurers, buffoons; there were swings, whirligigs, and stalls selling sweets to entertain the populace. The chief performance was the *zikr* of the dervishes or Sufi adepts. As Lane said, these involved the 'soul's being occupied in devotion' through chants and repetitive movements; during one of these Lane entered the circle of the Sufis and 'united in the performance'.[57] As interpreted by Derek Gregory, such scenes were not anomalies or aberrations, but suggestive of a dynamic wherein colonials oscillated between 'detachment and desire'.[58]

The question of Lane's attitude towards Egyptians is significant, given the importance of his cultural work. Artists and cultural explorers blurred the lines of cultural difference by their high degree of social integration in the locale. Robert Hay, an artist, set himself apart from what was already emerging as an annual corps of tourists who rushed through the sites and avoided social contact with Egyptians: 'Hurrying from the temples of Thebes to the Christian idolatry at Jerusalem – no accounting for taste.'[59] In such commentary there was evident a sense of expatriate life, long-term residence, privilege by proximity to Egyptians through initiation into local culture and knowledge. As already documented, Hay and the other British cultural workers had to defer to the authority of the Muhammad 'Ali and his officials, like the *kashif*. However, there was an underlying moral authority evident in descriptions of Egyptian state policies, in spite of Hay's dependence on the pasha. He was highly critical of Egyptian slave-trading, impressment of the fellahin, and excessive taxation, as well as the pasha's war against the Greeks. A proponent of 'liberty', he referred to the Greek War of Independence as the 'good cause'.[60] He expressed his support for the liberation of the fellahin and African slaves. On the slave market, he remarked on girls aged between ten and fifteen for sale, observing that it could not be known how they 'suffered inwardly'.[61] The topic resurfaced during his tour of Upper Egypt that winter when he encountered two French persons travelling to Sennar and Dongola to purchase slaves. He was struck by the irony that these men, who had fought under Napoleon in the name of liberty, were now to be 'found fighting under the Pasha of Egypt for the noble cause of slavery!!!'[62] In another episode, Hay encountered a Mr Bowe, who was employed by Muhammad 'Ali in the operation of a sugar refinery. Bowe had previously worked in the same industry in Jamaica, but he had come to Egypt because he believed it unlikely that Britain 'could keep liberty from the slaves'. The African slaves in Jamaica spoke openly of liberty, he said; moreover, profits were down by at least 50 per cent. Bowe described his impression that the African slaves possessed an innate sense of spirituality – that it was not something learnt or mimicked from the European masters, but rather had its roots in African traditions. He did not understand the terms used by the slaves, yet it was clear they represented spiritual ideas. Reflecting on the conversation afterwards, Hay recorded that the African belief in spirits might be compared to the popular Egyptian belief in 'afreet', genies or *jinn* and that these words probably had an African correspondent.[63] Likewise, in a conversation the following year with Colonel Charles Elwood, an officer in the East India Company, and his wife, Anne Catherine Elwood, Elwood claimed that *sati* or widow burning in India had not declined as much as expected under British influence. Female infanticide, however, was losing ground. The government had recently declared its intention to eradicate it. After listening to Elwood speak of the Christian missions in India, Hay recorded in his diary: 'The Bible Society seem to make as little progress in India as in this country and Syria and it is allowed that missionaries sent home over charge their accounts of the number of converts they have made and the progress of the institution in general.'[64] The commentary questions the degree to which a British 'moral imperium', as represented by the civilising mission discourse, held sway.[65]

The conversations involving Bowe and the Elwoods identified dominant themes in the liberal, reformist or civilising missions in the nineteenth century. Harbouring these ideas was not uncomplicated because the British colony's power was not formally established over the Egyptians, but acquired only in partnership with them. Muhammad 'Ali's state was at the height of its expansionist phase in the 1830s, occupying Palestine, Lebanon, and Syria, even threatening to topple the Ottoman sultanate. As a commercial client of Muhammad 'Ali, Samuel Briggs acted as Muhammad 'Ali's agent during the war in Greece when he organised the equipping of Egyptian warships. The Egyptian monopoly on cotton and grain was serviced by Briggs, his firm delivering these products to British markets as a security for financing the naval contracts. Indicative of colonial political influence in Egypt and England, Briggs arranged the appointment of his business partner, Robert Thurburn, as consul in 1833. Throughout the 1830s Briggs and Thurburn advocated a policy of British–Egyptian alliance, arguing that the advance of Egyptian power in the region would serve British state interests. Briggs's arguments in letters to Lord Palmerston were that it was necessary to counter French influence, block an Egyptian alignment with Russia, and thirdly, that a new caliphate under Egyptian patronage represented by a Sharifian dynasty in Arabia would have greater moral weight in the Muslim world than the Ottoman sultanate-caliphate.[66] Evoking a point of view held by the Utilitarian Jeremy Bentham, Briggs claimed that the Egyptian state was 'enlightened' in contrast to the Ottoman.[67] The policy was an obvious one to Briggs, but came up against the balance of power logic of Palmerston, who claimed that Muhammad 'Ali's motives were more 'carnal' than 'spiritual'.[68] Thus, in spite of Briggs's best efforts, a concert of European powers collectively intervened to prevent the Egyptian victory over the Ottoman Empire. The powers of the Ottoman sultan were restored in Syria. Palmerston removed Briggs's agents from the consulate, describing the company as a 'creature of Mehmet Ali'.[69] Briggs had, according to British government opinion, trespassed the borders of Britain's 'legal geography'.

In 1840 the British imperial state checked the ambitions of the British colonists. Although colonials developed a critique of the Egyptian state on issues such as monopoly, forced labour, slavery, and patriarchy, the colony was implicated in Egyptian politics and immersed in Egyptian society and culture. The colony had much invested in the state of Muhammad 'Ali and acted as lobbyist for him. Politically, the colony's power and influence was limited by the strategic thinking of Palmerston, which resulted in the restoration of the Ottoman sultan's powers in Egypt. The result was not embraced by the colonials. In 1840 James Gardner Wilkinson wrote to Hay describing the great change in the 'East' and claimed that he did not like 'our interference'.[70] Also in correspondence with Hay in 1843, Joseph Bonomi regretted the 'gradual decay' of the Egyptian governing institutions and the resultant overwhelming power of the French colony.[71] During her tour of Egypt in 1846, Harriet Martineau recorded a conversation she had while taking coffee with Selim Pasha, the governor of Qena, and his officers. When she expressed the hope that commerce would sustain friendly relations between the two countries, one of the pasha's officers exclaimed, 'How should that be, when you have robbed us of Syria?'[72] Grand strategy had made the colony vulnerable. Thus, in April 1853 Samuel Shepheard, hotelier, wrote that the 'handful of English' in Cairo viewed with misgiving the response of the British government to the crisis brewing in the Crimea. Shepheard implied that the only security for the colony was if the British government traded Russian power in Istanbul for British control in Egypt, otherwise, 'how we poor devils here shall fare only time will tell'.[73]

The second generation

In Lucy Duff Gordon's letters from Egypt the 'Turkish' ruling aristocracy was held to blame for Egypt's poverty. In this respect, nothing changed between the first generation of 'Oriental British' and the second, as represented here by Gordon and Blunt in the 1860s and 1870s. However, alongside the tyranny of the 'Turks', Gordon pointed to the rapacious foreigners (mostly Greek and French, according to her) so that the foreign colonies were part of the problem. Her letters were also a critique of the cruelty and insensitivity of the callous tourists, particularly the British. She was clearly pained by the common perception of the 'dirty Arab', 'lazy' and subservient to the 'Turk'.[74] The inverted commas were her own, indicating that these terms and perceptions were well established among the British public and that she disapproved of them. Gordon observed that the fault of all the English was to refer to Egyptian society 'as a lump'. Ironically, her perception of herself as advocate for the Egyptian people meant that she rendered the British colony in stereotypical terms. Gordon's letters underlined the absurdity of the 'English', a type laughingly entertained by Egyptians and self-reflective Britons like her. Gordon particularly resented the Anglo-Indians (British residents in India) for their exclusivist racial prejudice. She dreaded 'mail days', marking the arrival of liners at Suez or Alexandria on transit to or from India when Anglo-Indians were apt to make 'some new outrage'. On one such day, Gordon greeted a relation of the shaykh of the Abab'deh tribe in the open street in Cairo: 'Anglo-Indian travellers passed and gazed with fierce disgust'.[75] This type of racially driven exclusivity was the cardinal sin and her intention was to compose a narrative that would dissent from the conventions established by travellers like Harriet Martineau and the 'Anglo-Indians'.

Gordon made her home at Henry Salt's former residence in Luxor, a rambling villa with balcony and latticework parapet. During the hottest days its divan was the coolest place in the village and a desirable meeting place for the local notables, whom she befriended. There were spare bedrooms for guests, which meant that her family, friends, and tourists also participated in her social circle. Nearby was the colonnaded courtyard of the Luxor temple. The villa had served as a residence for the Egyptologists Belzoni, Champollion, and Rosellini and was a landmark of European cultural and social life in Egypt. By 1863, according to Gordon, Luxor had become 'an English watering-place' with the object of the tourist 'to *do the Nile* as fast as possible'. When tourists paused to 'make Christmas' at Luxor, Gordon pushed off to the 'little places', like Edfu or Esna, because 'the true poetical pastoral life of the Bible' exists 'where the English have not been, and happily they don't land at the little places'.[76] Gordon attributed this tendency to Martineau, who spoke with such 'bigotry' of the Egyptians, yet venerated Pharaonic Egypt.[77]

To rehabilitate Egyptians in the British imagination Gordon wanted to break down the perception of cultural difference through social mixing with Egyptians and her own representations of Egypt in her letters. She would 'see what no European but Lane had seen'.[78] Like Lane she attempted to place Egyptians in a familiar frame of reference and to counter 'the feeling of most English people here, that the difference of manners is a sort of impassable gulf, the truth being that their feelings and passions are just like our own'.[79] Gordon particularly found Martineau's 'attack upon hareems outrageous' because the implication was that they were 'brothels'.[80] Noting that Martineau's opinions were not based on observation, in spite of her pretence to scientific analysis, Gordon established her own expertise through first-hand observation.[81] Gordon recorded that Egyptian women were relatively well-off, with the power to sue their 'husbands-in-law' – without blame – for the full 'payment of debt' and divorce if the husband was 'in default'. On polygamy she said that men normally married a second wife only 'out of duty' to provide for a brother's widow and children (ignoring the contrary argument that women might be forced into such marriages).[82] She disapproved of taboos against cross-cultural sexual relationships because, as she said, love was 'a visitation of God' and not subject to cultural or communal closures: 'A poor young fellow is now in the muristan (the madhouse) of Cairo owing to the beauty and sweet tongue of an English lady whose servant he was. How could he help it? God sent the calamity.'[83] Gordon disapproved of colonial sexual taboos: 'I often hear of Lady Ellenborough, who is married to the Sheykh-el-Arab of Palmyra, and lives at Damascus. The Arabs think it inhuman of English ladies to avoid her. Perhaps she has repented; at all events, she is married and lives with her husband.'[84] In spite of the fact that Gordon said that the 'English' colony was overwhelmingly modelled on the 'Anglo-Indian', there is plenty of such evidence in Gordon's letters that British residents continued to integrate through marriage or other forms of social and cultural relations. Colonial exclusivity was more cultural production than social fact.

Indicative of the dominant cultural trend, Gordon was inclined to imagine Egypt as an empty tableau on which Biblical scenes were drawn or upon which she superimposed images taken from Lane's translation of the 'The Arabian Nights'. However, even this tendency was subject to her critique. One letter related that she and one of her acquaintances at Luxor, Shaykh Yusuf, laughed at the absurdity of a scene in a British illustrated journal showing the Biblical Rebecca and other women wearing 'fancy dress' while drawing water from a well. Abraham's 'old chief servant' was nearby, on his knees, without a turban. Gordon and Shaykh Yusuf put the scene in a local cultural context by noting that it was ridiculous that a distinguished elder would appear before a woman without his turban. Moreover, Gordon and Yusuf lampooned the practice of constructing a 'realistic' depiction of Biblical scenes by placing them in apparently authentic Middle Eastern settings. 'If the painter could not go to Es-Sham [Syria] and see how the Arab (Bedaween) really look', said Shaykh Yusuf, 'why did he not paint a well in England with girls like English peasants. At least it would have looked natural to English people, and the Vakeel would not look so much like a madman (majnoon) if he had taken off a hat.'[85]

The culturally reflective tone was also evident during a social gathering for the visit to Luxor of the Baron and Baroness of Kevenbrinc. Gordon 'sent for a lot of Arab Sheykhs' and other local notables for the amusement of her guests. The Baroness and 'Muawin' (an Egyptian official) danced the polka, which sent the gathering into hysterics. The 'Shaykh of Karnac' made a show of eating like a 'Bedawee', which involved dissecting and swallowing large portions of a smoking lamb whole; meanwhile the Baroness demonstrated how to curtsey before the Queen and the Sudanese shaykhs demonstrated the ritual debasement before an African king by throwing dust over their heads. The pantomimes seemed to suggest the absurdity of British and African or Arab social conventions in relative terms, with very little respect for decorum or the prestige of either the 'British' or 'Arab' lords in attendance.[86]

An 'Arab' entertainment or 'fantasia' was a required part of any tour, whether in Cairo, a village, or desert camp. During her first tour of Egypt in 1862, Gordon used the metaphor of 'The Arabian Nights' to explain the cultural impact of the 'fantasia', as it involved music, ululating, sweetmeats, pipes, and coffee: 'I was strongly under the impression that I was at Nurredin's wedding with the Vizier's daughter.'[87] The exotic tendency met with disillusion, however. On her way to take up residence at Luxor in the winter of 1864, Gordon's steamer stopped at Qena, where she was invited by 'a worthy old Arab' to his house, where 'we all sat around his copper tray on the floor and ate with our fingers'. Afterwards a Coptic notable invited her to a 'fantasia' with 'dancing girls'. She enjoyed the singing, but at first found the dance awkward. 'And then it was revealed to me.' The dancer's contortions were like those of a cobra about to spring, a 'serpent of old Nile', hypnotising its prey. The reverie thus created for the reader of her letters was shattered by her observation that one of the Egyptian men had quit entertaining foreigners with fantasia because two 'English gentlemen' had asked for the women to dance naked. The women objected and the Egyptian host was forced to turn the men out of his house.[88] The friendly reception of British on existing cultural grounds was compromised by the degradation of these customs through tourism.[89]

The new critique of the cultural impact of tourism and the debasement of Egyptians as cultural objects, rather than people, attended the familiar critique of the 'iniquity' of the Egyptian state. However, Gordon noted that state depredations were now done under the 'pretext of improving and civilising' and therefore drew the approval of colonial society. Yet, 'the poor Fellaheen are marched off in gangs like convicts, and their families starve, and (who'd have thought it) the population keeps diminishing'.[90] She said that the Egyptian people were in basic agreement in the 1860s on the proper cure for these ills: 'Let the English Queen come and take us.'[91] Gordon did not disapprove of this imperialistic impulse if, as she said, it was motivated by humanitarianism: 'I should like to see person and property safe, which no one's is here (Europeans, of course, excepted).'[92] Moreover, she noted that development projects had worsened conditions for the population, for instance the modern hydraulic systems had imposed a perpetual regime of cultivation upon the fellahin by creating two or three seasons of tillage, rather than the one season historically determined by the Nile flood. She underlined that this regime was not a natural condition of the Nile Valley, but one imposed by the modern state, beginning with Muhammad 'Ali, and accelerated by his heirs: 'What chokes me is to hear English people talk of the stick being "the only way to manage Arabs" as if anyone could doubt that it is the easiest way to manage any people where it can be used with impunity.'[93] The insight was twofold: one aspect was the manner by which Egyptians were represented in British popular culture; the other the irresponsible character of the Egyptian government. She made a straightforward plea to the British government in the name of the Egyptian people against their oppressors: 'Everyone is cursing the French here. Forty thousand men always at work at the Suez Canal at starvation-point, does not endear them to the Arabs. There is great excitement as to what the new Pasha will do. If he ceases to give forced labour, the Canal, I suppose, must be given up.'[94] As noted in Chapter 1, the new khedive, Isma'il Pasha, attempted to reform the forced labour system built into the treaty governing the Suez Canal Company, but was penalised for doing so in a case arbitrated by Napoleon III.

Gordon's letters were composed to counter Martineau's popular account and the generally negative perception of Egyptians disseminated in Britain. Wilfrid and Anne Blunt's writings are comparable to Gordon's.[95] In a sardonic aside Wilfrid Blunt observed that a Reuters' concession (a government grant to develop an industry) for regular news reportage meant the British colony was certain to have reliable information on the Oxford and Cambridge boat races, the Derby, and the Grand Prix. The Cairo Opera House, built at great expense to the Egyptian taxpayer, provided a venue for regular European entertainments, including the ballet, during the 'season'. On their tour the Blunts skirted the normal tourist routes, like Gordon, travelling by camel caravan along the old overland route from Suez to Cairo and camping near the pyramids of

Giza in the village of Tulbiya. Wilfrid Blunt wrote that the villagers had already become dependent upon the tourist trade and viewed tourists with some contempt. However, they extended the customary welcome and hospitality to weary travellers in spite of the 'straits of poverty' imposed upon them by the 'terrible years of Khedive Ismail's reign'.[96] Blunt said that the hardships of the people were the consequence of the financial pressure of Europe – the extreme exactions of tax collectors were driven by the need to pay off the 'coupons' belonging to the bondholders. Yet, as he said, in 1875 he was a 'believer in the common English creed that England had a providential mission in the East'.[97] The British government was regarded by Egyptians as relatively neutral, he said, because of Palmerston's policy of non-aggression towards the Ottoman Empire. Individual 'English' tourists were, he said, often disinterested, sympathetic and open handed in their relations with the Egyptians. Moreover, the Egyptian fellahin, although reduced to beggary, regarded Britain in terms of a 'bountiful and friendly providence'.[98] Like Gordon's, his opinion suggests an open appeal for British intervention to restore Egyptians, 'a good, honest people as any in the world', to 'a happy, well-to-do society'.[99]

Britain's civilising mission in the 'East', according to Blunt, could be traced back to Lord Byron's campaign for Greek independence. The British government, Blunt believed, had an obligation to support liberty against tyranny and misgovernment; against the prince who took government 'not as a public trust' but as a means of aggrandising 'private fortune'.[100] In his *Secret History of the English Occupation of Egypt* Blunt described 'barbaric' displays of extravagance witnessed at a fantasia in honour of the British-French financial controllers, which took place at the pyramids in the winter of 1876. The scene was emblematic. The dazzled guests failed to note the incongruity of royal plenitude alongside the misery of the fellahin, under whose very eyes the entertainment was spread. According to Blunt, the rich panorama of Egypt, ancient and modern, blinkered the British public – therefore his campaign to promote the idea of 'Arabian liberty'. He contrasted the misgovernment of the 'Turk' with the unspoiled freedom of the Arabs. In a report to Lord Salisbury, the foreign secretary, Blunt spoke of Egyptian and Syrian independence as a necessary consequence of misrule by Ottoman governors.[101] Blunt's opinions were ignored by Salisbury, who guaranteed Ottoman control of its provinces at the Berlin Congress of 1878.

Up until the winter of 1882, Blunt imagined an autonomous Egypt under British 'protection and supervision' as the best arrangement until a 'new generation has grown up used to a better order of things'.[102] Blunt was a Conservative, a political party that under Prime Minister

Benjamin Disraeli took an interventionist line; his views before the events of 1882 were not far removed from those later adopted by Lord Cromer as a justification for long-term military occupation after 1882.[103] However, political party lines are not the best indicator of colonial attitudes. Blunt held that British supervision would lead eventually, under British tutelage, to Egyptian representative government according to 'liberal' principles. These attitudes began to change after a chance meeting with Malkum Khan (an Iranian modernist) in London. Afterwards he was struck by the presumptions of the British civilising mission in the East.[104] It occurred to him that he had more to learn from the 'Eastern mind'.[105] In London, the pamphleteer and Arabist Louis Sabunji propagated the idea of an Arab caliphate to replace the Turkish, which Blunt attempted to insinuate into Gladstone's foreign policy. Rogers Bey, a British official in the Egyptian Ministry of Finance, introduced Blunt to reformist Muslims in Cairo during a visit in 1880. Blunt took Arabic lessons from Muhammad Khalil, a liberal-minded scholar from al-Azhar belonging to the school of Jamal al-Din al-Afghani and Muhammad 'Abduh. Blunt described the thought of Afghani and 'Abduh as 'Liberal reform' with a 'theological basis'.[106] His first meeting with Muhammad 'Abduh occurred on 28 January 1881 at 'Abduh's house in the Gamaliyya quarter of Cairo. At that moment, said Blunt, Egypt stood on the brink of 'political revolution' and 'Abduh was its 'intellectual head'.[107]

Blunt was referring to developments after Isma'il's forced abdication under the pressure of his European creditors in 1879, when 'Abduh was associated with a 'liberal party' later subsumed under the 'national party' led by Ahmad 'Urabi. Blunt's conversations with 'Abduh formed the basis of *The Future of Islam*, his study of modern Islamic ideology.[108] First published as a series of articles in late 1881, Blunt's work used the 'liberal' basis of 'Abduh's thought to influence public opinion in Britain by arguing for partnership rather than imperial 'crusade'. England, he said, should fulfil the 'trust' it had as heir to the Mughal Empire, the last Islamic government in India (the British Raj was in effect the largest Muslim state in the world). The objective of British policy should be 'developing, not destroying' Islamic liberalism, which meant support for the Egyptian revolution against Ottoman rule.[109] Blunt won few supporters in London. However, in *The Future of Islam* Blunt asserted that British agents were the natural allies of an Arab revival against the Ottoman sultan, 'Abd al-Hamid, and the 'extreme reactionary party of Islam' that the Hamidian court patronised. The British Empire, he said, was a new experiment in multiracial (he used racial categories) imperial government; thus, it needed to be guided by 'exceptional enlightenment'.[110]

Much of the narrative in his publications involves marshalling evidence that the Islamic reformist cause was practical and viable, against the contrary claims of the government (and later made a matter of colonial 'truth' by Lord Cromer in *Modern Egypt*). The official line highlighted the militarism of 'Urabi and the irresponsible and self-interested character of the landholding elites.[111] Blunt's evidence included letters from independent observers and his journal entries recording conversations with Egyptian and British leaders. His main point was that, by disregarding their own principles, the Liberal government in Britain lost the opportunity to found a legitimate, self-governing Egyptian government friendly to Britain. Blunt argued in *Secret History of the English Occupation of Egypt* that there might have been reconciliation with 'Urabi in the autumn of 1881. The British consul general, Sir Edward Malet, said that 'Urabi's call for a constitution was a sincere one and that the Egyptian ruler, Taufiq, was willing to work with 'Urabi, given the revolutionary temper of some of the military political groups.[112] Blunt said that when he interviewed 'Urabi in late 1881 he was satisfied that 'Urabi was motivated by liberal principles. The 'English element' in Cairo was generally agreeable to concessions to the Egyptian liberals, including Malet and the financial controller, Auckland Colvin, as well as some 'winter visitors', notably Sir William Gregory, Lady Gregory, and Lord Houghton.[113] The former viceroy in India, Lord Lytton, also supported Blunt's cause. Lady Gregory reported that during the winter of 1882 the Blunts left their rooms at the Hotel du Nil for a camp near Mataria, on Cairo's desert fringe. She visited in the company of Mrs Fitzgerald and Lord Houghton. The Blunts received them at the door of their tent in 'Bedouin costume'. Later Mr Moore and 'two or three Arab sheykhs' joined them for luncheon. There were sweets, incense, coffee, boiled lamb, rice, and coloured water. Lady Gregory recorded Blunt's ethnographic insights, 'W.S.B. said the chief sheikh is not a robber, but [only] ravages the villages near him.'[114] Colonial society delighted in these exotic entertainments, in which Blunt appeared as expert interpreter. Although there was nothing novel in such displays of 'Arab' culture, in this case it was probably an indicator of a political conversion. Thus, by March of 1882 Blunt described Egypt as his 'second *patria*'.[115] The purchase of the Shaykh 'Ubayd estate at Mataria by the Blunts was a symbol of that naturalisation.[116]

Blunt's campaign was one of the warning signs for interested parties in the British and French governments and financial circles. When in 1880 Sharif Pasha, who led the liberals in the Egyptian council of notables, announced the plan to draw up a constitution, the British and French governments advised the new khedive, Taufiq, not to sign the decree.[117] In the summer of 1881 Ahmad 'Urabi demanded constitutional government.[118] Reports in the London press claimed that constitutionalism 'was mere talk' or, worse, the justification for a military coup.[119] At this phase the leading British authorities, Edward Malet and Auckland Colvin, remained conciliatory. When the council of notables was convened in December 1881 to enact constitutional rule, Blunt acted as a go-between, providing information for the British officials by directly interviewing prominent Egyptian liberals and 'Urabi. Blunt attempted to inform opinion in London by forwarding the 'Programme of the National Party of Egypt' to Gladstone, and in January 1882 he published *The Future of Islam*. Meanwhile, the British and French governments issued the 'Joint Note' on 6 January 1882. The note demanded the continuation of khedival rule under Taufiq, legitimised by the Ottoman sultan, which, it said, was the best 'guarantee' for the present and future 'good order and general prosperity of Egypt, in which England and France are equally interested'.[120] And although Colvin recommended qualified support for the 'liberal movement' in communications with the Foreign Office immediately before the Joint Note was adopted, that advice was ignored by Malet and the Gladstone government. This was inexplicable for Blunt, given Gladstone's well-known antipathy for empire and that the Liberals had always declared their preference for self-government over empire. Blunt had misled himself and 'Urabi's supporters.[121]

The Joint Note fell like a 'bombshell' in Egypt.[122] Malet took cover in the consular residency. Blunt went to appraise 'Urabi's mood. He reported to Malet that the note was interpreted as a declaration of war.[123] This was one of his last services to the British authorities as intermediary.

According to Blunt the crisis of 1882 was manufactured by the British (and French) press, supplied with suitable misinformation by the Foreign Office. When Blunt pressed the foreign secretary on the intentions of Gladstone's government, Lord Granville assured him that the government would act in conformity with Liberal doctrine.[124] After the Egyptian council of notables published a draft constitution in January 1882, the press in London compared the act to the convention of the Third Estate on the tennis lawns of Tuileries in 1789. The revolutionary implications of this language goaded opinion in Britain. There was talk in London of an 'anti-Islamic crusade in the name of civilisation'.[125] Also, the press articulated the old prejudice, which Blunt credited to the Raj tradition of colonial rule, that the Egyptians 'had always been slaves, and slaves they would remain'.[126] There was also the 'Arabian Nights' motif that Muslims 'quailed' before the 'strong man' and the executioner's sword.[127] In rhetorical flourishes, Gladstone and Granville declared that 'Urabi represented a threat to the legitimate authority of the khedive.[128]

The *Pall Mall Gazette* and *The Times* published the most 'defaming' material on 'Urabi, entirely false, which described him as a thug threatening the Egyptian prime minister with his sword and torturing political prisoners in the cells of the citadel. He was also branded a 'rebel' against the Ottoman sultan.[129] On 1 June Gladstone said in parliament that 'Urabi had 'thrown off the mask' in a plot to depose the khedive.[130] Queen Victoria regarded 'Urabi as the leader of a revolt against legitimate monarchical authority.[131] On the mobilisation of the Egyptian army, John Morley wrote in the *Pall Mall Gazette*, 'The reserves are being brought up from the villages – in chains.'[132] When Blunt attempted to counter this impression in the press he was cast as treasonous.[133]

These events were the cause of Blunt's permanent 'disillusion'.[134] He argued persuasively in the *Secret History* that a body of opinion in Egypt and in Britain supported the encouragement of liberal reform in 1881 and 1882, rather than military invasion. It was his enemies, including Gladstone, who portrayed Blunt as a fanatical idealist, as the 'one unfortunate exception' among sensible Britons knowledgeable about Egypt.[135]

The invasion

Ideologically, Major General Garnet Wolseley's military campaign was represented as a restoration of lawful government. 'Urabi's followers were described as 'rebels' and the followers of the Egyptian ruler as 'loyalists'. On 19 August, while a portion of the fleet off Abu Qir made a feint towards Alexandria, the main fleet began the offensive at the Suez Canal. Strategic points were taken at Port Said and Isma'iliyya on 20 August.[136] At Port Said, Rear Admiral A.H. Hoskins, Commander-in-Chief of the Mediterranean fleet, presented himself as the agent of the khedive and allowed Isma'il Pasha Hamdi to resume his role as governor. An intelligence report said that 'loyal' police at Port Said were put under the authority of the governor.[137] Egyptian troops surrendered, pledged allegiance to Khedive Taufiq, and were confined to their barracks.[138] After occupying Port Said, British patrols operated alongside Egyptian police. At Isma'iliyya marines secured the surrender of the governor's guard early in the morning, followed by bombardment of the 'Arab town'.[139] Having occupied the town, mounted Egyptian officers galloped towards the British line under white flags; surrendering their swords and horses, they asked for British protection. In a proclamation, Wolseley declared:

> [The] object of Her Majesty's Government in sending troops is to re-establish the authority of the Khedive. The army is therefore only fighting

those in arms against His Highness ... religion, mosques, families, and property will be respected ... The General in Command will be glad to receive visits from the chiefs who are willing to assist in repressing the rebellion against the Khedive, the lawful ruler of Egypt appointed by the Sultan.[140]

The rhetoric resembled that of the Raj in India, where Queen Victoria as Empress stood for the former Mughal emperor, delegating power to local notables legitimated by customary authority and the emperor's seal.[141]

British and Egyptian forces met at short range for the first time at Kassassin on the British advance towards Cairo. The manoeuvre was an Egyptian counter-attack that took British forces by surprise. 'Urabi withdrew after British reinforcements arrived. In the early morning of 12 September, after neutralising the Egyptian forward positions, the British attacked 'Urabi's main force at Tal al-Kabir. Wolseley's plan involved a surprise attack. In preparation, Bedouin spies working with the British misled 'Urabi concerning the movements of the enemy and the commanders of Egyptian forces of cavalry, and infantry outside the lines of Tal al-Kabir were bribed to retire.[142] British forces were able to advance right up to the entrenchments under cover of darkness. When Egyptian sentries raised the alarm, British forces leapt over the entrenchments.[143] Once the Egyptians fell back, British batteries were put in position and 'inflicted considerable loss upon the enemy, in some cases firing canisters at short range'.[144] To ensure the annihilation, the cavalry of Bengal Lancers pursued the fleeing Egyptian forces through the village of Tal al-Kabir. 'Most of the enemy, however, threw away their arms, and, begging for mercy, were unmolested by our troops.'[145] The report of Caspar Goodrich, an American naval officer at the scene of the battlefield said:

> The trenches, after the battle, were found to be filled with dead, mostly bayoneted, and the ground in the rear, as far as the railway station, was dotted with the bodies of those shot down in retreat. The British cavalry, sweeping around the northern end of the entrenchments, cut down the fugitives by scores, until it became evident that the rout was complete. After that all were spared who had thrown down their arms and who offered no resistance.[146]

The official view was that, at least generally, the British army followed normal procedure, and numerous reports demonstrated the 'virulence' of the Egyptian wounded, who, lying on the field of battle, sniped at soldiers and stretcher-bearers, hence the slaughter of the wounded.[147] The report concluded, 'The object, to get at close quarters with the enemy and crush him, was accomplished. After the attack, Arabi's

['Urabi's] army ceased to exist.'[148] British casualties were 57 killed, 380 wounded, and 22 missing in action. Egyptian casualties given in official British reports were approximately 2,000 killed and 234 wounded. The official version did not square with Blunt, who numbered Egyptian casualties at 10,000, 'mostly killed, for little quarter was given'.[149]

Cairo was occupied on 14 September after a swift march along the delta fringe. In a report from the intelligence department of the War Office, Colonel J.F. Maurice insisted that the occupation of Egypt was more a restoration of order in the midst of rebellion than armed conflict.[150] Maurice described the manner in which British troops neutralised opposition by winning over local government officials and police, meanwhile disarming and sending home Egyptian regulars after a declaration of loyalty to the khedive. In Maurice's account the Egyptian population did not resist. Maurice described Drury Lowe's advance on Cairo with a British interpreter, Captain Wilson, and two Egyptian officers. From a forward base on the delta, whilst the army marched on the desert road, 'communication with the people' was established.[151] A proclamation in Arabic announced the end of the war, news of which ran ahead of the British columns. At 'Abbasiyya, Lowe met with the governor of Cairo, the police prefect, and the commander of the citadel. The prefect agreed to secure 'Urabi, who was at his home in Cairo, and advised that a force pass quietly through the 'tombs of the Khalifs' under the cover of night to gain control of the citadel. That evening a British cavalry force of 150 men entered Cairo through the Bab al-Wazir city gate and filed through the narrow streets surrounding the citadel. The inhabitants, 'many of whom were standing at the doors of their houses, regarded the troops with a look of dull curiosity, without demonstration of any kind, and with no apparent surprise'.[152] To emphasise partnership, rather than conquest, the manoeuvre was treated as a simple relief of Egyptian troops by the British, with the Egyptian garrison defiling out of the citadel gate, past Sultan Hassan mosque, to Qasr al-Nil barracks where they were disarmed the following day. At the same time, the prefect received 'Urabi's compliance with British demands in the company of Tulba Pasha, described by Goodrich as 'one of the leading rebels in arms against the Khedive'.[153] To stress the doctrine of rebellion, Maurice asserted that 'Urabi had intended to burn Cairo. Also included in the account was a telegram from loyalists underlining the theme of restoration of the khedival regime:

> The whole Egyptian Nation express their gratitude at the manner your Government have employed in supporting His Highness Tewfik [Taufiq] Pasha, our Khedive; therefore the Nation in general acknowledge your kindness, and beg, in the name of the Nation, to stop any further action on your part until you receive orders from His Highness the Khedive.[154]

Maurice concluded his account of the occupation by describing what would become a standard feature of British rule in Egypt – the military parade. The first grand parade took place on 30 September. In commentary rife with cultural stereotypes, Maurice said that there were few sights 'more calculated to impress an Eastern population than the display of the various arms ... Not the least effective was the march past of the Indian troops, representative of the many and various Eastern races who contribute to the might of Her Majesty's Empire.'[155] In this way the empire appeared as a community of 'races', with the British represented in this account as 'natural' leaders because of their success in the sub-continent as heirs to the Mughals. While not unlike Blunt's earlier description of the empire, the emphasis in Maurice's account was upon hierarchical authority and lordship, exhibiting typical motifs of Orientalist literature, such as when he described the British 'Giaour' (Christian) troops, a term made familiar by Byron and evoking the theme of Christians breaking free from the grasp of Oriental tyranny. But Maurice reflected the ethics of a later era when the British viewed 'Eastern' cultures as lesser orders in a hierarchy of race and civilisation. The theme was apparent in the passage from Maurice describing the British guard given to the 'ceremony' of the 'Sacred Carpet' (*mahmal*) attended by the khedive, already known from Lane's account. British troops provided security and an honour guard 'as a sign of respect to the Khedive and the faith of his people'.[156] The procession occurred on 5 October and its guard was the last act of the invading army before the troops were reduced to an army of occupation numbering ten thousand. It was highly symbolic as it identified the British Empire with hereditary authority and religious 'tradition', hierarchical and archaic: 'The sight presented by the streams of fanatical Mussulmans passing through the streets of Cairo, attended by the Giaour soldiers and the Indian Mahometan troops, alike wearing Her Majesty's uniform, was a striking and notable one.'[157] Maurice said that the appearance of British troops at the 'ceremony' caused considerable misunderstanding in Britain, but he defended the guard because it was necessary, he said, to allow the procession to avoid the impression of British obstruction of religious observance. Also, the ability to police and control any popular outburst was achieved by the British guard, albeit as respectful observers of the event. Security and governmentality were thus tied to respect for 'tradition'.

The year 1882 marked a major rupture for the British colony in Egypt. The events of that year saw liberal give way to conservative imperialism, with its security imperatives based on the Suez Canal and the balance of power in Europe. Diplomacy gave way to war. Wilfrid Blunt was disillusioned, to say the least, viewing the British invasion as driven by imperialistic self-interest and a complete abandonment of Britain's civilising mission in the world. Yet, Blunt's critique of Egyptian despotism had been characteristic of British discourses on Egypt over the previous half-century. For these, British liberty had been the signifier of the essential difference between Britain and Egypt. However, in a new development Blunt had bridged the supposed cultural gulf by defining the traits of Egyptian liberty in contradistinction to the Ottomans and hereditary pashas. He had found allies in Muhammad 'Abduh and others for the liberal critique of 'Oriental despotism'; he distilled Egyptian liberal political treatises and journalism into his writings for British consumption. In doing so, he promoted nascent Islamist arguments for a representative and responsible government. But for some this was apparently a line that could not be crossed and placed Blunt beyond the bounds of British legality. The real threat to British interests in Egypt was not military revolt and anarchy, but a constitutional government in Egypt that would limit British influence through the hereditary prince. The dominant idea in the imperial mind had evolved into something aristocratic and hierarchical, which is to say deeply conservative. That view had triumphed after the revolt in India of 1857 and preference for rule in India through the princely states. Liberal reform was regarded as dangerous, because in theory at least, it was held responsible for dislocating immutable, ancient cultures with the introduction of European ideas by Utilitarians and Evangelicals. In Egypt, these ideas were first articulated by the British colony, and checked by Palmerston. The British resort to monarchy and aristocracy was not entirely symbolic, it was not only a matter of self-definition: it involved the forging of bonds with collaborators in the Ottoman world. Thus, the respect shown to the Egyptian khedive, viceroy of the Ottoman sultan-caliph, and to religious ritual, all of which were offered as appeasement to Muslim opinion (and British) that political authority would follow customary, hierarchical lines. It goes without saying that those appeased were elitist and envisaged society in archaic forms to the exclusion of the proto-nationalists and Islamists, who had anyway already been dismissed as 'rebels' or 'fanatics'. It is indicative of the hardening boundaries in the 'legal geography' of empire that, by a logic that differentiated 'liberal' Britain from 'traditional' Egypt, the conservative imperialists also created ideological enemies within the colony, as represented by the 'incendiary' Wilfrid Scawen Blunt.

Notes

1 Philip Ziegler, *Omdurman* (London: Collins, 1973), p. 185 & Roger Owen, *Lord Cromer Victorian imperialist and Edwardian Proconsul* (Oxford: Oxford University Press, 2004), p. 301, who cites Blunt's letter to *The Times* (10 Sept. 1898) & Hugh

and Mirabel Cecil, *Imperial Marriage: An Edwardian War and peace* (London: John Murray, 2002), p. 90.
2 Wilfrid Scawen Blunt, *Secret History of the English Occupation of Egypt: Being a Personal Narrative of Events* (New York: Alfred Knopf, 1922, originally published in 1907), p. 302.
3 Edith Finch, *Wilfrid Scawen Blunt* (London: Jonathan Cape, 1938), p. 169.
4 Ibid., p. 169.
5 Blunt, *Secret History*, p. 7.
6 Edward W. Said, *Orientalism* (London: Routledge & Kegan Paul, 1978), pp. 232 & 231.
7 Harriet Martineau, *Eastern Life: Present and Past* (London: Edward Moxon, 1848).
8 Ibid., p. 50.
9 Ibid., p. 55.
10 John Barrell, 'Death on the Nile: Fantasy and the Literature of Tourism, 1840–60', in Catherine Hall (ed.), *Cultures of Empire: Colonizers in Britain and the empire in the Nineteenth and Twentieth Centuries* (Manchester: Manchester University Press, 2000), p. 193.
11 Ibid., p. 187.
12 Florence Nightingale, *Letters from Egypt: A Journey on the Nile 1849–50*, ed. Anthony Sattin (London: Parkway Publishing, 2002), p. 22.
13 Ibid., p. 34.
14 Eliga H. Gould, 'Foundations of Empire, 1763–83', in Sarah Stockwell (ed.), *The British Empire: Themes and Perspectives* (Oxford: Blackwell, 2008), p. 22.
15 British Library, Additional MS (hereafter BL Add. MS) 52283, Henry Westcar, 'Journal of a Tour through Egypt, Upper and Lower Nubia', 23 June 1824.
16 BL Add. MS 31054, Robert Hay, diary, 1824–7, 17 July 1824.
17 John Gardner Wilkinson, *A Handbook for Travellers in Egypt* (London: John Murray, 1867), p. 290.
18 BL Add. MS 31054, Robert Hay, diary, 1824–7, 17 July 1824.
19 Ibid.
20 Ibid., 1 April 1824.
21 Ibid., 3 April 1824.
22 Ibid., 11 Mar. 1824.
23 Ibid., Syracuse to Alexandria, 1 Sept. to 9 Nov. 1824.
24 Ibid., 17 Nov. 1824.
25 See, for instance, Barrell, 'Death on the Nile', pp. 193–4 & 200 & Khaled Fahmy, 'For Cavafy, with Love and Squalor: Some Critical Notes on the History and Historiography of Modern Alexandria', in Anthony Hirst and Michael Silk (eds), *Alexandria, Real and Imagined* (Aldershot: Ashgate, 2004), pp. 263–80.
26 BL Add. MS 2283, Henry Westcar, 'Journal of a Tour through Egypt, Upper and Lower Nubia', 7 Nov. 1823.
27 Ibid., 16 Nov. 1823.
28 Ibid., 17 Nov. 1823.
29 Ibid., 17 Nov. 1823.
30 Philippa Levine, 'Sexuality, Gender, and Empire', in Philippa Levine (ed.), *Gender and Empire* (Oxford: Oxford University Press, 2004), p. 151.
31 BL Add. MS 2283, Henry Westcar, 'Journal of a Tour through Egypt, Upper and Lower Nubia', 23 Nov. 1823.
32 Ibid., 26 Nov. 1823.
33 Ibid., 6 Jan. 1824.
34 Ibid., 3 Dec. 1823.
35 Ibid., 10 Dec. 1823.
36 Ibid., 15 Dec. 1823.
37 Ibid., 13 Dec. 1823.
38 Jason Thompson, 'Osman Effendi: A Scottish Convert to Islam in Early Nineteenth Century Egypt', *Journal of World History* 5/1 (1994): 99–123.
39 BL Add. MS 2283 Henry Westcar, 'Journal of a Tour through Egypt, Upper and Lower Nubia', 25 June 1824.

40 Ibid.
41 Ibid.
42 Ibid.
43 Leila Ahmed, *Edward William Lane: A Study of his Life and Works and of British Ideas of the Middle East in the Nineteenth Century* (London: Longman, 1978), pp. 95–6 & Timothy Mitchell, *Colonising Egypt* (Berkeley: University of California Press, 1988), pp. 23–8 & Said, *Orientalism*, pp. 159–64. The debate involves many responses to Said's *Orientalism*. Relevant to this discussion is John Rodenbeck, 'Edward Said and Edward William Lane', in Paul and Janet Starkey (eds), *Travellers in Egypt* (London: Tauris Parke Paperbacks, 2001), pp. 233–43.
44 BL Add. MS 31054, Robert Hay, diary, 1824–7, Moniers Inn, Cairo, 20 Nov. 1826.
45 Said, *Orientalism*, pp. 159–64.
46 Edward William Lane, *An Account of the Manners and Customs of the Modern Egyptians* (The Hague and London: East-West Publications, 1978), p. 115.
47 Ibid., p. 195.
48 Ibid., p. 562, nn. 10 & 11.
49 Suha Kudsieh, 'The Image of Edward Lane in the Arabic Sources', Middle East Studies Association Annual Meeting, Montreal, 2007. The reference is to 'Ali Mubarak, *Al-khitat al-tawfiqiyya*, vol. 11, p. 10. See also Geoffrey Roper, 'Texts from Nineteenth-Century Egypt: The Role of E.W. Lane', in Paul and Janet Starkey, *Travellers*, pp. 244–54.
50 Stanley Lane-Poole, *Life of Edward William Lane* (London: Gilbert and Rivington, 1877), p. 35. See also Lane, *Manners and Customs*, p. 562, n. 12.
51 BL Add. MS 25622, James Burton, diary, 15–18 July 1822.
52 Thomas Shaw, *Travels or Observations Relating to Several Parts of Barbary and the Levant* (Edinburgh: J. Ritchie, 3rd edn, 1808), vol. 2, p. 399.
53 BL Add. MS 25630/60, Burton.
54 Stephen Howe, 'Empire and Ideology', in Stockwell, *The British Empire*, pp. 164 & 170.
55 Lane, *Manners and Customs*, p. 425.
56 Ibid., p. 435.
57 Ibid., pp. 439 & 448.
58 Derek Gregory, 'Performing Cairo: Orientalism and the city of the Arabian Nights' in Nezar Al-Sayyad, Irene A. Bierman and Nasser Rabbat (eds), *Making Cairo Medieval* (Lanham, MD: Lexington Books, 2005), pp. 72–5.
59 BL Add. MS 31054, Robert Hay, diary, 1824–7, 9 Feb. 1825.
60 Ibid., 5–6 April 1826.
61 Ibid., 22 Nov. 1824.
62 Ibid., 12 Jan. 1825.
63 Ibid., 14 Feb. 1825.
64 Ibid., 21 May 1826.
65 Gould, 'Foundations', p. 33.
66 F.S. Rodkey, 'The Attempt of Briggs and Company to Guide British Policy in the Levant in the Time of Muhammad Aly Pasha, 1821–1841', *Journal of Modern History* 5/3 (1933): 324–51.
67 Ibid., 341.
68 Ibid., 339.
69 Ibid., 351.
70 BL, Add. MS 38094, Hay, letter, Wilkinson to Hay, 1840.
71 Ibid., Bonomi to Hay, 30 Jan. 1843.
72 Martineau, *Eastern Life*, p. 77.
73 Michael Bird, *Samuel Shepheard of Cairo: A Portrait* (London: Michael Joseph, 1957), p. 12.
74 Lucy Duff Gordon, *Letters from Egypt* (London: R. Brimley Johnson, revised edn, 1902), 7 Feb. 1864, accessed at the Gutenberg Project, www.gutenberg.org/files/17816/17816.txt (accessed 16 Nov. 2016).
75 Ibid., 21 Oct. 1864.

76 Ibid., 20 Dec. 1862.
77 Ibid., 7 Feb. 1864.
78 Ibid., 26 Feb. 1864.
79 Ibid., 7 Feb. 1864. See also Lane, *Manners and Customs*, p. 375.
80 Gordon, *Letters*, 7 Feb. 1864.
81 Ibid.
82 Ibid.
83 Ibid., 7 Mar. 1864.
84 Ibid.
85 Ibid.
86 Ibid., 30 Mar. 1865.
87 Ibid., 11 Nov. 1862.
88 Ibid., 13 Jan. 1864.
89 Karin van Nieuwkirk, 'Female Entertainers in Egypt: Drinking and Gender Roles', in Dimitra Gefou-Madianou, *Alcohol, Gender and Culture* (London: Routledge, 1992), pp. 35–47. Tourism's impact on the culture of female dancers was a factor throughout the history of the British colony. Nightclubs featuring 'belly dancing' and drink were established from around the turn of the twentieth century. These expanded during the world wars and provoked reaction from moral leaders like the Muslim Brotherhood. In 1949 and 1951 laws were passed that limited the culture of sex and drink that attended the dancers. Under 'Abd al-Nasir even the belly dance was curtailed.
90 Gordon, *Letters*, 21 May 1863.
91 Ibid.
92 Ibid.
93 Ibid.
94 Ibid., 11 Feb. 1863.
95 Daniel Martin Varisco, *Reading Orientalism: Said and Unsaid* (Seattle: University of Washington Press, 2007), pp. 228–30.
96 Blunt, *Secret History*, pp. 8 & 157.
97 Ibid., p. 7.
98 Ibid., p. 9.
99 Ibid., p. 10.
100 Ibid., p. 12.
101 Ibid., pp. 22–3.
102 Ibid., p. 74.
103 Michael D. Berdine, *The Accidental Tourist, Wilfrid Scawen Blunt, and the British Invasion of Egypt in 1882* (London: Routledge, 2005), pp. 13–14.
104 Blunt, *Secret History*, p. 65.
105 Ibid., p. 65.
106 Ibid., p. 79.
107 Ibid., p. 80.
108 Wilfrid Scawen Blunt, *The Future of Islam* (London: Kegan Paul, 1882). See Berdine, *Accidental Tourist*, for a treatment of this work, pp. 29–60.
109 Blunt, *Secret History*, p. 93.
110 Blunt, *Future*, pp. vi & 84.
111 Cromer, *Modern Egypt*, vol. 1, p. 107.
112 Blunt, *Secret History*, pp. 117 & 119–20.
113 The intermediate position of Malet is supported by a letter from Sir Charles Wentworth Dilke in Finch, *Blunt*, p. 380, n. 4. Auckland had served with Cromer (then Evelyn Baring) in India previous to his appointment to Egypt.
114 Finch, *Blunt*, p. 143.
115 Blunt, *Secret History*, p. 156.
116 Ibid., p. 157.
117 Ibid., p. 97.
118 Ibid., p. 120.
119 Ibid.

EGYPT

120 Earl of Cromer, *Modern Egypt* (London: Macmillan, 1908), vol. 1, p. 223.
121 Ibid., pp. 218–22 & 255–6.
122 Ibid., p. 229.
123 Blunt, *Secret History*, p. 145.
124 Finch, *Blunt*, p. 151.
125 Blunt, *Secret History*, pp. 122 & 157.
126 Ibid., p. 172, citing the opinion of the historian Henry Rawlinson, former minister to Persia.
127 Ibid., p. 230, quoting John Morley in the *Pall Mall Gazette*.
128 Ibid., pp. 206–10. Blunt argued that the Foreign Office was largely responsible for the misinformation in the run-up to the military occupation and that Granville, as well as officials in Egypt like Colvin, and in London like Dilke, were determined that Britain occupy Egypt, partly to secure financial and strategic objectives, but also to secure power in the British parliament.
129 Ibid., pp. 194–9. On the falsity of these accusations, Berdine, *Accidental Tourist*, pp. 127–8 & 166.
130 Finch, *Blunt*, p. 155.
131 Ibid., p. 166.
132 John Morley as cited by Blunt, *Secret History*, p. 219, whereas Blunt, *Secret History*, pp. 292–6, asserted that 'Urabi's prestige meant that volunteers and provisions flowed in from all sides. Auckland Colvin and John Scott had a hand in manipulating Morley's views, which did not change until after the invasion, see Berdine, *Accidental Tourist*, pp. 108–9, 145 & 188.
133 Blunt, *Secret History*, p. 209 & Finch, *Blunt*, p. 153 & Berdine, *Accidental Tourist*, p. 179.
134 Blunt, *Secret History*, p. 226.
135 Ibid., p. 325.
136 Caspar F. Goodrich, *Report of the British Naval and Military Operations in Egypt 1882, Office of Naval Intelligence* (Washington, DC: Government Printing Office, 1882), pp. 108–11. Goodrich was the executive officer of the US European fleet, thus the report was made to the US Office of Naval Intelligence.
137 Ibid., p. 125.
138 Ibid., pp. 111–13.
139 Ibid., p. 115, 'Captain H.F. Stephenson to Rear Admiral A.H. Hoskins'.
140 Ibid., p. 125, Wolseley's 'Proclamation to the Egyptians'.
141 David Cannadine, *Ornamentalism: How the British Saw their Empire* (New York: Oxford University Press, 2001), pp. 41–57.
142 Blunt, *Secret History*, p. 318.
143 Goodrich, *Report*, p. 151: Official Report, Wolseley, Cairo, 16 Sept. 1882.
144 Ibid.
145 Ibid.
146 Ibid.
147 Ibid., p. 137.
148 Ibid., p. 159.
149 Blunt, *Secret History*, p. 322.
150 J.F. Maurice, *Military History of the Campaign of 1882 in Egypt, Great Britain: War Office, Intelligence Branch* (London: J.B. Hayward & Son, n.d.).
151 Ibid., p. 98.
152 Ibid., p. 99.
153 Goodrich, *Report*, p. 158.
154 Maurice, *Military History*, p. 101.
155 Ibid., p. 105.
156 Ibid.
157 Ibid.

CHAPTER THREE

Projects

Project implies transformation.[1] The Church envisaged a complete transformation of colonised society through conversion, but in practice these ambitions had to be fitted to the agendas of imperial administrators and the way the colonised responded to the project. Similar observations could be made with reference to educational, technical, political, and other projects. An itinerary of sorts appeared coincidentally at the zenith of empire, with the publication of Lloyd's Greater Britain Publishing Company's catalogue in 1909: *Twentieth Century Impressions of Egypt: Its History, People, Commerce, Industries, and Resources*. The editor-in-chief was Arnold Wright, a journalist who had travelled widely across the empire, including Australia, India, and Egypt.[2] The volume contained articles by British officials employed in the Egyptian administration, as well as interviews with various British residents carried out by professional journalists employed by the publishing company. The catalogue was a kind of celebration of British administrative, technical, and commercial achievements in Egypt, yet the magnitude of the catalogue of items and the diversity of opinion it represented meant the publication lacked a singular vision of the British imperial mission or British colonial identity. The ideological dimension of the catalogue was to broadcast to the British public a world of opportunity beyond the seas: Egypt was integral to the world economy as a venue for investment enterprise and a hub in international transport and commerce. There were opportunities in the diplomatic service, the Egyptian administration, engineering, shipping, business, infrastructure development, and tourism. The catalogue was like one of those placards proclaiming a better life in the 'out-land', designed to entice colonists or simply sell the idea that Egypt was a part of the British Empire and thus a suitable locale for investment, work, or leisure.

The volume began with a history of Egypt from the ancient to modern periods, suggesting that the formation of the modern trade colonies was a consequence of the European rediscovery of Egypt's centrality in the world economy. After a French mission to Egypt in 1785, the British consul in Egypt, George Baldwin, alerted his government to Egypt's potential as 'emporium of the world'.[3] In an article by James Scott, legal adviser to the Egyptian council of ministers or cabinet, Egypt's greatness was connected with the rise and fall of world trade: Egypt lost its independence not with the Ottoman conquest in the early sixteenth century, but with the Portuguese interception of its Asian trade routes in the late fifteenth century. In the modern period, according to Scott, Britain was the catalyst for the restoration of Egypt's historical role in the movement of goods, as well as a leading producer of cotton, market for British manufactures, and regional power.[4] These arguments also underlined Egypt's strategic centrality, an obvious result of the 1882 invasion. The point was made by reference to the building of Britain's military bases in Egypt, the ports, canals, and railway projects, as well as the Aswan Dam. In sum, Egypt was the capstone of an African empire and sentinel to the East, controlling the Nile, Red Sea, and eastern Mediterranean.

Scott made his observations through a cultural perspective developed in the mid- to late nineteenth century by Edward William Lane and Stanley Lane-Poole. Scott wrote that the portrait of Egypt that emerged from Lane's translation of 'The Arabian Nights' was not only its exoticism and romance, but its 'worldwide commercial prosperity' and cultural diversity in the medieval period. As Scott observed, the tale of the Hunchback in 'The Arabian Nights' described Christian merchants lodged in Cairo's greatest khan, the Mesrur, demonstrating Egyptian openness to commerce and other cultures.[5] This representation of Egypt as an international society fitted colonial designs to incorporate permanently the European colonies into Egypt's political community. The retrospective glance was only partly romantic; it represented an imperial project to transform the political and social system. Yet, romance was not without value, it brought Egypt 'home' in popular culture.

It was equally important to carry Britain 'out', to realise its extraterritorial existence. References in Lloyd's catalogue were made to the 'Commercial Community' of Alexandria, which was represented as inclusive of diverse national and religious groups. The British were constituent parts, diverting attention from the fact of British paramountcy, and thus suggesting a region wide open to commerce and settlement. The impression given in the catalogue was of a colonial society defined by the individual's willingness to separate from 'home' and connect with a world of professional networks. These took many forms. The catalogue included portraits of the diplomatic staff, church, military, police, and business people, as well as other professional categories that included lawyers, journalists, teachers, artists and craftspeople, engineers, technicians, doctors, tourist industry entrepreneurs, all of whom were from diverse national and religious backgrounds. In many of the biographical treatments of these people, it was evident that motivations included professional and personal interest, family and career ambitions. The idea that British colonials shared a sense of imperial duty was not absent. Yet, it was not the sole or even primary motivation. The imperial project was not singular, but involved multiple types and sites; moreover, some of these projects were contradictory, with one interest sometimes cancelling out or competing with others. In Church records, the archbishop of the Church of England had an entirely different view of the imperial mission from that of the British proconsul in Cairo, with Lord Cromer arguing that 'traditional' Egyptian culture was of some value and that its preservation ensured social and political order necessary for colonial rule. Other projects were equally self-contradictory, either through frustration and failure, as in the religious missions, or that their successes created the conditions for Egyptians to overthrow British domination, as in the development of a modern Alexandria municipality that represented diverse social and cultural sectors.

The official imperial mission

The British arrived in Egypt, said Lord Cromer, with the 'fixed idea that there was a mission to perform': to raise the mass of the population morally and materially.[6] As it had with the ryots (peasants) of Bengal and Madras, the British would bestow civilised conditions of life upon the Egyptian fellahin. Drawing a comparison to India, Cromer wrote in 1908 that the existence of 'Brahmins' complicated things, by which term he meant 113,000 Europeans and the 'Turco-Egyptians', elites whose privileges were wholly inconsistent with 'Benthamite principles'.[7] The reference to Jeremy Bentham underlined Cromer's opinion that Egyptian self-government would not bring happiness to the majority, only to the few, an enduring argument among the imperialists.[8] Thus Cromer distrusted the educated, particularly Western-educated, Egyptians, or as he said, 'Brahmins'. Racial theory underlined these imperialistic principles: British officials like Cromer feared the educated Egyptian, finding the 'primitive' mentality more reliable or trustworthy. Prejudice was confirmed by practice. The British preferred Sudanese ('black' or 'Berberin') servants and subalterns, just as Punjabis were preferred to Bengalis in India.[9] There was, according to Lord Cromer, the 'imperial race' and the 'subject races'.[10] These racial arguments justified a long-term military occupation premised on the threat to

British imperial interests from 'rebels' ('Urabi), 'fanatics' (the Mahdi), and rival European powers.

The dominant theme in the official narratives was that the 'imperial race' exported technical expertise to the benighted 'races'. Alfred Milner's *England in Egypt* (1893) represented imperialism as 'duty and drama, a burden and an exciting, if unsought, opportunity'.[11] 'It is not only, or principally, upon what Englishmen do for Egypt that the case for England rests. It is upon what England is helping the Egyptians do for themselves.'[12] But there was also the imperial romance of the 'Christian hero' in the figure of Charles George Gordon, a legend promoted by missionary societies in Africa.[13] Gordon died defending Khartoum against the forces of the self-professed Mahdi, Muhammad Ahmad, in 1885. According to legend, indomitable imperial virtues were pitted against the occult forces of 'fanaticism'. In 1889, General Francis Grenfell, sirdar or Commander-in-Chief of the Egyptian army, scored the first victory in the reconquest of the Sudan at the Battle of Tushki. Herbert Kitchener led an Egyptian cavalry unit against the Sudanese in that battle. There was also the sensational account of Rudolf Carl von Slatin in *Fire and Sword in the Sudan* (1896).[14] It told of his long imprisonment by the Mahdi and his successor Abdullah al-Tassi, as well as Slatin's daring escape with the assistance of Reginald Wingate, an intelligence officer serving under the new sirdar, Major General Kitchener. The English-language edition of Slatin's book was translated and edited by Wingate. Because Slatin had served under General Gordon, his story was like an unfinished sequel to the tragic tale of 'Gordon of Khartoum'. The portrait drawn of the regime of the 'Khalifa' was one of slavery, tyranny, massacre, cruelty, terror, and corruption. More fantasy than fact, the point was to vilify the Sudanese in the run-up to the Khartoum campaign to destroy the Mahdist state.[15] The campaign was an essential part of the European scramble for African territory; Kitchener's forces eventually checked the French attempt to control the entire Sudanic area of Africa, from Senegal to Abyssinia. That campaign was celebrated in Winston Churchill's *The River War* (1899), wherein he described the 'haunting nightmare' of the Egyptian regime and the 'Khalifa'.[16]

The vituperative rhetoric stirred up had no less an impact on the military operations in the Sudan than the press campaign against 'Urabi. The conquest of the Sudan was a public event, covered by journalists from all the leading British papers, most notably Winston Churchill, who also served as cavalry lieutenant. Another public figure, Edward Cecil, served as aide-de-camp to Kitchener. Cecil was the younger son of the Conservative prime minister, Lord Robert Cecil, third marquess of Salisbury. Cecil arrived in Cairo in April 1896.[17] At Wadi Halfa he lodged with Slatin Pasha and dined in full evening dress, which Cecil found rather 'rot'.[18] Hugh and Mirabel Cecil, who had access to Cecil's private papers, claimed that Cecil had hardly a word of criticism for either the Egyptian or Sudanese troops in the Anglo-Egyptian army, 'only wonderment or occasional exasperation'.[19] His exasperation was later highlighted in his *Leisure of an Egyptian Official*, a memoir in comedic form published after the First World War.[20] Suggesting something of the prevailing zeitgeist, he preferred Sudanese units to Egyptian in the Anglo-Egyptian army, but approved of the summary execution of Sudanese prisoners of war.[21] The Sudanese soldiers were referred to collectively as 'Sambo', a generic label applied to dehumanise the 'type' as either loyal dog or brave lion.[22] As Catherine Hall has said of the use of this term: 'Sambo is part of the scenery, not a real person. Sambo has been named by his masters ... He has no past or future.'[23]

Philip Ziegler reviewed the diaries and memorabilia of British soldiers and officers involved in the expedition to Khartoum and, according to him, officers generally regarded the Egyptian and Sudanese soldiers with equal contempt. 'They were, if not sub-human, decidedly sub-British.'[24] Egyptian officers were treated similarly, as Ziegler noted, in spite of the fact that they had the status of 'gentlemen'. The Egyptian *bimbashi* (major) or *kaimakam* (colonel) had to endure inferior British officers (such as sergeants) as military instructors. In 1898, Ernest Bennet, a correspondent for the *Westminster Gazette*, referred to these Egyptian gentlemen as 'Gyppy officers'.[25] Bennet Burleigh of the *Daily Telegraph* wrote of the 'Arabs': 'A fine specimen of a man, though his usefulness in the economy of things is not apparent.'[26]

Exclusivist or supremacist attitudes in the military were partly a consequence of the practice of segregating military personnel from the Egyptian population as a security precaution.[27] This is referred to in the early twenty-first century as reducing the military 'boot print'. Historically, it had negative consequences. One infamous example was when a British officer insulted Muhammad Mahmud, Oxford graduate and future prime minister of Egypt, at the Gezira Sporting Club: 'Who is the bloody nigger?'[28] The comment was made in the dressing room by one subaltern officer to another, but within Mahmud's earshot. Mahmud refused to attend the club for at least ten years, indeed, not until he became prime minister in 1929. The Sporting Club was not technically racially exclusive, but British members clearly employed techniques of informal, if not institutional, exclusion. Muhammad Mahmud liked to recount another episode, which occurred when he was a young inspector in the Egyptian administration. As was customary when touring the provinces, he had his horse stabled and took a room at the villa of the *'umda* (mayor) of a provincial town. In this instance, after retiring to the villa, Mahmud heard a great commotion in the stables where British officers, also on a provincial tour, were outraged that the horse of an Egyptian official should be stabled alongside the horses of the British. Mahmud later reflected that while he was familiar with the racism of the British, he had not assumed that these theories had been extended to horses.[29] Such caste-like conceptions of social relations were particularly characteristic of British officers, said Henry Keown-Boyd, son of Wingate's private secretary, Alexander Keown-Boyd. According to him, the British soldiery was 'openly and cheerfully' racist, employing terms such as 'nigger', 'wog', and 'gyppo' to refer to Egyptians of all classes and types.[30]

Military culture certainly had an impact on cross-cultural relations and shaped the general impression of the British colony. Many British officials began their careers as soldiers, like Cecil and Keown-Boyd, and presumably they carried military culture into the civil service. Yet, the British-led Egyptian administration had diverse sub-sets, with differing values and even loyalties. Malcolm Yapp's discussion of the culture of imperial officialdom pointed to the difficulty of identifying the motives of the British official. Arguably, a commonality was racism, not unrelated to a paternalistic sense of imperial duty to the fellahin, which inspired Foreign Office personnel at the 'Residency' and in the Egyptian administration from the era of Cromer into the mid-twentieth century.[31] The degree of commitment to the ideal, if any at all, is difficult to determine and probably would require a case-by-case study. However, Cecil's ironic self-description as 'Serious Under-Secretary' in his memoirs indicated that, at least ideally, the British officials were supposed to be defined by imperial duty to safeguard the welfare of the Egyptian people. Indeed, in some cases British officials in the Egyptian service were hardly trusted by the British government because of suspicions that their advice was designed to meet local interests, not metropolitan.[32] On a more mundane level, the British officials were perhaps not motivated by principle or prejudice, simply devoted to the idea that the Egyptian administration was a field for career advancement, and therefore keen to block Egyptian or French or German or Italian.[33]

Kitchener, Wingate, and Keown-Boyd developed credentials as Arabists. Cromer and Cecil did not. For the latter, Arabic was the language of servants.[34] However, towards the end of the nineteenth century a professional colonial service was initiated through the recruitment of Oxford and Cambridge graduates who had completed two terms of Arabic. The new recruits initially took up posts at the Department of Education before transfer to other departments or ministries. At the same time, restrictions were placed upon admissions of Egyptians from private (mostly French) schools into the higher schools of law, engineering, and agriculture that served as training grounds for civil servants in Egypt.[35] This policy had the effect of reducing the number of Egyptians eligible for higher education, while anglicising the educational system. At the same time, courses at the law school were anglicised.[36] Such policies resulted in protests from Egyptian nationalists and Radical Liberals in the British parliament or press. The attitudes of the British recruits in the Department of Public Instruction ('PI') were infamous in nationalist literature. Salma Musa testified to the humiliation felt by Egyptian students at the schools under the tuition of British instructors.[37] Naguib Mahfouz and Salma Musa portrayed the British staff at the law school as patronising, stern, and brusque.[38] 'Abd al-Rahman al-Rafi'i described the protests of students at the law school against the British educational policies.[39] Egyptians in the public service and schools were referred to as 'walads' (boys) and 'wogs'. The former term was patronising, at best, and signified subaltern status in the administrative and social hierarchy. 'Wogs' carried a pejorative meaning although in origin a descriptive acronym ('workers on government service').[40]

Even these supposed norms of colonial culture could be tested in practice. At the agricultural school William Wallace, also head of the Public Works Department, funded a journal published in Arabic, *al-Zira'a* (Cultivation). The editor, Yaqub 'Awn, regarded the British-run schools as instrumental in creating a 'new Egypt' by training a class of 'civilised' Egyptians capable of taking up the task of building a modern Egyptian society and economy. The rising Egyptian elite of technicians and bureaucrats, known as the *effendiyya*, was just as obsessed as were the British with the problem of how to modernise Egypt without upsetting a social order founded upon paternalistic social relations wherein the new technocratic elite directed the fellahin towards 'civilised' endeavours.[41] British imperial mission and Egyptian nationalism could find common ground, something also evident in British legal instruction at the law school. Maurice Sheldon Amos was director of the law school until 1915, after which he was employed at the Ministry of Justice, ultimately becoming the judicial adviser. At the school, British constitutional law was taught to underline the point that political modernity and responsible self-government were the result of a long evolutionary process. The rule of the pashas would not disappear in a day, nor would the British, given that Egypt's constitutional development was comparable to England at the time of Edward I: the assembly and councils were relatively powerless and their duties ill-defined in law; only the ruler and premier wielded effective power.[42] Such ideas appealed to the conservatism of some Egyptians, more fearful of the lower classes than of British advisers. Nascent Islamist political theory was essentially conservative, envisaging a consultative council of notables with religious credentials.[43] Among sectors of the Egyptian elite and colonial officialdom there were similar visions of state-building and social relations. Therefore, it is not easy to imagine Amos or Wallace using terms like 'walad' and 'wogs' in consultation with associates or students because political collaboration had a deep cultural and theoretical basis, and was not simply functional. Indeed, Egyptian elites recalled the professionalism of British 'technocrats' and valued collaboration on intellectual grounds. The idea of cooperation on the principle of 'progress' was held by some of the most prominent Egyptians of the colonial era, including Ahmad Lutif al-Sayyid and Muhammad Husayn Haykal, and 'good relations' were particularly characteristic of engineers, like William Willcocks, according to Chafika Soliman Hamamsy.[44]

A central project of the colonial administration was financial, reordering Egypt's finances from bankruptcy to solvency. That project was built upon the export of cotton. Therefore, agricultural and hydraulic works were crucial to the imperial mission and a central theme in Milner's *England in Egypt*. The greatest of the hydraulic projects was the Aswan Dam, planning for which was undertaken by Willcocks, who chose the Aswan site for its geological characteristics. The dam created a reservoir of water for agricultural development and increased production, which, incidentally, brought pests and waterlogging that have continued to plague agriculturalists. Writing before the completion of the dam in 1902, Milner noted that British engineers from India were brought to Egypt and established as inspectors over five agricultural districts. Their most important work in the period before 1900 was the restoration of the delta barrages constructed in the pre-1882 period by French engineers, which involved improving what was an already fully developed system of irrigation canals, sluices, and drains, in some cases of ancient origin and thus, as it was observed, not constructed on 'scientific principles'. The engineers intervened in an ancient system, with unpredictable results, and often against the hostile resistance of the fellahin. As Milner put it, the engineers had to confront 'private interest', which he said was the greatest impediment to scientific advance. Another way to view private interest is customary usage, something lost at an environmental cost. Yet, according to Milner, the engineers were the 'saviours of Egyptian Irrigation'.[45]

Milner celebrated the triumph of science; nevertheless, the object was political control. As Cromer said, economic growth and the resultant material prosperity of the masses was the surest antidote to 'race hatred and religious fanaticism'.[46] British rule reformed finances, supported the free flow of capital into Egypt, increased agricultural production, and developed the export economy. One result was the expansion of a relatively prosperous middle stratum of Egyptian agricultural producers in the period before the First World War. Members of this group found their way into the administration alongside the old Ottoman ruling aristocracy. The British did not renounce the elements of the civilising mission that targeted the harsh extractive regime of the pashas in the pre-colonial period and as a result had the support of elements in the Egyptian population. One paradox, however, was that the liberal economy ravaged those at the bottom of the social scale and threatened social disorder. For the British, political conservatism overrode free market theory so that Kitchener passed a law forbidding the mortgaging of any property of less than five feddans (2.1 hectares), which was designed to safeguard the small property holders. Also, a state-run savings bank was created for deposits and loans at guaranteed interest rates. The point of these reforms was to buy the quiescence of the rural masses. The larger landholders objected, as did the 'Levantine' (mostly Greek) moneylenders. The result was to multiply the opportunities to compound the indebtedness of the poorest.[47] Another paradox was that neither the colonial administrators nor the Egyptian elite could fully depart from the old Ottoman world of caste-like distinctions between the pasha and the peasant, elite and mass. The imperial dream of a politically indifferent rural 'squirearchy' to check the influence of urban nationalists was not realised, largely because of myopic administrative policies that blocked Egyptians from school and civil service positions. It is not hard to see the underlying tensions even in Lord Cromer's official reports: a fear of modern change and the way it eroded the caste structure of Egyptian society. Meanwhile, nationalists continued to embrace French or British political theories on liberty.[48]

Being theoretical, the conservative vision of colonial social relations bore little resemblance to reality. Egyptians elites recognised the 'arrogance' of imperial administrators, particularly Cromer and Kitchener, as well as the range of opinion and disagreements within colonial circles. The fissure between consular staff and those employed in the Egyptian administration was one source and, as a result, those British dedicated primarily to the Egyptian public service were recalled as 'good men' by some Egyptians.[49] It is not surprising that many British in the Egyptian service rejected outright the dogma of benignly paternalistic social relations between British and Egyptians, particularly after the Dinshawai incident of 1906 revealed the disparity between liberal doctrine and authoritarian practice. Opinion within the British colony split along those lines. The incident involved a group of unfortunate British officers accidentally setting a barn on fire and injuring a local woman while on a bird hunt. In the ensuing melee one officer, Captain Paul, was struck and later died of sun-stroke. The beating of a British officer was viewed by Cromer and others in the ruling caste as a violation of the customary taboos of colonial society. Afterwards, a trial presided over by Egyptian officials, but driven by Cromer, convicted fifty-two villagers – four were hung in the village on 28 June 1906 and dozens were publicly whipped. This provoked an outcry. One of the newly recruited British officials, Thomas Russell, wrote in a letter to his parents that Egyptian demonstrations against the trial of the villagers created 'some excitement in the House [Cromer's official residence] with the Boyles [a reference to Cromer's Oriental Secretary, Harry Boyle] & Co it's a nasty eye opener for everyone. We in the districts have always disbelieved in the theory of the "dear native".'[50] Russell thus questioned the entire premise that, by regularising taxes and irrigation, the British won the eternal gratitude of the rural masses. Russell's opinion also marked a fissure between officials in the 'districts' (those employed in the Egyptian administration) and the diplomatic staff in Cairo. Some suggested that Cromer was out of step with political change: one might expect insensitivity from soldiers isolated in barracks and sporting clubs, but not from the master of the political game. Wilfrid Blunt said that the trial and punishment of the villagers was a 'judicial crime of the largest dimensions committed by our representative in Egypt, the thing hardly denied, quite undeniable and defaming the fair face of British justice throughout the world'.[51]

Wilfred Edgar Jennings-Bramly lived near Blunt's estate in Cairo while employed at the Giza Zoo. In 1906 he drafted a letter to the *Daily Mail* that recorded the complete failure of the imperial mission to bring economic growth and prosperity. He said that the original justification for Britain's occupation was strictly financial: 'it was not to make Egypt fit Britain's conception of the civilised – if Egypt can pay her debts and secure capital investments Britain has no cause to occupy'.[52] Jennings-Bramly went on to imagine a future free of the cotton-brokers when, he said, a decline in cotton production would transform Egypt into a producer of stuff for its own consumption and free itself from its dependency on cotton exports and British manufactured imports: 'She will export less Pashas to Paris.'[53] He thus identified the colonial system with the misrule of pashas and British officials, driven by the export economy. Like Blunt, he ridiculed imperial mission; like Russell, he questioned the veracity of the official ideology of imperial mandate over the fellahin, which in effect empowered the ruling class of pashas. In short, he exposed the hollowness of the rhetoric of imperial mission, echoing nationalist claims that the Egyptians were quite capable of working out their own version of the 'civilised'.

Mabel Caillard's memoirs also recalled colonial opinion on the subject. Her father worked in the Egyptian postal service and customs house.

As she said, he was exasperated at Egyptian misrule before the British occupation. She praised Cromer for the entrenchment of Egypt in the imperial system and the shaping of a cohesive ruling group. She appreciated that Cromer regarded Egypt as 'an important piece in the broad game of empire' and, as a result, it was only fitting that he should impose a strict code of conduct and order upon colonial society. Cromer's era marked the most 'brilliant period of the British regime in Egypt'.[54] The last decade of the nineteenth century was a period of colonial confidence, she said, referring specifically to the reforms of Edgar Vincent in finance and Colin Scott-Moncrieff in irrigation. Caillard saw the imperial mission as essentially technocratic and strategic. Yet she dismissed the myth of the 'bovine' fellah, corralled by disinterested British administrators. 'Only partly true to life', the fellahin had a 'fanatical' interest in politics.[55] Again, the theory of cultural exclusions to ensure the natural evolution of the 'races' was questioned because, as she said, Cromer's construction of the 'Anglo-Egyptian' ruling caste from the late nineteenth century created a gulf between the British and Egyptians; between rulers and ruled.[56] Old hands from the collaborative period, such as Edgar Vincent, John Scott, and Alfred Milner departed Egypt at the end of the century when Cromer established the 'Anglo-Egyptian' civil service based on the Indian model. According to Caillard, 'the Lord' became intolerant and arbitrary.[57]

This interrogating of Cromer's legacy in letters and memoirs was not only a matter of political principle between conservatives and liberals, although that was a factor; the issue was also one of colonial location and its attendant duties, successes, and failures. Russell was distinctive in this regard, with an appreciation of Egyptian sensibilities and interests to such an extent that at critical moments some British associates thought he verged too far towards the Egyptians.[58] Russell came to Egypt in 1902 because he was impressed by the 'high sense of duty' that inspired his cousin, Percy Machell, then an employee of the Egyptian administration. A central theme in Ronald Seth's biography of Russell, *Russell Pasha*, was his loyalty to the Egyptian state. Russell was, Seth claimed, regarded by Egyptian associates as 'an impartial friend and adviser who put the general good of Egypt before anything else'.[59] Unlike Cecil, Russell reconciled service to the British Empire with the idea of the public interest of the Egyptians. Unlike Cecil's wife, Dorothea Russell remained in Cairo. While their two children were born in England, they were brought up in a Russell household that included an English nanny, an English maid, an Egyptian cook, and three Egyptian servants. Thomas Russell's leisure hours were spent riding, hunting, and gardening, while his wife pursued her interest in Cairo's mosques and great houses (she wrote a book on the subject). His view of imperial service was significant because he was clearly inspired by the mission to 'civilise'. Yet, for Russell this did not mean unwavering agreement with his government's policies. When Eldon Gorst was appointed as Cromer's successor, Russell remarked, 'It's pretty certain to be "Egypt for the Egyptians". The interesting thing will be to see if possible from his face whether he really believes it himself. No one does but we must do as we are told.'[60] His observations suggest that the British officials did not simply follow the lead of the British agent and consul general, but constituted something like an independent constituency that, in Cromer's case, censured a too aloof consul general or, as with Gorst, one tending too much towards appeasement of the nationalists. Russell was not alone; Ronald Storrs recorded that many officials considered Gorst's policy 'weak'.[61]

One of the new recruits contemporaneous with Cecil and Russell, Humphrey Bowman, documented in his diary the negative consequences of the rapid expansion of British personnel under Cromer because of the 'jingo sentiment' of new arrivals.[62] Typically, Bowman's first position was in 'PI'. He spent his leisure hours at the Gezira Sporting Club and the Turf Club. There was also the Church; yet 'it seems not many go to Church in Cairo, except during the season! What a strange thing.'[63] Bowman found Cecil 'mannered', whereas he recorded that Gorst 'waxed eloquent over the language question here and told me how important it was to know Arabic'.[64] Gorst alerted Bowman to the cultural tensions between the British and French, noting the growth of the use of English in the administration after Fashoda, a reference to the final act of Kitchener's Omdurman campaign. Bowman's ambition, like that of other recruits, was to advance out of public instruction into one of the prestigious ministries, such as finance. The ladder up involved advance from instruction to school inspector and the promise of 'prestige, leisure time, etc.', but the path involved passing exams at Cambridge for certified teachers.[65] Also, it meant taking a post held by an Egyptian. In Bowman's case, the British adviser in PI, Douglas Dunlop, promised to appoint him as sub-inspector in the school board after the retirement of an Egyptian official. By 1907 this policy was advocated to such a degree that the mouthpiece of the British colony, the *Egyptian Gazette*, supported a policy of 'anglification' or the 'denationalisation' of the Egyptian public service.[66] Dunlop blocked the appointment of Egyptians to the teaching staff at the government law school. Thus, imperial mission and its stalwarts must have appeared to some as little more than careerism and cronyism. Yet, Bowman confided in his diaries that the future of British officialdom depended upon 'collaboration' and therefore recorded his support for the appointment of an Egyptian, Sa'd Zaghlul, as minister of education. Bowman's diaries also followed the contest between Dunlop and the French rector of the government law school, Lambert, who resisted the appointment of young graduates from England in place of 'excellent collaborators of long-standing'. When copies of Cromer's official farewell speech appeared on 6 May 1907, a retirement provoked by the Dinshawai scandal, it was duly noted in the press that Cromer had made great achievements in the 'material' sense of finances and technical development, but Bowman commented in his diary that opinion among some of the officials in Egypt was that Cromer had failed on a 'moral' level.[67] Also he noted that Wilfrid Blunt had always been a bitter foe to 'Lord Cromer and his school' suggesting there was some legitimacy in Blunt's recent pamphlet, *Atrocities of Justice in Egypt under British Rule*.[68] But Bowman was not a liberal on political principle or a supporter of Egyptian self-government, nor was he at all pessimistic about the imperial project. He was an imperial careerist. Not long after the Dinshawai trial, Bowman commented: 'I feel strongly that what we want here is firmer rule, but a more sympathetic one: and I believe that this can only be produced by obtaining full sovereignty over the country. European complications no less than Turkish are now as ever, the chief obstacle.'[69] On a more pedestrian level, he observed, 'Natives were no longer polite in the street, and direct insults were offered to Englishmen on more than one occasion.'[70]

The Church

During a conversation in the summer of 1906 between the archbishop of the Church of England, Randall Davidson, and Lord Cromer, the latter argued that proselytising missionary work in Egypt had to be avoided. While Cromer supported the educational services of the Church and its missionary arm, the Church Missionary Society (CMS), he did not support conversion or the teaching of Christian subjects in Egyptian schools. Referring to the efforts of Anglican chaplains to have courses on Christianity part of the curriculum, Cromer said, 'If I were to introduce that plan I should need 10,000 more troops in Egypt. It would be the way to raise a religious war.'[71] Besides these security concerns, there were ideological underpinnings to his position. Cromer did not believe in the possibility of converting Muslims to Christianity. Or, as Archbishop Davidson put it in his diary, Cromer did not 'greatly believe in its [Christianity's] usefulness in the present state of Egypt'. This was a remarkable position for the head of what was ostensibly a Christian colony. To make his point, Cromer told the story of a twenty-two-year-old Egyptian who had been converted to Christianity by one of the leading figures in the CMS, Douglas M. Thornton. The father of the young man had pleaded with Cromer to act as an independent intermediary and restore his son to the Muslim fold. By doing so, Cromer inverted the missionary discourse of the Church, premised on conversion. The Church clung to the idea of a universal mission, with all persons the object of conversion and, in spite of racial theory, capable of acceptance of Christian teaching. Cromer, on the other hand, had an immobile vision of social order founded on the idea of impermeable boundaries in an unchanging hierarchy of civilisations. He spoke on the subject with Davidson, claiming that the Muslim world was one of the 'civilised regions' in that hierarchy. In Davidson's record of the conversation, Cromer offered as evidence that 'fanaticism' was 'abating, not increasing' in the Muslim world. The implication was that hierarchical imperial rule had 'naturally' appeased Muslim opinion by a policy of segregation. There was thus no cause for fanaticism or communal friction. The British had a genius for this type of rule. So far the argument was cultural, yet Cromer betrayed the racial underpinnings of the theory when he said he regarded the 'heathen south' as a perfectly valid object of Christian missionary activity, speaking of the work of the CMS in the southern Sudan.[72] That region was, apparently, beyond the realm of the civilised.[73]

While the archbishop appeared to endorse Cromer's view, it was hardly surprising that several chaplains and missionaries serving in Egypt strongly objected. Douglas Thornton complained in a letter to Davidson that British authorities in Cairo, directed of course by Cromer, failed to support Christian activity or raise funds for the Church in spite of the fact that, as he said, 'over 20 English residents in Cairo get over 200 per annum'. He pointed the finger at Lord Cromer, who refused to take part in services associated with missionary activity and as a result the lower-level officials also failed to show any interest. In short, there was 'official disfavour of our mission to Mohammedans'.[74] Missionary educational services found support from 'even Prime Ministers and Viceroys', he said, and would have appealed to British officials in Egypt if Lord Cromer had not been obstructive. 'Of course where no public English opinion exists, except when it emanates from our plenipotentiary, it is not likely that any Church opinion is ever formulated. But worse, there is no corporate Church life also.'[75] Confirming Bowman's opinion on the relegation of the Church to the social background, Thornton also seemed to strike at the hierarchical system that underpinned Cromer's rule and, continuing this critique, pointed to the efforts of the bishop in Jerusalem and chaplains in Egypt to create an independent bishopric in Egypt. Cromer blocked it. Alluding to the overwhelming power and influence of Cromer, Thornton said he risked the charge of 'disloyalty' by his efforts to form a meeting of clerics in Cairo in concert with Algernon Ward, also involved in the project for a bishopric. As Thornton said, 'I am not disloyal I am sure in saying so ... We need him [a bishop] to teach us the very elements of Christian truth and church teaching. We need to organize church life from the very foundations ... instead of the present independent regime.' Thornton envisaged a bishop resident in Egypt as advocate with 'the powers that be' and allying with the patriarchs of the Greek and Coptic Churches, with the object of freeing missionary work of territorial or political boundaries. For Thornton, imperial and Christian mission must be one and the same.[76]

Unlike the chaplains, Archbishop Davidson's view was more pragmatic. He could boast that Church educational services were expanding, thanks to the missions, with courses offered in both Arabic and English. While falling short of conversion, missionary work had beneficial outcomes. He agreed with Cromer's view that the Egyptian population was 'increasingly free from bigotry, and there is a wider intellectual outlook'.[77] Davidson conceded that the Egyptian population was unreceptive to the Christian message and pointed to the tourist industry as, 'unfortunately, anything but a help to the Spiritual progress of Egypt'.[78] Unlike Thornton, he could agree with Cromer that the 'British Administration' was in a 'most peculiar position'. While the permanence of the British occupation secured commercial confidence and political stability, the British consul general's political legitimacy was linked to the authority of the Egyptian sovereign, titular head of a Muslim society. Politics led Cromer to forbid open evangelisation. Street preaching in Cairo was not allowed. The government schools had Muslim instruction only. The British national Church served the British colony, expressly not the Egyptian people.[79] Thornton however imagined the Church as a vehicle for greater social engagement and cultural interaction with Egyptians, principally through schools and hospitals, with the ultimate goals of conversion and the extension of the Anglican congregation among Egyptians.

Thornton lamented that much had changed from an earlier period marked by ardent proselytising. Church records documented sponsorship of missions from 1806 with the first official missions to the Coptic Church in Egypt occurring from 1840 when the Alexandria chaplaincy was founded. Most activity in the period before the 1870s was riverside missions conducted by the CMS, as well as the Presbyterian Saint Andrew's Mission and American United Mission. Mary Louisa Whately, the daughter of Archbishop Whately of the Church of England, spoke of the CMS's role in founding medical and educational missions in 1875 with the explicit goal of conversion. She requested in that year that an ordained clergyman be sent out and that schools with Christian instruction in Arabic were expanded. The CMS School in Cairo had nearly 350 children by 1880. She noted that although few in number, the students were from the 'more educated and influential' classes. The same year she also referred to the possibility of setting up an 'English-Arabic Church'. She justified the expense as a corollary of the immense public interest in Egypt and that the region was 'teeming with population'.[80] She underlined this point again in a letter sent to her superiors at Lambeth Palace in the summer of 1880 when she asked for support for a medical mission because Egypt 'has a special claim on our countrymen (as being so very much linked in quest of health and pleasure)'.[81] Operating through the patronage of the earl of Shaftesbury, Whately's medical mission treated over two thousand patients suffering from 'poverty and disease', particularly eye disease. The school expanded to include more than five hundred children after 1882 – boys and girls – with 'the larger number being Mohammaden'. Instruction was in the 'Scriptures as well as in all useful branches of Education'.[82]

Mary Louisa Whately was active in Egypt from the mid-nineteenth century; her *Ragged Life in Egypt* (1863) recounted British cultural and humanitarian work among Egypt's lower classes.[83] It was to this tradition of conversion that Thornton referred in 1906 on the centenary of the first missions. In a letter to Archbishop Davidson, Thornton emphasised his efforts to reach young 'effendis and shaykhs' (signifying both the educated classes from government and religious schools). The point in his instruction and preaching was to demonstrate the theological ascendancy of Christianity over Islam: the CMS published works in Arabic on the 'Moslem controversy with Christianity'; there were also regular seminars, held at the CMS headquarters in the 'Arabi House' (Bait al-'Urabi), the former residence of the Egyptian national leader in Cairo. Thornton chose this setting for the seminars because, as he said, it was a 'traditional type of house' with a central hall from which there were divans or meeting rooms on either side. Thornton noted that by choosing a setting and style of discussion characteristic of Egypt's indigenous middle and upper classes, the CMS created the conditions for interacting socially with Egyptians. Lectures were given on moral and intellectual matters in English and Arabic each Friday afternoon. Reading rooms were open throughout the week. Thornton admitted that Egyptians attended not so much for the religious instruction, but because English-language proficiency was a requirement for career advancement in government services. However, Thornton insisted that the meetings had an impact. He noted that the CMS published Dr Tidsah's 'Sources of Islam' in Arabic, which, he said, was the most 'destructive work yet written on Islam'.[84] Other topics included 'The

Emancipation of Women', 'Temperance', and 'The True Sacrifice'. The missionary agenda was ideologically driven and not conducive to the cultural distance, or even separation, preferred by Cromer.

On the centenary year of the Anglican mission in Egypt, Thornton organised the Cairo Conference. Held at Bait al-'Urabi, it was a comprehensive discussion of missionary activity across the Muslim world, involving such topics as dogma, population, regional variations, and various missionary activities in education, health, conversion literature, and missions to Muslim women. All of these subjects were presented in a manner designed to prove the supremacy of Western civilisation and Christianity over Islam.[85] Nevertheless, the CMS was forced to repudiate conversion of Muslims, focusing instead on missionary activity among Copts.

The Coptic policy of the British authorities involved preferential treatment for Christians in government services, including Armenians and Syrians. The rationale was to create social distance between the 'ruling caste' and the majority of Egyptian Muslims. In arguments that combined cultural and racial motifs, Cromer credited the Christian Arabs of Syria and the Copts of Egypt with more aptitude than Muslims. As a result, by 1910 the Copts, who accounted for approximately 5 per cent of the Egyptian population, held 45 per cent of civil service positions.[86] Church papers, reproducing a doctrine attributed to legal expert Sheldon Maurice Amos, represented the Copts as genealogically linked through language and traditions with the ancient Egyptians, the ultimate fount of Western civilisation.[87] The Coptic policy began immediately following the British occupation with the founding of the 'Egyptian movement', an Anglican enterprise dedicated to strengthening ties with the Copts. It began with the formation of the Association for the Furtherance of Christianity in Egypt (AFCE), inaugurated at a meeting in the Jerusalem Chamber at Lambeth Palace on 22 February 1883. A special committee was appointed to establish formal ties between the Church of England and the Coptic Church, while avoiding any impression of interfering with Coptic doctrine.[88] In a communication with the archbishop, a proposal was made to send envoys to the Copts, with letters of introduction in Greek and Arabic, for the purpose of the 'amelioration of the condition of the Christians in Egypt'.[89] An expert in the Greek Testament, Reverend George Greenwood of Trinity College, Cambridge, was one of the envoys; his goal to reform the Church 'from within' through education. The AFCE regarded the Copts as a distinct people manifest in an unbroken line of Christian teaching and therefore echoed elements of Cromer's cultural/racial approach. The AFCE therefore differed from other missions, such as the Presbyterian, which sought to convert by deprecating the Coptic Church.[90]

By adopting a policy of respecting the cultural distinctness of the Copts and the official repudiation of converting Muslims, alongside missionary work through educational and charitable foundations, the Church of England aligned its policies with the strategy of Lord Cromer's administration. When an 'English School' was founded in 1884 in Cairo, known as Gordon College, it received Christians, Jews, and Muslims with the objective of 'raising their moral tone', not conversion.[91] The school's instruction was secular, indicating the sort of compromises demanded by official policy. The project had the support of Lord Dufferin, Lord Cromer, Henry Drummond Wolff, and Nubar Pasha, the Egyptian prime minister. Yet, the Church chafed at these restrictions. At the second meeting of the AFCE, held in the Jerusalem Chamber in 1886, Dean Butcher (chaplain of All Saints in Cairo) reported that although the British schools were not strictly religious the 'great object' of conversion had not been set aside. He spoke of the convening of the AFCE as an augur of former kings dreaming of crusade. 'The temper and manner of the age had changed; but the spirit that animated their meeting was not alien from the traditions of the Jerusalem-chamber.'[92] Unsurprisingly, Muslim opinion was not neutralised and British official policy was regarded as a sectarian policy with political implications: the Copts were targets of nationalist attacks in the press in 1910 as a result of the Coptic Congress. The Christian prime minister Butros Ghali was assassinated in that year.[93]

An alternate area for missionary activity was the Sudan after its conquest in 1898. The nationalist paper *Al-Liwa* rightly interpreted the efforts of the AFCE in the Sudan as conversion.[94] Cromer and Kitchener also complained of the unchecked activities of various missionary societies in the Sudan. Bishop Blyth, from his seat in Jerusalem, responded in a letter to Cromer that the Church had an interest only in education, not proselytising, noting that this had been shown to be the proper way to establish friendly relations, or as he said, 'kindly intercourse' in regions like Egypt where there was a large British presence. At the same time Blyth reminded Cromer that the 'duty of England' was multidimensional – commercial, civilising, imperial, and religious.[95] However, indicative of the Church's limitations, in the final draft appeal for a bishopric in Egypt and Sudan, Bishop Blyth clearly distinguished between the Muslim regions of northern Africa and those of sub-Saharan Africa: missionary activity was restricted to 'heathen' peoples south of Fashoda. The purpose of the bishopric in Egypt was to confer 'dignity' on the British colony and reflect the increasing number of British personnel in government, commerce, and engineering projects. The bishop's private comments to Cromer suggest that the Church regretted these limitations, which meant effectively abandoning the Christian project in the Muslim world.[96]

Church policy was subject to the civilisational discourse, as articulated by Lord Cromer, which placed Africans at the bottom and Arab or Muslim 'civilisation' in an intermediate position. Copts and Christian Syrians had a higher status than Muslims. This theory was applied to hiring practices, with the result that a caste-like policy of racial and/or religious exclusions was applied to the colonial administration. The crusading mission was reined in to stabilise the hierarchy, with the strange outcome that Cromer and Kitchener appeared as defenders of Islam. In spite of the complaints from the CMS and AFCE that the colony, if not irreverent, was indifferent, the Church was an important venue for colonial social life. Services on Victoria Day and Saint George's Day at All Saints in Cairo or Saint Mark's in Alexandria were quasi-national events. The very exclusivity of the British evident in such performances averted any appearance of cultural interference with Egyptian or Muslim society. Therefore, the Church of England in Egypt was highly symbolic of imperial ideology and obscured the diverse functions of the Church, which included various types of Christian orientations and institutions inclusive of other faiths. Reports from 1887 show that All Saints 'Consular' Church in Cairo held services for 'English Church people' only; however, there was a CMS schools for boys and girls in the Cairo quarter of Qasr al-Dubra. The students were mostly Coptic and upper class, but not exclusively. In the 1880s and 1890s Mary Louisa Whately openly proselytised in Arabic to Egyptian Christians and Muslims at her 'British School' and in gatherings at her home. There was also the Bulaq Church School, founded for the education of the children of lower-class British workers in the nearby railway yards, but also inclusive of Egyptians, and of course Bait al-'Urabi. Edward Said fondly recalled memorising the Common Book of Prayer and the Gospel of John in the Anglican Church in the 1940s. He was instructed by Padre Fedden and Bishop Geoffrey Allen, who instilled in him a 'love' for the Gospels and a shared 'enthusiasm for religious substance'.[97] He recalled that the CMS opened a hospital on Qasr al-'Aini in Cairo that admitted Egyptians at little or no cost.[98] At Anglican churches weekly services were given in Arabic.[99]

It is difficult to pin any simple tag on British religious institutions in terms of race, class, or missionary orientation. While some institutions toed the official line, clearly there were dissenting voices, and even the Church of England chaplains were critical of the narrowly defined political and social objectives of Church and consular policies. Nor was the exclusionary boundary separating Christian and Muslims very effectively policed by the heads of the British colony. Nevertheless, official doctrines inspired an ideology of rule wherein the Coptic Church would be the vehicle of conversion and collaboration, with the Copts serving as partners in the civil administration. Penelope Lively recalled that the term Copt was synonymous with elite and ancient ancestry, rather than religious identification.[100] Emphasising class and culture, rather than race or communalism, Edward Said observed that it was not uncommon for members of the Westernised elites in Egypt to convert to Christianity.[101] Peter Mansfield has said that unlike Britain in Ireland, 'religious differences were never seriously involved' in Egypt. The British did not support a 'religious minority against the indigenous majority'.[102] The sectarian bias of official policy questions that conclusion.

The Anglican Cathedral of All Saints was one of the few monumental structures produced by the British colony in Egypt. Bishop Geoffrey Allen observed at the opening of the new cathedral in 1938 that the edifice stood as a testament to British imperialism. Allen highlighted the imperial narrative by identifying the British colony with a 'Christian ideal' of 'service': officials, soldiers, administrators, and professionals had served in schools, hospitals, and government for the 'love and sympathy' of the Egyptians.[103] As a memorial to the British imperial project, the cathedral was the scene of special commemorations and services during the Second World War. Sir Miles Lampson attended regularly. General (later Field Marshal) Bernard Montgomery addressed the congregation. After the war a stained-glass window was installed commemorating the 8th Army's campaign in North Africa.[104] Predictably, the cathedral became the object of Egyptian wrath as British–Egyptian relations broke down during and after the war. Unloved, the structure was demolished to build a flyover for a new thoroughfare in the late 1980s.

Schools and hospitals

The British campaign to anglicise the Egyptian higher schools of law, engineering, agriculture, and medicine ultimately failed. British staffs in these schools declined in number after the First World War as the higher schools were integrated into the national university, initiated in 1908, and established as a state institution in 1925. It was named after its patron, the first Egyptian king, Malik Fu'ad al-Awwal, and after 1952 was known as Cairo University. English-language instruction and British staff remained a prominent part of the university in the interwar period. There were also British-staffed private schools servicing the colony and Egyptians. Victoria College was founded in 1902, elitist in design, like an English public school; also, the 'Dean's Building School' was founded in 1903, catering to the poorest elements of the British population; most of its students were described as '50%' British (of mixed parentage). There were as many as thirty-seven mission schools in 1916, but only nineteen of these were regarded as genuinely 'English'; many, including the CMS and Church of Scotland, taught in Arabic.[105] The High Commission surveyed the schools during the war after proposals were made to create an 'English School'; the British Union lobbied for the government to fund such a school in 1926, arguing that it would shape British residents into 'citizens of Empire'.[106] The implication was that self-identification with empire was not a given, but required fostering and reconstructing.

According to Edward Said, British cultural institutions, like schools, were designed to discipline colonial subjects and produce collaborating elites.[107] These elites lived in 'artificial' worlds, such as Zamalek in Cairo, divorced from 'Egyptian and Arab surroundings'. The lives of these elites resembled a set photograph where the Egyptian and Arab milieu was only hinted at by the occasional 'camel, gardener, servant, palm tree, pyramid, or tarbushed chauffeur' in the background.[108] Schools and other elite cultural institutions sponsored by the British were a microcosm of this society. British schools were an 'experiment' in the formation of a 'mock little European group' trained to identify British culture as the universal standard.[109] Students of the schools became bureaucrats or teachers or worked in European or American businesses. A resident of Egypt in the 1930s and 1940s, Said was speaking from personal experience, having attended preparatory schools in Zamalek and the Victoria College campus in Cairo, the pre-eminent British teaching institution. A 1947 pamphlet advertising the college's mission claimed that the school educated 'mainly young Egyptians with a thorough knowledge of Arabic and English'. Its purpose was to 'win respect for English ways of thought and life, and provide the most successful means of strengthening friendly and commercial ties between England and Egypt and Near East ... [and] that the training of character is best achieved by means of a British education'.[110] There were ample references in the document to the British Empire; particularly that empire depended upon the construction of British cultural pillars. The pamphlet did not necessarily contradict Said's interpretation. This iconic British institution was originally promoted by Jacques Levi de Menasce. Lawrence Durrell used the Menasce family as the model for the fictional Hosnani family in *The Alexandria Quartet*. Of Egyptian ancestry, the family had acquired Austrian protection under the Capitulations in the first half of the nineteenth century, but the family's business offices were in Liverpool, Manchester, and London, as well as Marseilles, Paris, and Constantinople.[111] Jacques Levi de Menasce was born in Cairo in 1850 and educated in England, afterwards employed in the Liverpool and London offices of the family cotton brokerage. Although associated with the Levantine milieu of Alexandria, the Menasces had a British governess, Polly O'Meara, who nurtured generations of the family between 1901 and 1950. O'Meara ensured that the first language of the children was English.[112] Egyptian Jewish families of this class were culturally oriented towards Britain, hence when the foundation stone of the college was laid in 1901 Menasce read the dedicatory address to Lord Cromer.

The college was not an official British institution, but found its cultural models in England and had the practical purpose of teaching the necessary skills for participation in a global marketplace dominated by British finance, industry, and transport. Victoria College found support among merchants, bankers, and shipping magnates of various cultural backgrounds. Six of the founding members were British, including Sir Charles Cookson, G.B. Alderson, Henry Barker, Sidney Carver, Harry Pugh Kingham, and Robert Moss; also mentioned in the Lloyd's catalogues description of the college was Jacques Levi de Menasce, 'Austro-Hungarian' president of the Jewish Community of Alexandria.[113] The college was free from British consular control; in fact, Cromer refused to provide private or state subventions.[114] Students entering Victoria College in its first year 1902 were defined as Syrian, Greek, 'Egyptian Moslem', 'Israelite', and 'English'. In that year there was only one British student in a class of twenty-six.[115] Victoria College was a civilian project, directed by the Alexandrian elites.

Classes were taught in English, but Arabic and French were mandatory. In keeping with its mission to impart a British education, there was also cricket, soccer, and hockey. In his memoirs, *Out of Place*, Said observed that British staff at the Zamalek preparatory school taught 'English' history and literature to instil within the children identification with 'home' and pride in the empire, although the students in the school were composed of diverse national groups, including upper-class Egyptians. By defining 'home' as a faraway island that few in the classroom had ever visited, Said recalled that the British-run schools in Egypt imparted more a sense of dislocation than of belonging.[116] Of Victoria College campus in the 1940s Said recalled that very few students were British. The first rule was a ban on the speaking of Arabic. For Said, the rule had to do with identity. His example was of an 'anglicised' Egyptian, later well known as the actor Omar Sharif, who as head-boy would lord it over the other schoolboys, his ridicule and insults delivered in the best of British accents.[117] Omar Sharif of course played the archetypal 'Arab' in *Lawrence of Arabia* and Egyptian nationalist in

Fi baitina rajul, so his function as 'enforcer of the hierarchy and its rules' was ironic.[118] As Said recalled, the atmosphere in the schools was one of 'unquestioning assent framed with hateful servility by teachers and students alike'.[119] Said characterised the British as haughty, cold, lame, spastic, gnomic, bedraggled, ugly brutes and pederasts marooned in Egypt or forced out of Britain by their quirks and deformities.[120] These passages have the flavour more of schoolboy taunts, than academic analysis. Others observed that college curriculum and activities bred a primary identification with the school, not Britain or empire, 'blurred ethnic and religious differences and created an atmosphere of tolerance'.[121]

Edward Atiyah's memoirs suggest that the teaching of English language, history, and literature created a commonality among the diverse groups at the college. A Syrian, he and his Egyptian friends shared a common perception of themselves as 'civilised boys', with England as the source of 'civilised' attitudes.[122] Atiyah recalled that he viewed Egypt through a colonial and elite lens; therefore, those Egyptians demonstrating in nationalist rallies in the interwar period were 'rabble'. He identified with his teacher, R.W.G Reed, a graduate of Oxford who was headmaster at the college between 1922 and 1945. Atiyah liked his teacher and did not want to disappoint him, thus his identity as 'Arab' was not primary, rather, 'civilised'. Elite cultural distance differentiated the Victoria College students from the mass, with elitism signifying the shared values upon which social order was founded. Tolerance or inclusion was not extended to the masses. Atiyah recalled that he deferred to the opinions of his schoolmaster that the 'Egyptians could not govern themselves'.[123] The school thus sustained a cultural discourse on difference that enabled accommodation across racial lines within the elite structure of colonial society. Eventually, however, exclusivity turned on Atiyah and he had to resort to his Arab identity: the crisis of identity occurred when he was posted to the British administration in the Sudan, where his alienation from the British was a consequence of British racism.[124]

Atiyah's testimony neither entirely supports nor refutes Said's claim that the schools represented an 'organized system set up as a colonial business by the British'.[125] Yet, Atiyah's and Said's memoirs equally represent the typical dilemma of the colonised – whether to identify with the coloniser through assimilation, acculturation, and collaboration or to resist within the bounded categories of Arab or Egyptian. As Atiyah memoirs demonstrate, self-identification within the school was not 'racially' exclusive, but became so with his employment in the colonial administration. For Said, conversion to nationalism occurred only in the 1950s and 1960s; his identification of the college as racially exclusive, a cultural arm of imperial power, was more retrospective than historical. Memoirs, like fictions, are subject to these sorts of distortions. Take, for example, another commentary on the British educational system, also from the 1940s, in Olivia Manning's *Levant Trilogy*. Manning and her husband R.D. (Reggie) Smith arrived in Egypt in 1941, with Smith taking a lecturing position first at Alexandria University and later at the British Council. Olivia Manning's representation of the Egyptian classroom inverted the encounter between teacher and student as described by Said and Atiyah. Whereas Said and Atiyah provided insight into the contradictory alienation/identification of the student, Manning set up the internal dialogue of a fictional university professor, closely modelled on her husband, who felt that by teaching English literature and language he 'had been peddling the idea of empire to a country that only wanted one thing, to be rid of the British for good and all. And to add to the absurdity of the situation, he had himself no belief in the empire.'[126] Just as Said identified the schools with an overarching and pervasive discourse on empire and race, so did Manning.

Similar conclusions were drawn by yet another prominent literary figure, Robert Graves, who accepted a position at the reorganised 'Egyptian University' after the First World War. Indicating continuity with the pre-war British-run educational system, the medicine and science faculties were predominantly British staffed, whereas the arts were mainly French or Belgian. However, most of the students had been educated in the government secondary schools in English, not French. Graves's portrait of colonial Egypt focused on dislocating juxtapositions. Thus, the university buildings were from the exterior a 'harem-palace' and from the interior a 'harem boudoir', as if the 'true' Orient wanted to break the spell of the dull and insidious modernity of English instruction and committee meetings.[127] Graves's friends and family (like many others, his emigration to Egypt was a consequence of family connections) lived in a 'brand new dead town on the desert's edge' (Heliopolis) where RAF planes droned overhead; meanwhile, housewives wrote novels and painted in watercolours.[128] Graves recalled, 'British officials at the Ministry of Education begged me to keep the British flag flying in the Faculty of Letters.'[129] For a brief spell Graves obliged them, not so much to keep the Egyptians down or to serve as an 'ambassador of Empire', but to check the 'semi-political activities of the French professors at the university'.[130] Essays written by Egyptian students at the Teacher Training College demonstrated the way colonial doctrines on race infiltrated and were internalised by Egyptians: On evolution, Egyptian students learnt not only that Egyptians' essential difference from others was a product of environment, but that even 'dear Europeans', normally strong and tough, were subject to fatigue and an excess of leisure in Egypt. On the proper use of leisure time a student reflected that hours spent in cafés longingly observing and desiring women was corrupting, whereas the spectacle of 'happy peasants, toiling afar from town life' purified social manners.[131] Egyptian nationalists had distinctly British-drawn virtues. One student that he befriended owned a copy of Samuel Smiles's *Self Help*, whose doctrine had been emulated by the Egyptian nationalist, Mustafa Kamil, to regiment and indoctrinate students in the national struggle.[132]

Egyptian nationalists used various European literary forms to construct a narrative of a uniquely Egyptian national character, as for instance in the contemporary literary works of Muhammad Husayn Haykal, which idealised the rustic peasantry in his novel *Zaynab* (1913). Critical literary method was applied to the study of the Qur'an in Taha Husayn's *On Pre-Islamic Poetry* (1926). Taha Husayn taught at the university; Graves described him as 'one of the few Egyptians with fame as an orientalist'.[133] While race nationalism was a dominant discourse, Graves identified the high degree of cultural dialogue between colonials and Egyptians, albeit at an elite level. This trend was underlined by the translations of Egyptian texts into English. E.H. Paxton translated Taha Husayn's *An Egyptian Childhood*, a loving description of life and folklore in an Egyptian village. Collaboration between Herbert Howarth and Ibrahim Shukrallah resulted in *Images from the Arab World* at the end of the Second World War. Hilary Wayment brought out an anthology of translations, *Living Egypt*. Denys Johnson-Davies began a distinguished career as translator of Egyptian novels and short stories while working at the university in the 1940s. The English section of the university also included the poets Bernard Spencer, Terrence Tiller, and Robin Fedden, members of the literary group 'Personal Landscape' that formed during the Second World War. These poets consciously shirked the obligatory flag-waving of propaganda departments and developed an aesthetic founded on individuality as shaped by specific locales. As Robert Furness observed of these expatriate authors, even the writings not specifically about Egypt 'owed something to Egypt'.[134]

Graves's memoirs recalled the fragile proximity of Europeans and Egyptians at the new university (Taha Husayn's work resulted in controversy and a religious backlash). The interwar period witnessed confrontation along these cultural fissures, but also efforts to build bridges across communal and national lines. This was the founding purpose of the British Council, or as it was known in 1934, the British Council for Relations with Other Countries. Egypt was identified as a key site in its mandate to enhance Britain's cultural profile internationally. A Foreign Office initiative, the British Council disseminated information about Britain's role in the world through literary, artistic, and educational projects: 'Still more serious is the situation in Egypt, where English studies have not kept pace with French and Italian in spite of our special position in that country.'[135] The British had a 'moral duty' to promote an understanding of British culture, its contribution to the arts and political theory and offer an alternative to the 'tyrannies of the Left and the Right'.[136] The cultural initiative was strategic; responding to a revived Italian imperialism in Libya and Ethiopia and, as it was said, the seductive attraction of Bolshevism to the British Left. The British Council was founded to 'spread the light of British culture', conceived in its liberal format.[137] The threat posed by Italian fascism and Communist ideologies probably accounted for the rapid expansion of the Council's activities and its attraction to Conservative politicians like Lord Lloyd. The Council addressed the issue of imperial 'prestige'. It was argued in the mainstream press that the 'national identity of British communities abroad' flagged because of the paucity of schools.[138] Whereas in 1932 the University of London's Institute of Education provided teaching and research for the Commonwealth, the Council was created in 1934 to reach beyond the Commonwealth. The Council coordinated educational policy with the University of London and funds were made available for schools teaching British curriculum. By 1941, the British Council owned three schools and supported another eleven in Egypt. The Council assisted in establishing the Cairo branch of Victoria College in 1940. There were funds for lectures, recitals, concerts, and art exhibits, as well as courses in the arts and sciences leading to degrees at the University of London. But the main business of the schools was the teaching of English language.[139]

The British Council muted empire and underscored the ordinary cultural pursuits of international relations. The Council was designed to meet the needs of English-speakers in Egypt, not primarily British residents, and counteract the decline of British influence in the Egyptian government. Herbert Addison documented the changing pattern of employment in the Egyptian administration since 1922. Only in the Ministry of Education did British numbers hold up, largely because of the need for teachers of English as a foreign language. After the First World War the number of British in the Egyptian administration fell precipitously, so that from 1,671 in 1919 there were 483 British officials in the Egyptian civil service in 1926. Of these, there were 183 serving in the Ministry of Education, two of which were British women.[140] In 1937 there were 570 British officials, with 317 in the Ministry of Education. In 1939 there were in total 511 British officials, with 392 or 70 per cent serving in the government school system. Of these, seventy-one were British women. Schools were a growth area for the British in

Egypt, a sign of the use of English in business and professional life; the need for female educators was an indicator of the increasing number of Egyptian women seeking education and employment. These interwar trends confounded Egyptian legislation that restricted the use of European languages and personnel in government. Although the running down of the British colony by 1945 was evident in the total number of British officials – 224, mostly teachers – the fact that 'many women' were working in the schools was an indicator of the changing nature of the colony.[141] The outright ban on foreign personnel in government was not made until 1951.

Marginalised in governmental institutions after 1919, the British administration, particularly under Lord Lloyd, sought to expand cultural institutions as a check on declining influence with the rise of nationalism and imperial rivals, like Germany, Italy, Japan, and France. Robert Furness recorded that in 1930–1 there were 35,459 Egyptian students attending foreign schools, but only 2,374 attended British schools. The majority were in French schools (20,207), followed by American schools (6,573), and Italian (4,305). French schools were the most diverse and Greek the most homogenous, not a result of a specific policy, but of the social need among Egyptians for English- and French-language instruction. Furness at the university, and Lloyd at the High Commission, found common ground in the new cultural policy; each advocated for the British Council. Lloyd also proposed the establishment of a British Institute to compete with the French Institute.[142]

While united in advancing British influence, there were tactical disagreements within British colonial opinion. The rival visions were evident in debates surrounding the future of the 'New English School'. The idea for such a school began in 1914 with the Anglican nun, Sister Margaret Clare, renowned for her social work among the poorer sections of the British colony.[143] The school's original patron was Edward Cecil, the leader of the British colony at that time. Specifically designed as an institution for the children of 'British in-land or Dominion parentage', candidates of non-British parentage were limited to 20 per cent of the student body in the early proposals. In keeping with the racially exclusive mentality of the era, Egyptians were explicitly barred from attending the English School from its opening in 1914. The 20 per cent non-British referred to Levantines, Syrian, Greek, Italian, Jewish, and so on, to the exclusion of Egyptians. The school was funded also to meet the needs of a less affluent sector of the British community, as an official memorandum from 1916 said, like those in England who would have sent their children to grammar schools: clerks, officers, commercial agents, policemen, and engineers. The English School had 115 students in 1916 and occupied the palatial residence of the former German School (many

Britons had sent their children to the school in the absence of alternatives) and was described as '100%' British (English, Scottish, Irish, colonial and American). Highlighting the nationalism of the era, official reports recorded that members of the British colony feared a 'lapse into the class of Levantines'.[144]

The purpose of the English School as envisioned by Clare, Cecil, and later by Lord Lloyd, was not to spread British cultural influence, but to consolidate colonial identity and solidarity. In 1928 Lloyd lobbied for British state subventions for the English School by pointing to the 'imperial task' it was performing in a climate where French influence was in decline and the German, Austro-Hungarian, and Ottoman had been eliminated. The British colony was also changing, with an increase in the poorer British population because of the replacement of other foreign personnel in government services, particularly the police force, short-term contract work, as well as demobilised soldiers who had then taken up contracts at government headquarters. These soldiers had often married locally, which had created a class of people whose children were just then coming to school age. Also, the British had an important place in financial services, increasing the number of middle-level resident Britons. Lloyd's examples included those employed at Egyptian Markets Co., Shell Co., Gresham Insurance Co., alongside those in the British consulates and Egyptian state services. Lloyd's concern echoed those voiced during the First World War. He said that children of '50%' British ancestry would otherwise attend the French and Italian schools and be culturally absorbed into the Levantine social category. With 200 students at the New English School in 1928, up from 120 students in 1924–5, Lloyd's appeal for funds was justified with the claim that the English School was the 'largest wholly British institution in the country'.[145] The chauvinistic tendencies were probably an index of social change, wherein the British colony was less distinctive and more a constituent part of the foreign community, a trend Lloyd abhorred.[146] Other British officials read the changing circumstances as an opportunity to adapt and renew the colony, represented in the use of terms such as cultural 'interchange'. The British Treasury's power to direct policy through funding allocations threw its support on the side of a more inclusive cultural policy by insisting that the English School should foster cultural links with the Egyptians and not limit these by an exclusive, racially inspired admission policy. The British government blocked funding for reconstruction of the New English School until it terminated its prohibition on Egyptians.[147]

Lloyd's attempt to create distinctly 'British' cultural institutions was a rearguard action, without support from the British government. Race solidarity had never much inspired the colony. Official reports credited the British community with a 'laissez-faire' attitude, relying on services organised by private charities and, after forty years of military occupation, the British were the only important European community in Cairo without a national hospital. The British colony remained indifferent when Cromer initiated a campaign for a British hospital in 1901, the Anglo-American, which was never very popular with the community. The Victoria Diamond Jubilee subscription had resulted in the naming of the Victorian Deaconesses Hospitals in Cairo and Alexandria; however, these were staffed by German nurses from the Kaiserwerth Hospital in Germany. The war had some impact on people's attitudes. Italian nurses replaced German at the Victorian Deaconesses.[148] Kitchener's untimely death resulted in a committee to administer a fund in his memory, which proposed a hospital for women and a school for women doctors. The committee included Egyptian and British government officials, and notable private citizens, British and Egyptian. The term 'Kitchener Mission' was applied to those Egyptian women sent to England to study medicine; and in 1922 a women's hospital was set up in the premises of the former Austrian Hospital in Shubra. However, the Egyptian government took over the funding and as a result the control of the enterprise fell out of the hands of the committee and its identity as a British initiative and memorial to Kitchener was lost.[149] Health services remained in the hands of private and Egyptian state hospitals.

After the war, British nurses taught and practised in Egypt through the Overseas Nurses Association. ONA nurses were employed by the Egyptian Public Health Department and various private hospitals, notably French and Swiss. The nurses, known as 'sisters', served Egyptian women because the custom of 'hareem' meant the women would not consult European doctors; most cases dealt with pregnancy. The official correspondence of Susan Odair to the ONA headquarters showed that before her posting she had studied Arabic at the School of Oriental Studies, Finsbury Square, London. Reporting in 1920, she said that the remote towns of Upper Egypt remained subject to banditry and that during the 1919 revolt against the British the local police and troops had been targeted, but not the 'Sisters'.[150] Respected among Egyptians in the interwar period, nurses were employed in the government hospitals and those affiliated with the university, notably the Qasr al-'Aini Hospital. In the government hospitals the primary role for British nurses was training Egyptian nurses in up-to-date methods; however, the British nurses also served in the operating theatres in all capacities. Six British nurses were employed at the Qasr al-'Aini Hospital in the 1940s. In the children's hospital in Cairo a British 'matron' oversaw the work of an Egyptian staff.[151] By the 1950s even nurses faced obstruction because of anti-British feeling.[152] Professionally committed as these nurses were, and in many cases deeply attached to their professional duties in the Egyptian setting, their correspondences indicate that politics could ruin a posting in Egypt.[153]

Law and order

The problem addressed first by Lord Dufferin in 1883 and afterwards by Lord Cromer was how to reform the Egyptian administration without dismantling it entirely. Dufferin developed the theory that Britain served the interest of the fellahin against the privileged classes. As he said, the Egyptian assembly of notables represented privilege, and thereby might be legitimately bypassed. Instead, he regarded the local village councils, 'elders of the land assembling round their Chief', as at least having a basis in Egyptian society. From that basis, self-government might 'evolve'.[154] A similar critique was applied to the judiciary. Dufferin described Egyptian civil law, codified in the 1870s, as simply the 'laws of Muhammad Ali' and the civil courts as 'courts of summary justice', implying they lacked legitimacy. Moreover, the application of Egyptian civil law was restricted by the consular, mixed, and Islamic courts. Effective authority was invested in the executive branch of government. The director-general of reform and adviser to the Ministry of the Interior, Clifford Lloyd, proposed a radical reform along the lines of the administration of Bengal (English and customary law administered by British commissioners and Indian subalterns). But the model of the Indian princely states was preferred, and thus the introduction of English law was blocked in preference to the customary authority of the notables. The British-advised Egyptian minister of the interior instructed judges through various mechanisms, such as committees of surveillance and superintendents of the police, with local courts falling under the authority of the rural notables, whose powers were largely inherited. To supervise the Egyptians, the British concentrated power in the hands of British inspectors. Inspectors in the Ministry of the Interior were responsible to the inspector-general, initially Colonel Valentine Baker and later Colonel Herbert Kitchener. The police force was reorganised, with the mostly new recruits marshalled into three districts, encompassing a total force of 7,310 in 1883. There were European police for the European quarters of the cities, under two European officers and two deputies, with the Cairo force numbering thirty-five. The director-general of police was a British officer, taking orders from the British adviser in the Ministry of the Interior. Most Egyptians were policed by a *ghaffir*, a local watchman, numbering 50,000. The ghaffirs came directly under the authority of the Egyptian provincial governors (known as the *mudir*) and the prefect (ma'mur) of districts, all of whom were representatives of large landholding families. The governors and prefects were instructed by the British inspectors, who communicated to the British director-general of public security, and the British director of personnel within the British supervised Ministry of the Interior.[155] British overall ascendancy was wielded by a council of British advisers to the Egyptian ministers after an unsuccessful attempt to impose British ministers. In practice the most powerful British official was the financial adviser. By the First World War the advisers dictated government policy, and the financial adviser of the day, Edward Cecil, was essentially the Egyptian prime minister.[156]

Given that the British in Egypt adopted something like the Raj tradition of administration, the dogma developed that British interference in local affairs should be minimised. Cromer identified British rule with the Egyptian peasantry, the ancient village system, and Islamic law, while explicitly blocking the reformist policies of Clifford Lloyd.[157] Direct authority was left in the hands of local notables, who oversaw civil and criminal cases held in intermittent courts resembling the assize courts of England and Wales. Theory and practice did not always meet. Problems arose when British inspectors attempted to introduce new agricultural techniques that either upset the customary practices of the fellahin agriculturalists or the 'feudal' rights of the notables over the fellah. Each was an inevitable consequence of British inspectors intervening between fellahin and notable with innovative techniques. There was also the problem of indebtedness with the opening of the rural provinces to the unrestricted activities of moneylenders, local and European. The fellahin fell into debt and their properties were foreclosed upon in the courts. The British-run administration interposed itself upon rural life further by restricting credit, as already described. Thus, the attempt to maintain the 'ancient' village system broke down the customary social relations of small and large landholders. British policy defeated itself, or at least, the British were the target of blame in a rural society experiencing the dislocations of rapid change.[158]

Nevertheless, there were various areas of policing that uniquely suited the British sense of imperial mission.[159] These were those that touched upon imperial security and 'prestige'. The first of these was the consumption of hashish and opium, secondly prostitution, and thirdly political violence, each regarded as evils that reflected particularly badly upon the British as a 'ruling race'. Race and sex were connected because of the perceived threat posed by the marriage of British women to Egyptian men, and, more notoriously, the white slave trade that marketed Europeans to the prostitution rackets in the Near and Far East. Drugs, particularly opium and its derivatives, were also regarded as a threat to

British status when the result was the ruin and degradation of a British national in the colonial setting. The main obstacle to reforming sex and drugs trades was that the Capitulations enabled traffickers to avoid prosecution under Egyptian law. The consular authorities of 'certain' European states protected nationals engaged in smuggling, trafficking, and prostitution; therefore, there was considerable obstruction among these states (particularly France) towards British attempts to reform the Capitulations. Although they were identified as problems early in the administration, there was a degree of tolerance because prostitution was not illegal under Egyptian law and hashish had been consumed for centuries. Hashish was also the principal source of extra income for the poorly paid Egyptian Coastguard and Camel Corps Section of the Coastguard. Rewards were paid for contraband seized. Contraband was sold by auction at the Alexandria Customs House, with the provision that resale was for export only. Much of the contraband was turned around at sea and smuggled back in: 'Needless to say, the coastguard officers raised no protest against this practice.'[160]

The gameplay between smugglers and coastguard changed with the First World War. The British navy's interception of all coastal shipping under wartime conditions reduced the flow of illicit drugs and drove up prices. Military provision ships were therefore the next target of smugglers, with military vehicles the unconscious accessories. Drug smuggling next emerged as a security threat and the military intervened. The introduction of martial law on 2 November 1914 enabled military authorities to supersede regulations under the Capitulations, wherein smugglers faced only a fine and confiscation of property. Heavy fines and lengthy prison sentences under martial law meant that smuggling decreased and prices of the drug increased beyond the capacity of the average Egyptian. Profits for drug traffickers did not necessarily decrease, although many switched to opium or heroin, where the odds and returns were more in their favour.[161]

Similar military policies were applied to the sex trade. The Egyptian Expeditionary Force after the catastrophe at Gallipoli was based at Port Said, a town notorious for vice of every sort, servicing tourists, transients, and sailors. Survivors of Gallipoli eagerly found consolation in the town's diversions. The result was to incapacitate the British army on the eve of its offensive into Palestine and Syria. In April 1916 admission to hospital for venereal disease in one unit of the army had risen to an annual ratio of 25 per cent and the average rate for the entire Expeditionary Force was at 12 per cent. Military authorities concluded that the Egyptian government's supervision of the legal prostitution houses was unsatisfactory and intervened to declare the district devoted to this trade 'out of bounds'.[162] The business moved to 'Arab Town', a bidonville on the outskirts, where even rudimentary inspection was absent and conditions for prostitutes and clients were much worse. The army therefore campaigned against the gangs responsible, imposing fines, imprisonment, and whippings. As it turned out, the military's methods were illegal under English law and had to be suspended. As Lieutenant-Colonel Elgood observed, 'The troops continued to frequent the quarter, and the hospitals to be filled with victims.'[163] The military authorities had therefore pause to consider the larger causes and implications of the matter, noting that disciplinary and moral points of view were sometimes at odds with each other. The moral arguments of the 'purity committees' were useless on soldiers daily confronting their mortality or simply freed from the normal constraints of family and community. Disciplinary measures were tried and failed. Medical measures of a prophylactic nature were one remedy, but the moral dilemma involved in promoting the safe conduct of something that ought to be discouraged altogether befuddled military command.[164] Wartime measures did temporarily end the international traffic in prostitutes to and from Egypt, but not prostitution in Egypt. Rather, the war expanded the sex trade and produced acute health hazards.[165]

The post-war situation offered little respite when the problem was restored to the Egyptian government and the consular courts. A former soldier-turned-consul, Thomas Rapp, noted the 'post-war spirit of indiscipline and insubordination producing a steady flow of defendants'. There were cases of lunacy, suicide, and drug addiction – what Rapp described as 'tragic casualties of the East'.[166] Shattered versions of his former self, discharged soldiers and sailors were viewed by him as 'weaker brethren'.[167] There is in the commentary a sense of the cultural threat posed by the 'East' to British prestige on moral grounds. Many British, men and women, caught up in drugs and sex trades retreated to the 'native' quarters to avoid the eye of the British colony. Also in the post-war period, Port Said continued to serve as a transit centre for the 'white slave trade' and there was also a 'black slave trade' between Arabia and Africa. Responsible for policing the smuggling rackets, the Egyptian government officials, often British nationals, were nevertheless frustrated by a division of loyalties and interests between British in the diplomatic service and those in Egyptian service. Rapp recorded his campaign to defend the 'freedom' of the British colony at Suez to engage in sports fishing after an Egyptian patrol led by 'Jarvis Bey' (C.S. Jarvis) fired on fishing parties suspected of hashish smuggling. It was a common problem that legitimate activities provided a cover for smugglers. There were many scandalous examples of respectable members of the community falling under suspicion.[168]

Throughout the colonial period, Cairo's red-light districts were adjacent to the grand colonial hotels at Azbakiyya Gardens. One of these, known as Wasa'a, was described by Rapp as involving 'second and third class prostitutes of all hues, ages, and contours' who 'offered their wares seated in open shacks on both sides of the street filled with a jostling crowd of prospective clients, pimps and mere sightseers'.[169] Egyptian government regulations made legal the operation of 'safe' brothels, largely to service the demands of foreigners or Egyptians seeking cover in a European setting. British women were prohibited from working in these districts. A question of race prestige, the necessity of the prohibition against British women suggests that British sex workers were active. Wigh al-Birka was another street adjacent to Azbakiyya where European prostitutes were available and under the operation of a European gang, whereas the Wasa'a was run by an Egyptian gang. These areas were made out of bounds to troops after the 'battle of the Wassa' in 1915 when British (mostly Australians, but not entirely) soldiers ran riot in the region. One account of the incident noted that a British soldier from a Manchester unit had found his sister working in one of the houses in the district, but was unable to convince the brothel keepers to release her. An altercation ensued. The soldier was thrown out of a window and sought the assistance of Australian soldiers with their own 'grievance'. The account of a member of the constabulary force sent out to restore order, Private John Jensen, recorded that the woman in question had been brought to Egypt as a servant to 'some lady', but was abandoned in Cairo, and, as Jensen said, went from 'bad to worse'.[170]

Commentary on drug and sex trades reflected the desirability of cultural distance between the British colony and the Egyptians. However, colonials crossed the boundaries regularly. Sex trades were tolerated in the interwar period, drugs were not. The British officer leading the campaign against drugs was Thomas Russell Pasha, Cairo police chief from 1917 to 1946; his 'crusade' ultimately brought about narcotics laws against heroin production in Egypt in 1926 and understandings with foreign governments that enabled the Egyptian police to circumvent the Capitulations and bring the campaign to Europe and Asia, the sources of exports to Egypt. In short, the British-directed police in Egypt initiated the global war on drugs. As an officer in the Egyptian police service, Russell's perspective differed from Rapp's. His chief concern was the impact of drugs upon the Egyptian population, not British. Certainly, Russell's views reflect the prevalent culture of imperialism wherein drug addiction was regarded as a peculiarly 'Eastern' vice. Yet Russell regretted that this vice was exploited by European drug traffickers shielded from Egyptian law enforcers by the consular courts, with the resultant victimisation of the Egyptian population. That is the dominant line in his narrative, rather than the threat posed by Egyptian vices to the British.[171] Rapp, however, was responsible for British subjects and therefore regarded British drug addicts as 'casualties of the East', not drug casualties. There was of course nothing new about drug addiction, but the war had amplified the problem with the influx of soldiers. Like riotous drinking binges, drug consumption by British subjects was an affront to the propriety and prestige maintained by the official residents and the military establishment. After the war Rapp recalled that many demobilised soldiers were unwilling to forsake the life they had grown accustomed to. 'Among them were many who had failed to make good and some who had succumbed to Cairo's temptations.'[172] In the following years British consular authorities were involved in sweeps designed to rid Cairo of these undesirables. 'British subjects could not be exempted from the consequences of anti-social conduct we criticized in others; hence our Consular Court made full use of its authority to deport undesirables who had become involved in Cairo's underworld, occasionally as addicts or traffickers in heroin or cocaine.'[173] Rapp mentioned the example of a British doctor of a 'well-known family' who on his return voyage from Singapore left ship in Suez to seek the drugs he had become addicted to in China. An Egyptian police informant ('Tegs') found him 'sick and penniless in a sordid hovel after he had disposed of his watch and personal papers for his last shot of heroin'. Heroin and cocaine, said Rapp, came to replace the 'much less harmful hashish, hitherto the traditional dope'.[174]

The shift from 'black' to 'white' drugs was the result of the success of the campaign to eradicate the import of hashish, begun during the First World War. Russell, 'Hammer of the Drug Barons', turned his attention to heroin addiction in Cairo after the war. While hashish had been a drug of the working classes of Cairo and Alexandria, heroin reached all classes. Introduced by a chemist in 1920, intravenous use was first reported in the mid-1920s. The practice of sharing needles led to a spike in the incidence of malaria. To counteract the traffickers, Russell created the narcotics 'Intelligence Bureau' to intercept smugglers and obstruct dealers in Egypt. He employed the venue offered by the League of Nations to give public exposure to the legal, yet as he described it, morally repugnant drug industry in Europe. His campaign at the League began in 1930 and brought European countries, sometimes reluctantly, into a concerted effort to interdict the production of heroin in Europe, mostly in France, Switzerland, and the Balkans. The success of this campaign shifted production to Turkey, the major source of the international heroin supply in the 1930s, when it was legally exported until international pressure meant that the Turkish president, Mustafa

Kemal, shut down the heroin factories. Manufacturers moved to Bulgaria, China, and so on. Nevertheless, by 1935 figures for arrests and convictions indicated that heroin consumption in Egypt was much reduced.[175]

Rapp and Russell shared a similar regard for the ill-effects of drugs and sex trades, one informed by a modern regime of health and social welfare, as well as moral propriety. E.M. Forster's narrative in *Pharos and Pharillon*, on the other hand, bemoaned the assault of imperial authorities on the exotic customs of the 'East', attractive to him and tourists alike. His taste for the exotic was evident in his account of 'The Den'. In that article, which appeared in a popular journal published in Alexandria, Forster recounted his efforts to observe hashish smokers. When at last a suitable venue was found (operated by a British subject of Maltese ancestry), the police spotlight was turned upon it and promptly shut it down. Forster regretted yet another casualty to the forces of modernity.[176] Similar observations were made by Evelyn Waugh during his visit to Wigh al-Birka quarter in Cairo in the 1920s. Waugh reported that troops had been prohibited from entry into the district since the war because, as he recorded somewhat sceptically, a prostitute had been thrown out of a window of one of the houses of ill-repute and killed (a distorted reference to the battle of the Wasa'a in 1915).[177] But the taste for the exotic had not been quenched among Britons like Forster and Waugh; the flouting of convention was characteristic of the interwar period. Without explicitly saying that such attitudes threatened imperial prestige or British colonial identity, Thomas Rapp's narrative implied the underlying menace involved in cultural or social mixing between British and Egyptians. Rapp said that the consular courts were called upon to perform many marriages of British soldiers to local women, normally women belonging to one of the national or religious minorities (mostly Greeks). This was not purely a wartime phenomenon – there were three such marriages a day when Rapp was consul in Cairo between 1922 and 1924.[178] Desertion of these wives, he said, seemed the rule rather than the exception. The Anglican Benevolent Fund spent much effort on the 'abandoned wives and children of the soldiers'.[179] The Anglican nun Sister Margaret Clare dedicated her charitable work to the 'welfare of British women who fell on evil times'.[180] Many of these women clung to their newly acquired British passports and attempted to integrate into British society, which Rapp described as 'pathetic efforts to bring up their children decently'.[181] Less often, British women married Egyptians, in many cases Egyptian students studying in Britain. Rapp claimed that in most instances these women found the conditions of Egyptian society 'intolerable' and that Muslim family law left them with 'no rights or protection, a fact that an Englishwoman who has differences with her husband soon discovers'.[182]

Rapp tempered his commentary with the observation that although intermarriage was rare and often troubled, there were examples that contradicted the supposed norm. Two important political figures, Hasan Nasha'at and Amin 'Uthman, as well as the industrial magnate Ahmed 'Abud, married British women. Egypt also had its version of what was known in India as the 'Fishing Fleet' – the winter migration of British women in search of husbands among British officials in the Egyptian government, diplomatic service, or the army of occupation. These women sometimes formed liaisons with Egyptian men frequenting the hotels and clubs, although such relationships did not normally lead to marriage. Official attitudes were to discourage such social mixing and intermarriage, particularly the marriage of British women to Egyptian men. It was unimaginable to many official colonials that a British woman would knowingly consent to such a fate.[183] John Young's memoirs record this sentiment with a reference to an encounter he had with a British woman and her son while conducting official business with the *'umda* of the village of Galubiyya. Young was informed by the *'umda* that the woman had married an Egyptian engineer. The two had met while her husband was studying in London (she was his landlady's daughter). Young's enquiries were met with assurances that the engineer loved his wife and treated her well. Young responded, 'I hear he beats her,' to which the *'umda* responded, 'Of course he beats her ... I love my wife but I frequently beat her.' Young observed that the woman's husband had 'probably given her an utterly false description of his rank in life and of her future home'. The woman had thus found herself 'leading the life of a peasant'. For Young, this was intolerable. He reported the case to the British Consulate in Cairo where her 'marriage papers were shown not to be in order and she was sent back to England'.[184]

Rapp viewed mixed marriages, particularly those involving middle- or lower-class Britons, as undesirable, if not a threat.[185] John Young's attitudes went further because he strictly delineated the cultural line between British and Muslim on the question of the status of women – even a woman who had chosen to live among Egyptians was judged a captive, bereft of rights, and in need of rehabilitation into 'civilised' norms. Needless to say, Young's position was as much ideological as it was based on a reading of actual social conditions.[186] The anecdote shows that there was social mixing, both in Britain and Egypt, and that the engineer, the young Egyptian in question, was not a 'peasant'. It is thus possible to imagine the children of cross-cultural marriages attending government or private schools, conversant in English and

Arabic, according to lifestyles that defined Egypt's middle classes, local or foreign. The type of cultural and social interaction described as taboo in Young's recollections probably occurred more often than official accounts of the colony suggest. From the post-war generation of colonials, Rapp was more inclined to admit that fact.

The other area of law and order that British authorities took particular interest in was political violence, or 'terror'. Like sex and drugs, terror represented to imperialistic sensibilities something inherently aberrant, the result of unregulated modern change in an Oriental society. There were racist assumptions in the belief that Egyptians were unbalanced by nationalist ideologies and unfitted for political modernity. The arguments were premised on the idea that Egyptians had an essential nature, suited to despotic rule and assent, and that change created an inauthentic or deviant character. On the contrary, political violence was a predictable outcome of competing international forces in the region. Before his death in 1908, Mustafa Kamil, a nationalist ideologue, found patrons in France and in the Ottoman capital, Istanbul, to put diplomatic pressure on the British in Egypt. The 1904 *entente* with France removed the French counter to British power, with the result that various radical, nationalistic societies were formed to seek other avenues of protests against British 'tyranny' (*zulm*).[187] Germany was regarded as an alternative patron and, particularly in the years immediately before and during the First and Second World Wars, German intrigues and financing provided an ideological and organisational base for radical political groups. The situation in Palestine significantly complicated political trends after the First World War; British control of the Sudan was a running sore from 1899, and more so after the elimination of Egyptian partnership in its administration after 1924. Also, the social changes created by the British regime meant that young men, particularly first-generation recruits into the modern school system (and thus often frustrated in their career ambitions), were susceptible to radical political ideologies.[188]

These factors produced two distinct periods of 'political crime' during the British military occupation of Egypt: the first began in 1910 with the assassination of Butros Ghali and lasted until 1925. The second period lasted from 1937 until the British withdrawal in 1956. The first period saw the murder of twelve British officials, including the commander of the Anglo-Egyptian Army, Sir Lee Stack. Twenty-one assassinations of Britons were attempted. In the same period there were fourteen attempts on Egyptian officials identified with the British, and two killed, including a serving prime minister. In the second period, three British army personnel were murdered and four attempts in the years between 1937 and 1946; Prime Minister Ahmad Mahir was the victim of a 'suicide murder' in 1945, Amin 'Uthman, a known collaborator with the British, was assassinated in 1946, and Prime Minister Ahmad al-Nuqrashi in 1948.[189] The period after 1948 was more like a war of attrition between the British military and Egyptian paramilitaries (with the assistance of Egyptian police and military), therefore terms such as 'terror' or 'political crimes' are perhaps inappropriate; violence increased on both sides in that final phase.

In police reports the assailants were always described as young men of the urban classes, which provided the pseudo-sociological insight into the causes of political violence, as described above. Mustafa Kamil's Watani or Nationalist Party was credited with influencing Ibrahim al-Wardani, Butros Ghali's assassin. Al-Wardani belonged to the class of Egyptians educated in the modern school system that had been politicised by British educational policy and the increasing anglicising of the schools and administration. Watani ideology extolled the virtues of self-sacrifice and struggle in the national cause, without, however, explicitly calling for political violence. The latter was the work of nationalist cells, independent of political parties like the Watani. The immediate cause of Butros Ghali's assassination was the proposal to extend foreign control over the Suez Canal, an affront to nationalist sensibilities. In the case of the assassination of Sir Lee Stack, the prominent figure in the political cell held responsible was Shafiq Mansur, probably influenced by the Wafd Party propaganda that had been driven to stridency by the failure of treaty negotiations with the British in 1924. Mansur's motives included his exclusion from the Wafd government of the day, a not-uncommon complaint among the more radical supporters of the Wafd Party, which had come to power on a wave of popular street battles and protests. The Wafd government, though, took a moderate line on its formation in early 1924. Mansur, like others, sought to pressure the Wafd leadership into a more radical posture. Or perhaps he thought political violence was the road to his personal power.[190] While these rational interpretations of motive can be made, police and press reports at the time emphasised the deviant character of politicised Egyptian youths in the 'effendi' or modernised sector of Egyptian society. Students exposed to European nationalist ideology were particularly susceptible to 'extremism', detached from the customary hierarchical system of political authority and respect that the British imperial system had attempted to maintain with the formation of an Egyptian monarchy and aristocracy in the years since the military occupation of 1882.[191]

Discipline in the British-run administration of Egypt was severe. Long prison sentences under conditions of hard labour (rock cutting at the Tura prison camp) and whippings were meted out to all sorts of prisoners. Ten years of such treatment at Tura turned one of the members of a cell into a police informant. The cell was credited with political crimes, including the attempt on the British-appointed Sultan Hussein in 1915 and Butros Ghali's assassination. Whether or not there was a cohesiveness cell, the informant assisted in uncovering those prosecuted for Sir Lee Stack's assassination. In return, the informant was given amnesty in Britain. The affair uncovered the existence of a militant 'secret apparatus' of the Wafd Party, although the cell might have had dual allegiances and fell under the patronage of the monarchy by November 1924.[192]

Martial law during the First and Second World Wars resulted in the imprisonment of thousands of Egyptians and foreign nationals suspected of spying or unpatriotic actions or beliefs; many were subject to the 'horrors of internment' on unsubstantiated accusations that had the character more of personal vendetta than political intelligence or criminal activity.[193] Political prisoners in the 1920s spent twenty-two hours a day in fetid two-metre cells.[194] In high-profile and sensitive cases, such as the assassination of political figures, police methods included surveillance, subterfuge, whispering campaigns, and feigned arrests or confessions to break the code of silence.[195] Expert police methods did not always bring about the expected results. In one of the most high-profile cases, the murder of Sir Lee Stack, the evidence indicated that two of the suspects hanged for the assassination, Mahmud Isma'il and Shafiq Mansur, were part of a palace plot interested in advancing the king's political agenda, whereas it had been assumed that radical members of the Wafd were responsible. That line of enquiry was dropped as it would have been politically damaging for those in the British administration championing the monarchy as a check on the Wafd.[196]

During the Second World War the British military interrogated political prisoners at the Combined Services Detailed Interrogation Centre, annexed to a British base in the Cairo suburb of Ma'adi, where refined methods of torture were allegedly used.[197] Egyptian political violence also developed more sophisticated methods; however, assassination and sabotage were the usual approaches. There was very little subtlety in British analysis of 'terror' in the Foreign Office files; it was uniformly denounced, its perpetrators pursued and tried by British military and Egyptian state police, not surprisingly as British 'imperialism' and Egyptian 'feudalism' were the primary targets.[198] As events played out, political violence increased over the course of the British military occupation, spiking in the 1940s and 1950s. Police reports record that political assassins were regarded as 'national heroes' by many Egyptians, had public sympathy, expert legal advice, and the funds to assist their cases in courts.¹⁹⁹ Egyptian courts were often loath to impose heavy sentences.²⁰⁰

The municipality

Alexandria has been romanticised as a 'cosmopolitan' utopia where multiple cultures and religions coexisted. That view has been much criticised as a nostalgic and distorting representation of colonialism because, in fact, Alexandrian society was riven with racial and religious divisions. Yet, the picture in colonial ledgers of the time supports neither of these views; on the contrary, evidence suggests that Alexandrians did share a common social ethic founded on porous communal boundaries where opportunism was the norm and the market and profits a common motivator across cultural lines. Of course, these opportunities were available at different rates according to social position, sometimes determined by religious or national identification. The usual colonial reports on Alexandria spoke of the banality of its modernity, of an urban culture obsessed entirely with business. Improvements to the municipality's infrastructure were purely utilitarian, with an eye to maximising and rationalising optimal productivity and efficiency. In short, Alexandria's culture was homogenously modern, oriented towards improved living standards and revenues, and the diverse ethnic and religious groups mixed together like a swirl of colours turning into a uniform grey. For this reason, E.M. Forster loathed it upon first impression. Lawrence Durrell said that most Europeans considered it 'dull'.²⁰¹ Yet its very banality may have been strategic, as Robert Mabro has observed: Alexandrians knew that politics and religion were a source of conflict and therefore avoided discussion of these topics. Such restrictions ensured a social ethic founded on opportunism and mobility; therefore, colonial social life revolved around sports, entertainments, and business.²⁰²

These values sustained the Levantine orientation of the city throughout the period of British political domination. Even in the years after the military occupation, the British did not overawe the city. There were few obvious monuments to British imperial power in Alexandria: St Mark's Church erected in 1855, the Ptolemaic column that commemorated Kitchener's victory at Omdurman, and the complex of race tracks and sports fixtures known as 'Sporting'. It has been observed that the British were 'insular' and stood at odds to the 'cosmopolitan' or 'Levantine' society of the city.²⁰³ According to this interpretation, the tennis, polo, horse racing, golf, bowls, croquet, and cricket identified with British colonial culture failed to rank alongside the cosmopolitan cultural pursuits of the 'Levantines'. It was not uncommon that the British were ridiculed for their 'shabby gentility', as compared to the polished entertainments of the francophone elites celebrated by Lawrence Durrell in *The Alexandria Quartet*.[204] Oswald Finney, reputedly the richest Briton in Egypt, patron of the arts and gracious host, was one of the leading lights in the British colony in Alexandria. He was a benefactor, providing funds for the synagogue and the Greco-Roman Museum. His entertainments were renowned, the annual costume ball an institution of colonial life. It was attended by a wide range of Alexandrians, including the Peels, Barkers, and Carters. Arguably, Finney was more Alexandrian than British, more cosmopolitan than British national. During the Second World War he fled rather than stand with the British in Egypt. Forster and Durrell were attracted to such types as a reaction against the nationalistic culture prevalent during the world wars, when they sought alternative identities in pacifism, internationalism, classicism or exoticism. Yet, the theory of the insular British can hardly be supported if some of the more eminent cultural figures of 'cosmopolitan' Alexandria were British: Forster and Durrell. The divergence between the 'British' and the 'Levantine' can be too starkly drawn because the 'Levantine' or 'cosmopolitan' was, as Mabro argued, in its very banality accessible to all. Indeed, according to Lloyd's 1909 catalogue, Alexandria's residents were all primarily concerned with money and lifestyles and betrayed a basic conformity, rather than divergence. The catalogue admitted the town's tedium, its obsession with the market, and credited the successful coexistence of multiple national communities to its very dullness. The principal municipal works undertaken in the twenty years between 1886 and 1909 were the widening of streets and the construction of public squares, the Corniche or seaside promenade, sewage system, abattoirs at Mex, housing for the working classes, the Greco-Roman Museum, a disinfection establishment for the sanitary department, the demolition of ancient fortifications, the removal of unsanitary neighbourhoods, and the creation of public gardens such as the Municipal Gardens along the ruined Arab walls and the Nouzha and Antonniades Gardens. The authors of the catalogue found these developments vapid, 'All considerations of science, art, and archaeology are choked by the city's strenuous commercial activity.'[205]

According to the catalogue, Egyptian and European members of the upper classes lived in 'harmony' side by side. There was intermingling even across cultural lines among the lower classes, 'something they would never dream of doing in Cairo'.[206] The description is not nostalgic, but probably optimistic, designed to promote British finance, commerce, and settlement by advertising a welcoming social setting. However, its description of Alexandria before the First World War as a city divided along class lines, rather than religious or national, is not inaccurate. As Robert Ilbert has said, divisions did not follow communal lines, Alexandria's urban social structure was more modern than 'Islamic'. Only the old 'Turkish' city of Alexandria was sometimes dubbed the 'Arab' or 'native' quarter by colonials. Colonial legend held that rue Ibrahim (also referred to as rue des Soeurs and al-Sab'a Banat) was the dividing line between Christian and Muslim, foreign and Egyptian, and therefore the site of confrontation (most notably in 1882). However, the street's notoriety had no ethnic or linguistic characterisation. It was polyglot. Rather than dividing, it linked various groups.[207] Across Alexandria, Muslim, Christian, and Jewish were found in elite and lower-class milieus. The British were a minority even within the elite commercial community. The majority of the British were Maltese, and although mostly lower class, some had access to elite status through business or profession. The new quarters of Manshiyya and 'Attarin to the east of old Alexandria and rue Ibrahim housed the elite British, alongside others, whereas the majority of British (Maltese) occupied a quarter to the west, over-crowded, with higher rates of poverty and crime. As a result, Maltese British mixed with locals more than with 'in-land' British, that is to say, of 'metropolitan' origin.[208]

A 'metropolitan' urban landscape emerged in what was in the nineteenth century a more remote area in the eastern district of Stanley Bay, the inception of neighbourhoods like Bulkeley and Mustafa Pasha, the heart of residential Ramla or 'Sands'. The summer residence of the British consul general was on the ridge above Stanley Bay, known as Abu Nawatir, and the Anglican Church of All Saints was in the adjacent Bulkeley. In 1876 Robert Moss, a cotton broker, was one of the first British to make his residence at 'Ramleh', when only a few summer villas dotted the coastline – the Moss villa was known as 'The Cloisters'. In an interview with the Lloyd's cataloguers Moss recalled that in the 1860s there were 'no gaslights, no footpaths, no paved roads, no police, no running water, no breakwater, no quays, no steam tugs or launches; and, no taxation in Alexandria'.[209] He was referring to colonial Alexandria before the formation of the municipality In 1869, the result of a set of compromises between the Egyptian ruler and the 'mercantile community'.[210] In the mid-1860s the Alexandrian merchants, including British concerns like Henry Bulkeley, Barker & Co., and the Carver Brothers, demanded unrestricted public access to the Egyptian state railway, water transport, and docks. The merchants argued that the Egyptian 'Viceroy' had a preferential monopoly.[211] The merchants complained that goods were detained by customs agents because of a want of inspectors and storage space, merchandise was damaged and pillaged, and unpaved roads left carts stuck in the mud to the ruin of merchandise. There was graft on the railway and at the customs house. The merchants proposed a shift of responsibility to the locality, rather than depend upon the Egyptian state. The result of these demands was the creation of the Alexandria municipality, which, ironically perhaps, led to some concessions on colonial privilege, as Moss bemoaned, principally with a tax on cotton and grain exports. After the creation of municipal government, Alexandria fell under a dual authority, unique in Egypt, with the municipality having powers to construct roads, issue rules and regulations for public well-being, with the assent of the Egyptian government.[212] This partnership meant that the municipality was able to widen the tax base, pave roads, and install drainage in the vicinity of the docks. As a sign of its growing autonomy, a municipal council was formed in 1890 of appointed and elected members, with the provision that no more than three persons from any one communal group stood for election. 'The preponderating influences in the Council may best be described as the native [a reference to local Egyptian] influence, the Israelite influence, and the Greek influence.'[213]

Described as a 'city of notables', the great urban monumental structures were those buildings constructed by banks, financial companies, and professional associations, like the Cotton Exchange on the 'Square'; the nearby neoclassical Banco di Roma, modelled on the Farnese Palace in Rome, was said to be the finest building in Alexandria; the palatial quarters of the British Union and the British Consulate were comparable monuments to the British colony. According to Robert Ilbert, in its hybridity Alexandria was more 'Mediterranean' than colonial.[214] Various attempts to give Alexandria a recognisable urban façade, on the scale of the planned colonial cities of Khartoum or Rabat, failed. The forces of a liberal market economy frustrated municipal planning; also, the rapidity of demographic change outran the urban planners who sought to harness it. Plans for large-scale urban renewal were drawn up, but delayed. The main stumbling blocks were the lack of funding from the central government and that the big property holders, Egyptian and foreign, blocked the necessary expropriations.[215] As a consequence, Alexandria's growth was anarchic and unplanned, particularly the ad hoc construction of roads and overcrowding of the urban centre – a cause of complaint because it impeded the movement of goods. After filling every space in the urban core, migrants built informally on the southern fringe of the city. The dwellings were built on land that had not been zoned for housing and without any infrastructure for traffic, sewage, water, or electricity. Known as the *hishash*, the acutely unsanitary conditions therein were made obvious in 1891, a year of a cholera epidemic. An official inquiry proposed the destruction of the *hishash* and the construction of workers housing in line with public health standards. The municipal council entrusted technicians to draw up plans. Years passed before building commenced, on a much reduced scale because of speculation on proposed sites. In spite of claims to the contrary, the results were impractical and the *hishash* grew apace.[216]

In the 1907 report by the municipality's chief engineer, a grand scheme for urban development was proposed with Paris and Vienna as models.[217] Ten years later the same engineer, David Ernest Lloyd-Davies, concluded that these schemes had to be abandoned because of the usual obstructions – speculators driven by profit from rent.[218] Municipal councillor G.B. Alderson's scheme to destroy the bidonvilles and replace them with apartment blocks foundered in council discussion. As if the problem of accommodating the lower classes did not even exist, some councillors proposed that the slums should be replaced with public gardens.[219] Others spoke of future development in a green belt, a 'garden city'.[220] The failure of planners meant that a parallel city of migrants stood as a rebuke to the city of notables. The class divisions were ramified by cultural differences because, by the twentieth century, most migrants to Alexandria were from rural Egypt. In other words, these developments questioned the idea of a multicultural city divided only along class lines because the preponderance of the lower classes, known as *baladi*, were Muslim Egyptians. Most were first-generation residents of the city. Given that the social ills that attended urban development were not cured, nor went away, these served as an indictment of the elites and marked a significant process in the political evolution of Alexandria and Egypt.[221] For one, the result was a shift of authority from the notables to a managerial class of technicians after the First World War. The emerging middle class of functionaries regarded the failed experiments in urban renewal as indicative of an elite society incapable of meeting the needs of a city composed predominately of workers. The experiment in municipal government was instructive because the municipality articulated the interests of a community that had come to represent, at least symbolically, the middle- and lower-class Egyptians.

In sum, the British colony produced wealth, its engineering feats impressive, the municipality a political model; however, it was unable to control the political and social forces these projects set afoot. Ultimately, the best-laid plans of the colony were self-defeating. These themes were reflected, whilst being critiqued, in E.M. Forster's celebrated guide to Alexandria. Nostalgically, he disapproved of the erasure of the city's Mediterranean identity, noting that Alexandria had become more

Egyptian after 1922, with national governments erasing old place names. He regretted this on historical grounds because, as he said, the national project broke 'the few links that bound their city to the past'.²²² The past he referred to was the city of Alexander and Cleopatra, Arius and Plotinus. His aversion to Egyptian nationalism did not mean that Forster had any attachment to the British Empire, because, like Rome, it was 'solid but unattractive'. Imperialism and nationalism were not opposed, not opposite, but identical. It is hard not to read Forster's description of the Roman conquest of Egypt as a commentary on the British invasion:

> She then came forward with studied politeness as the protector of liberty and morals in the East. Legal and self-righteous, she struck a chill in the whole Hellenistic world. She was horrified at its corruption – a corruption of which she never failed to take advantage, and the shattered empire of Alexander fell piece by piece into her hands.²²³

The Ptolemaic stood in for the Levantine in this parable. In it, Forster identified with the fragile compromises of the Ptolemies, inclusive of Egyptians, Greeks, Jews, as well as the melding of all the various gods, rituals, and temples. Identification with Hellenistic Alexandria was a sign of his rejection of the excesses of racial and ethnic exclusions evident in the 'Great War' in Europe and the emerging nationalisms of Africa and Asia. Forster interpreted history as a conflict between the Levantine and its antithesis, nationalism; thus of the religious controversies of late Roman Egypt he said there was the 'nucleus of a national movement' that 'permeated the whole country, even Alexandria, and as soon as it found a theological formula in which to express itself, a revolt against Constantinople broke out'.²²⁴ Here civilised life, 'truth and beauty', was destroyed by 'racial trouble' manifested in the anti-Greek violence of the Egyptian mob led by 'a regular Egyptian monk, poor, bigoted and popular'.²²⁵ In such commentary colonial critiques of Egyptian nationalism were echoed, a distorted reflection of the imperial mission. Forster's *Alexandria: A History and a Guide* offered a historical framework that made colonial Alexandria heir to the legacy of the ancients: Egypt, Greece, and Rome. Focusing on 'Graeco-Roman' Christian Egypt in his history had the effect of denying that Arab and Muslim cultures were capable of sustaining civilised life. Forster's historical narrative was bound up with an imperial culture that imagined that Hellenic-Christian civilisation was 'destroyed' by the 'Arabs'. Referring to the Muslim conquest of Alexandria, he enunciated one of the commonplace myths of popular history: 'Though they had no intention of destroying her, they destroyed her, as a child might a watch. She never functioned again properly for over 1,000 years.'²²⁶

This observation voiced the dominant imperial narrative because, in Forster's logic, modern European colonisation reactivated civilisation. In the late nineteenth and early twentieth century the orthodox view was that the Arab invasions had destroyed Greco-Roman, Christian civilisation, as for instance in A.J. Butler's *The Arab Conquest of Egypt*.[227] Forster acknowledged Butler as an important source, whose views were also endorsed by members of the colony. The son-in-law of Wilfred Jennings-Bramly, Anthony De Cosson, argued in 1933 that late Roman antiquity 'was the last civilising force to affect the land [of Maryut, the Roman province surrounding Alexandria], and from A.D. 600 it gradually declined from prosperous civilisation to neglected desert.'[228] Of course the seventh century witnessed the Arab invasions, confirming the historical timeline of antique civilisation followed by Muslim degeneration. In line with the culture of official imperialism, the arguments were racialist so that De Cosson referred to Oric Bates's argument that the Arab conquests meant that 'the ancient inhabitants' of Egypt and North Africa were 'more and more Semeticised, both in speech and blood'.[229]

The culture of imperialism was not consistent, however, and Forster's position was ambiguous. His story fell short of explicitly serving imperial doctrines, which he despised. His guide corrected some colonial legends, arguing that the Arabs brought a different type of civilisation – 'Oriental', landed, not maritime – resulting in a shift from Alexandria to the new capital at Cairo. As he said, the monuments of medieval Cairo were a testament to the grandeur of a civilisation neither fanatical nor barbarian.[230] The undying legend that the Arabs destroyed the greatest library of the ancient world was, as Forster said, false: It had already been destroyed by the Christians.[231] To this degree Forster provided a critique of popular Orientalist legend, whereas De Cosson was insistent that Arab culture had to be blamed for the destruction of classical Egypt.[232] While it was recognised that the coastal provinces west of Egypt were populated and cultivated for three centuries after they fell under Arab domination, De Cosson said that in those centuries the decline set in, 'for with the Arabs came the wild Beduin and the disappearance of the Roman master farmers. The land must have suffered progressively with increase of the lawlessness of the Beduin, farms and villages would have become deserted, and wells and cisterns neglected, as security was less and less guaranteed.'[233] For seven hundred years, according to De Cosson, the region of Maryut was subject to Bedouin marauders, infiltrating the ruins of ancient monasteries, temples, and cities, besieging the very gates of Alexandria. 'Thus did neglectful government and Beduin lawlessness replace the patient planting of the thousand years of Greco-Roman civilisation. The wind, rain, and sand of continuous seasons completed the destruction, leaving only the foundations of countless building to tell the tale of this once prosperous land.'[234] Gertrude Caton-Thompson, well-known for her work on sites such as Abydos or Zimbabwe, reversed De Cosson's conclusions through her archaeological work in the region of Maryut ('Mareotis'). Her research showed that there had been continuous settlement in the region from 5000 BCE to 1000 CE, after which cultivation and permanent settlement disappeared. She pointed to the environmental causes of degradation, published in an article on the 'Kharga Oasis' in *Antiquity*, June 1931.[235] Together with her discovery of ancient irrigation systems, Caton-Thompson's environmental history marked a break with the cultural arguments of De Cosson. Also, the 'Desert Club' of explorers, given a fictional treatment in Michael Ondaatje's *The English Patient*, revealed the dramatic environmental changes over millennia.[236]

These discussions were not purely academic. The British army transformed the region of Maryut by the pacification of the Bedouin of the Western Desert. A process begun by Muhammad 'Ali, it was completed during the First World War after the Sanusiyya had been won over by German agents and raised a general revolt in the Western Desert as far as Mersa Matruh. As a consequence, the British mobilised as many as thirty-five thousand Egyptian and imperial troops in the Western Desert during the First World War when Wilfred Jennings-Bramly served as an intelligence officer with the Egyptian Frontiers Administration. He was involved in organising a system of depots for the RAF from Aswan to Alamein, as well as building the first desert road from Alexandria, through Maryut, towards the western frontier with Libya. The British line of defence cut the Bedouin off from their crops and pastures and as a result by the winter of 1915–16 the Bedouin were forced to choose between 'starvation with Sanussi or to return broken to the British camp'.[237] After the war Jennings-Bramly absorbed many of the survivors into 'Burg El Arab' (or Burj al-'Arab, Arab Tower), a new town near Abu Sir designed as a 'cultural centre' to promote commerce, manufacturing, and state education.[238] The entire complex was built with the intention to make it fit an imagined 'Arab' cultural landscape. A carpet factory included cloister, tower, and two halls; the nearby walled town had a beautiful court house. It was a kind of fantasy on the theme of a revived Arab civilisation; Francis Rennell Rodd described Jennings-Bramly, its builder, as 'one who loved, and was loved by, the Bedawin of the Western Desert'.[239] As Forster said, Jennings-Bramly cleverly incorporated ancient stone and statuary into a structure of a 'most interesting' design. It was, he wrote, along with the Greco-Roman Museum in Alexandria, 'one of the few pieces of modern creative work to be seen'.[240] Jennings-Bramly's daughter, Vivien, provided a detailed discussion of the significance of Burg El Arab in the 1938 edition of Forster's guide. The region around the village was planted with olive, vines, carobs, and other trees of commercial value. The development of the region made manifest the doctrine of imperial reconstruction of an ancient landscape, according to a colonial vision of that past. The restoration of the ancient 'signal tower' at Abu Sir, after which Burg El Arab was named, fitted the classicism of colonial scholarship. The tower was described by Forster in the guide as the last concrete evidence of the design of the Pharos, Alexandria's lighthouse.[241] As De Cosson said, the point was 'to transform the vast desert into a flourishing country ... inhabited as in antiquity'.[242]

Burg El Arab and the Greco-Roman Museum, Forster's two significant projects in the region, each fitted a colonial vision of Egypt's past and future. The museum was given an extensive and detailed description in Forster's guide and in Lloyd's catalogue. The idea for the museum was initiated in 1892 by the Athenaeum, a literary society that published a journal in Italian, with funds from the municipality and under the directorship or Guiseppe Botti. The uncovering of large numbers of collectible items as a consequence of rapid development of the urban landscape necessitated the museum's expansion at the site at rue Musée (al-Muhtaf) in 1895. As Forster observed, many of the best antiques had fallen into private hands by that date or else had been transferred to museums and public sites in Europe and America. E. Breccia, Botti's successor as director, regretted the loss of so many objects to foreign collections and regarded the museum as necessary to ensure that Egypt's material culture remained in Egypt. He noted that it was incorrect to assume that the museum was principally interested in the collection of monuments in Alexandria illustrating 'Graeco-Roman' history. On the contrary, he said it consisted of various material objects representative of Greek, Roman, and Christian art and civilisation. Such fine distinctions support the impression that the museum celebrated a colonial version of Egyptian history.[243]

Forster, Butler, and De Cosson created a historical narrative that made the Arab period of lesser, if not negligible, cultural or historical value. Nevertheless, Forster's scepticism marked an idiosyncratic slant on the official culture of colonialism. In the guide, he commented, by reference to the neighbourhood of Camp de César, that 'Caesar never camped here'.[244] He defied popular legends, like the idea that the British barracks at Mustafa Pasha was also the site of the encampment of Octavian's legions, with the obvious association of the British as successors to the Roman imperium in Africa.[245] Whilst working on the second edition of the guide, with the assistance of Vivien Jennings-Bramly, Forster concluded that his earlier judgements on the Arabs were incorrect, saying that 'medieval Alexandria was more important than I knew'.[246] Forster's responses to editorial suggestions for the 1938 reprint suggest that it was difficult to break with conventional historical narratives; however, he did reconsider the phrase that the clock had stopped in Alexandria with the Arab invasion.[247] For sure, the idea of a classical cultural stamp on Alexandria represented a colonial barrier against Egyptian and Muslim culture, not unlike the urban social divisions. But these divisions and barriers were permeable. The urban divisions were not cultural constructs, but the product of a pitiless liberal market that did not discriminate by nationality or religion, only profits. The market broke down cultural difference. Born at the intersection of European imperialism and the Ottoman Levant, the Alexandrian locale engendered a liberal market and self-governing political autonomy inclusive of diverse groups. The municipality perpetuated the conditions for the coexistence of subjects of multiple states and beliefs. Forster's imagined historical landscape captured the Levantine orientation of that project.

Notes

1 Nicholas Thomas, *Colonialism's Culture: Anthropology, Travel and Government* (Princeton: Princeton University Press, 1994), p. 105.
2 Robert Bickers, 'Britains and Britons over the Seas', in Robert Bickers (ed.), *Settlers and Expatriates: Britons over the Seas* (Oxford: Oxford University Press, 2010), p. 5.
3 Arnold Wright, 'History', in Arnold Wright and H. A. Cartwright (eds), *Twentieth Century: Impressions of Egypt: Its History, People, Commerce, Industries, and Resources* (London: Lloyd's Greater Britain Publishing Company, 1909), p. 35.
4 John Harry Scott, 'The Capitulations', in Wright and Cartwright, *Twentieth Century*, pp. 109–15.
5 Ibid., pp. 109–10.
6 Earl of Cromer, *Modern Egypt* (London: Macmillan, 1908), vol. 2, p. 130.
7 Ibid., p. 131.
8 Eric Stokes, *The English Utilitarians and India* (Oxford: Clarendon Press, 1959).
9 Peter Mansfield, *The British in Egypt* (New York: Holt, Rinehart, and Winston, 1971), p. 138 & Alfred Milner, *England in Egypt* (London: Edward Arnold, 3rd edn, 1893), pp. 182–3.
10 Earl of Cromer, *Political and Literary Essays, 1908–1913* (London: Macmillan, 1913), p. 3 & Mansfield, *British in Egypt*, p. 313 & Roger Owen, *Lord Cromer: Victorian Imperialist, Edwardian Proconsul* (Oxford: Oxford University Press, 2004), pp. 243–52.
11 Owen, *Lord Cromer*, p. 148.
12 Milner, *England in Egypt*, pp. 392 & 407.
13 George Barnett Smith, *General Gordon: Christian Soldier and Hero* (London: S.W. Partridge & Co., 1896). A contrasting portrait of this complex individual was drawn by Lytton Strachey in his *Eminent Victorians* (New York: Modern Library, 1918).
14 Rudolph C. Slatin Pacha, *Fire and Sword in the Sudan: A Personal Narrative of Fighting and Serving the Dervishes 1879–1895* (Leipzig: Bernhard Tauchnitz, 1896).
15 Philip Ziegler, *Omdurman* (London: Collins, 1973), pp. 14–15.

PROJECTS

16 Winston Churchill, *The River War* (New York: Skyhorse Publishing, 2013, originally published 1899), p. 90.
17 Hugh and Mirabel Cecil, *Imperial Marriage: An Edwardian war and peace* (London: John Murray, 2002), p. 87.
18 Ibid., p. 88.
19 Ibid., p. 91.
20 Lord Edward Cecil, *The Leisure of an Egyptian Official* (London: Hodder and Stoughton, 1921).
21 Hugh and Mirabel Cecil, *Imperial Marriage*, p. 90.
22 Churchill, *River War*, p. 93.
23 Catherine Hall, 'Culture and Identity in Imperial Britain', in Sarah Stockwell (ed.), *The British Empire: Themes and Perspectives* (Oxford: Blackwell, 2008), p. 208.
24 Ziegler, *Omdurman*, p. 51.
25 Ibid., p. 52.
26 Ibid., p. 51.
27 Mansfield, *British in Egypt*, p. 87.
28 MECA GB 165-0295, Gordon Waterfield, Box 5, File 1, letter, Gerald Delany to Waterfield, 27 Jan. 1974.
29 Ibid.
30 Henry Keown-Boyd, *The Lion and Sphinx: The Rise and Fall of the British in Egypt* (Durham: Memoir Club, 2002), p. 27.
31 Malcolm Yapp, 'Introduction', in Malcolm Yapp (ed.), *Politics and Diplomacy in Egypt: The Diaries of Sir Miles Lampson 1935–1937*, (Oxford: Oxford University Press, 1997), p. 43.
32 Ibid., p. 11.
33 Mansfield, *British in Egypt*, p. 184 & Milner, *England in Egypt*, p. 172.
34 Ibid., pp. 93 & 319.
35 Robert Tignor, *Modernization and British Colonial Rule in Egypt: 1882–1914* (Princeton: Princeton University Press, 1966), p. 336.
36 TNA FO371/249 24583.
37 Ami Ayalon, *The Press in the Arab Middle East* (New York: Oxford University Press, 1995), pp. 162 & 237.
38 Naguib Mahfouz, *Palace Walk* (New York: Doubleday, 1990), pp. 357–8 & Salma Musa, *The Education of Salma Musa*, trans. L.O. Schuman (Leiden: E.J. Brill, 1961), pp. 27–37.
39 'Abd al-Rahman al-Rafi'i, *Mustafa Kamil ba'ith al-haraka al-wataniyya* (Cairo: 1939), pp. 195 & 251.
40 Donald M. Reid, *Lawyers in Politics in the Arab World* (Chicago: Bibliotheca Islamica, 1981), p. 41, n. 5 & Jacques Berque, *Egypt: Imperialism and Revolution*, trans. Jean Stewart (London: Faber & Faber, 1972), p. 204, n. 1.
41 Michael Ezekiel Gasper, *The Power of Representation: Publics, Peasants, and Islam in Egypt* (Stanford: Stanford University Press, 2009), pp. 175–6.
42 Sir Maurice Amos, *England and Egypt: Cust Foundation Lecture* (Nottingham: University College, 1929), pp. 12 & 66.
43 Zaki Fahmi, *Safwat al-'asr fi tarikh wa rusum mashahir rijal misr min 'ahd sakin al-jinan Muhammad 'Ali pasha al-kabir mutajan bi rasm sahib al-jilalat Fu'ad al-awwal malik misr wa sudan* (Cairo: Matba 'at al-i'timad, 1926), p. 116.
44 Chafika Soliman Hamamsy, *Zamalek: The Changing Life of a Cairo Elite, 1850–1945* (Cairo: American University in Cairo Press, 2005), pp. 53–5, 84–6, 130 & 149.
45 Milner, *England in Egypt*, p. 289.
46 Owen, *Cromer*, p. 286.
47 P.G. Elgood, *Egypt and the Army* (Oxford: Oxford University Press, 1924), pp. 35–6.
48 Cromer, *Modern Egypt*, vol. 2, pp. 172–3 & 186.
49 Hamamsy, *Zamalek*, p. 130.
50 MECA GB 165-0247, Sir Thomas Wentworth Russell, letter, 7 July 1906.
51 Edith Finch, *Wilfrid Scawen Blunt* (London: Jonathan Cape, 1938), p. 329.

EGYPT

52 MECA GB 165-0160, Wilfred Edgar Jennings-Bramly, Box 1, Folder 4, draft letter to *Daily Mail*.
53 Ibid.
54 Mabel Caillard, *A Lifetime in Egypt, 1876–1935* (London: Grant Richards, 1935), p. 106.
55 Ibid., p. 124.
56 Ibid., p. 148.
57 Ibid., p. 149.
58 Keown-Boyd, *Lion and Sphinx*, pp. 22 & 109.
59 Ronald Seth, *Russell Pasha* (London: William Kimber, 1966), pp. 20–1.
60 MECA GB 165-0247, Sir Thomas Wentworth Russell, letter, 30 Oct. 1907.
61 Ronald Storrs, *Orientations* (London: Nicholson & Watson, 1937), p. 77.
62 MECA GB 165-0034 Humphrey Bowman, Box 3, diary, Sept. 1905–Mar. 1910, cutting from *Egyptian Standard* (1 Oct. 1907) & letter, 1 Jan. 1905.
63 MECA GB 165-0034 Humphrey Bowman, Box 3, diary, Sept. 1903–Dec. 1904.
64 Ibid., 4 Dec. 1903.
65 Ibid., 21 April 1905.
66 *Egyptian Gazette* (1 Oct. 1907).
67 'Cromer's Farewell', *The Times* (6 May 1907); on financial reforms, *Mail* (28 Oct. 1907).
68 Wilfrid Blunt, *Atrocities of Justice in Egypt under British Rule in Egypt* (London: T Fisher Unwin, 1906).
69 MECA GB 165-0034 Humphrey Bowman, Box 3, diary 27 Sept. 1906.
70 Ibid., 27 Sept. 1906.
71 Lambeth Palace Library (hereafter, LPL), Davidson papers, 12 ff. 4–6, 'Interview with Lord Cromer at Lambeth, Friday, July 13th 1906'.
72 Ibid.
73 Ibid.
74 LPL Davidson papers, 93 ff. 191–5, letter, Douglas M. Thornton to Davidson, 25 Feb. 1904.
75 Ibid.
76 Ibid.
77 LPL Davidson papers, 112 ff. 395–419 'Missionary Work in Egypt'.
78 Ibid.
79 Ibid.
80 LPL Tait papers, 214 ff. 144–9, 'Letters on Missionary Work in Egypt', 1879.
81 LPL Tait papers, 264 ff. 163–5, 'M. L. Whately, Medical Missions and Schools in Cairo, Egypt'.
82 LPL Tait papers, 264 ff. 163–5, letter, 'Medical Mission and Schools in Cairo, Egypt, under M. L. Whately.
83 Mary Louisa Whately, *Ragged Life in Egypt* (London: Seeley, Jackson and Halliday, 1863).
84 LPL Davidson papers, 93 ff. 191–5, 'Political and Religious Situation in Egypt, Feb. 25 1904'.
85 LPL Davidson papers, 112 ff. 409–10, 'Egypt, 1906'.
86 British Parliamentary Papers Accounts and Papers, vol. cxii, *Egypt*, No. 1 (London, 1910) and Cromer, *Modern Egypt*, vol. 2, pp. 211–13 & 229.
87 LPL Benson, 9 ff. 151–62: 310, 'The Copts as a Political Factor', attributed to Sheldon Amos.
88 LPL Benson, 9 ff. 151–62: 265, 'The Egyptian Movement Inaugurated in Meeting of Jerusalem Chamber, 22 Feb. 1883'.
89 LPL Benson, 9 ff. 151–62: 279, 'Blakiston to Archbishop'.
90 LPL MS 2335 ff. 1–104: 20–21, 'Association for the Furtherance of Christianity in Egypt', est. 1883, Chairman, Archbishop of York (Oct. 1897).
91 LPL MS 2335 ff. 1–2, letter of Charles Bromage, warden of Gordon College, Saint George's Day, 1887.

PROJECTS

92 LPL Benson, 40 ff. 247, *Guardian* (28 July 1886), '2nd Public Meeting of AFCE – Jerusalem-Chamber'.
93 Egyptian National Archives, Majlis al-Wuzara' (Council of Ministers), Box M/3/1, Ministry of Interior, reports on political speeches in Asyut in 1915, which made reference to the violence in 1910.
94 LPL MS 2335 ff. 34, *Al-Liwa* (7 Feb. 1900).
95 LPL MS 2335 ff. 37, letter, Bishop Blyth to Cromer, 15 Feb. 1900.
96 LPL MS 2335 ff. 53–5, draft appeal and memo on draft appeal, 1900.
97 Edward Said, *Out of Place: A Memoir* (New York: Vintage, 2000), p. 144.
98 Ibid., p. 122.
99 'Bishop's Letter', *Diocesan Review* 15/3 (1936).
100 Penelope Lively, *Oleander, Jacaranda: A Childhood Perceived* (London: Viking, 1994), p. 89.
101 Said, *Out of Place*, pp. 263 & 280
102 Mansfield, *British in Egypt*, pp. 323–5.
103 'Bishop's Letter', *The Diocesan Review*, 17/5 (1938).
104 Ibid., 31:4 (1951).
105 TNA FO141/1, British Institutions, note by McMahon to FO.
106 TNA FO141/1, note, British Union to HC (Lord Lloyd), 1926.
107 Said, *Out of Place*, pp. 185–6.
108 Ibid., p. 75.
109 Ibid.
110 MECA GB 165-0002, Herbert Addison, pamphlet, 'Victoria College', p. 2.
111 Wright and Cartwright, *Twentieth Century*, p. 448.
112 Michael Haag, *Alexandria: City of Memory* (Cairo: American University in Cairo Press, 2004), p. 148.
113 Wright and Cartwright, *Twentieth Century*, p. 448.
114 Sahar Hamouda and Colin Clement (eds), *Victoria College: A History Revealed* (Cairo: American University in Cairo Press, 2002), pp. 19–20.
115 Ibid., pp. 13 & 251.
116 Said, *Out of Place*, p. 39.
117 Ibid., pp. 200–1.
118 Ibid., p. 184. David Lean, dir. *Lawrence of Arabia* (1963); Henry Barakat, dir. *Fi baitina rajul* (1961).
119 Said, *Out of Place*, p. 42.
120 Ibid., pp. 43–5, 104, 145 & 182–5.
121 Alain Silvera and William Cleveland, 'Victoria College', www.encyclopedia.com/doc/1G2–3424602826.html (accessed 16 Nov. 2016).
122 Geoffrey Nash, *The Arab Writer in English: Arab Themes in a Metropolitan Language* (Brighton: Sussex Academic Press, 1998), p. 110 & Edward Atiyah, *An Arab Tells his Story: An Study in Loyalties* (London: John Murray, 1947).
123 Nash, *Arab Writer*, p. 110.
124 Ibid., p. 111.
125 Said, *Out of Place*, p. 42.
126 Phyllis Lassner, *Colonial Strangers: Women Writing the End of the British Empire* (London: Rutgers University Press, 2004), p. 37.
127 Ibid., pp. 266 & 278.
128 Ibid., pp. 278–9.
129 Robert Graves, *Goodbye to All That* (London: Penguin, 2000, originally published 1929), p. 267.
130 Ibid., p. 267.
131 Ibid., pp. 272–4.
132 Timothy Mitchell, *Colonising Egypt* (Berkeley: University of California Press, 1988), pp. 108–10.
133 Charles D. Smith, *Islam and the Search for Social Order in Modern Egypt* (Albany: New York University Press, 1983), p. 268.

EGYPT

134 MECA GB 165-0115, Robert Allason Furness, Box 3, Folder 2 (hereafter 'MECA Furness 3/2'), item 1 & G.S. Fraser, *A Stranger and Afraid* (Manchester: Carcanet New Press, 1983), pp. 153–9 & Roger Bowen, *'Many Histories Deep': The Personal Landscape Poets in Egypt 1940–1945* (New Jersey: Associated University Presses, 1995), pp. 40–1.
135 *The Times* (20 Mar. 1935).
136 *The Times* (16 Nov. 1936).
137 MECA Furness 3/ 2, letter, British Council to Furness, 22 Sept. 1937.
138 *The Times* (16 Nov. 1936).
139 TNA FO924/851, 'Cultural Relations Dept. Report on the Main Work of the British Council'.
140 MECA GB 165-0002, Herbert Addison, 'List of British Officials in the Egyptian Service, 1926–1945'.
141 Ibid.
142 MECA Furness 3/2, 'Egyptian Students at Foreign Schools 1930–1' & item 24, letter, Embassy to Furness, n.d.
143 E. Yaghdijan, 'The English School Cairo 1916–1956', www.esc-obog.org/1916–1956.html (accessed 16 Nov. 2016).
144 TNA FO141/1, 'Schools, Church, Hospital'.
145 TNA FO141/679/5, 'Private' letter of Lloyd to Churchill, 18 Nov. 1928. Churchill to Lloyd, 13 Dec. 1928, promising the £2000 grant to the New English School. In 1928 there were seventy-two British children under school age.
146 'The English School', *Egyptian Gazette* (12 Mar. 1938), p. 2.
147 Ibid.
148 TNA FO141/1, 'Need for a British Hospital in Cairo'.
149 TNA FO141/607, 'Lord Kitchener Memorial, 1916'.
150 Rhodes House, Oxford (hereafter RH), MSS Brit. Emp. s 400, Box 139 File 3, f. 1, letter, 23 Jan. 1920, Sohag, Upper Egypt, Susan Adair to ONA.
151 RH MSS Brit. Emp. s 400, Box 134, File 7, ff 26–7.
152 RH MSS Brit. Emp. s 400, Box 134, File 7, f. 36, 4 Jan. 1952 & f. 55, 1962.
153 RH MSS Brit. Emp. s 400, Box 129.
154 TNA FO78/3568, 'Lord Dufferin Scheme for Reorganisation'.
155 Ibid.
156 C.W.R. Long, *British Pro-Consuls in Egypt, 1914–1929: The Challenge of Nationalism* (London: Routledge Curzon, 2004), p. 24.
157 Cromer, *Modern Egypt*, vol. 2, p. 481.
158 Elgood, *Egypt and the Army*, pp. 9–11 & 37.
159 Karen van Nieuwkirk, 'The Pleasures of Public Space: Muhammad 'Ali Street and the Nightclubs in Cairo (1900–1950), in Dimitra Gefou-Madianou (ed.), *Alcohol, Gender, and Culture* (London: Routledge, 1992) & James H. Mill, *Cannabis Britannica: Empire, Trade, and Prohibition 1800–1929* (Oxford: Oxford University Press, 2003) & Nathan Lambert Fonder, 'Pleasure, Leisure, or Vice? Public Morality in Imperial Cairo, 1882–1949' (PhD dissertation, Harvard University, 2013).
160 Thomas Russell, *Egyptian Service 1902–1946* (London: John Murray, 1949), pp. 18–19.
161 Elgood, *Egypt and the Army*, pp. 281–2.
162 Ibid., p. 258.
163 Ibid., p. 260.
164 Ibid., p. 261.
165 Mansfield, *British in Egypt*, p. 214.
166 MECA GB 165-0234, Sir Thomas Cecil Rapp, memoirs, p. 14.
167 Ibid., p. 20.
168 Ibid., p. 49 & Elgood, *Egypt and the Army*, pp. 281–2.
169 MECA GB 165-0234, Sir Thomas Cecil Rapp, memoirs, p. 36.
170 Australian Light Horse Studies Centre, Desert Column, 'First Wassa', account by 955 Private John 'Jack' Jensen, 1st Battalion, H Company, written on 28 Aug. 1915, England, commenting on events 5 April 1915, http://alh-research.tripod.com/

PROJECTS

Light_Horse/index.blog/1973775/first-wassa-egypt-april-2-1915-john-jack-jensens-account (accessed 16 Nov. 2016).
171 Seth, *Russell Pasha*, pp. 169–95.
172 MECA GB 165-0234, Sir Thomas Cecil Rapp, memoirs, p. 32.
173 Ibid.
174 Ibid., p. 37.
175 *The Times* (5 June 1934). Russell, *Egyptian Service*, p. 222.
176 E.M. Forster, *Alexandria: A History and a Guide and Pharos and Pharillon*, ed. Miriam Allott (London: André Deutsch, 2004), pp. 238–40 & Seth, *Russell Pasha*, p. 169.
177 Evelyn Waugh, *Labels: A Mediterranean Journal* (New York: Penguin, 1985), p. 60.
178 MECA GB 165-0234, Sir Thomas Cecil Rapp, memoirs, p. 37.
179 Ibid., p. 39.
180 Ibid., p. 37.
181 Ibid., p. 39.
182 Ibid., p. 37 & TNA FO141/463/1411, British Consulate, 1924, 'Report of the Committee of the British Charitable Fund' & TNA FO141463/1229, 'Memo, Consulate', reporting on the 'sore of mixed marriages' because of women becoming British subjects, abandoned by the men, and turned into the streets.
183 Philippa Levine, 'Sexuality, Gender, and Empire', in Philippa Levine (ed.), *Gender and Empire* (Oxford: Oxford University Press, 2004), pp. 140–1.
184 MECA GB 165-0310, John Young, 'A Little to the East', ch. 7, 'Early Days in Egypt', pp. 4–10 & Hanan Kholoussy, 'Stolen Husbands, Foreign Wives: Mixed Marriage, Identity Formation, and Gender in Colonial Egypt', *Hawwa* 1/2 (2003): 206–40.
185 MECA GB 165-0234, Sir Thomas Cecil Rapp, memoirs, pp. 37–8.
186 The prevalence of the theme of the 'degraded' woman in colonial discourse is discussed by Catherine Hall, 'Of Gender and Empire: Reflections on the Nineteenth Century', in Levine, *Gender and Empire*, pp. 52–8.
187 Malak Badrawi, *Political Violence in Egypt 1910–1925: Secret Societies, Plots and Assassinations* (London: Curzon, 2000), p. 5.
188 Elgood, *Egypt and the Army*, pp. 219–21.
189 Russell, *Egyptian Service*, pp. 214–15.
190 Seth, *Russell Pasha*, p. 166.
191 TNA FO371/10020 1727/22/16 & TNA FO371/10887 2237/29/16: British intelligence reports on Wafd radicalism and the assassination of Stack. Press reports on Ghali's assassination: *The Times* (22 & 23 Feb. 1910).
192 TNA FO371/10887 2337/29/16. The evidence showed that the assassins of Stack had links to the chief political agent of King Ahmad Fu'ad.
193 Elgood, *Egypt and the Army*, p. 59.
194 Hanna F. Wissa, *Assiout: The Saga of an Egyptian Family* (Sussex: Book Guild, 1994), letter, Esther Fahmy Wissa to Lord Allenby, 1 Sept. 1922, pp. 369–70.
195 Russell, *Egyptian Service*, pp. 214–21 & Seth, *Russell Pasha*, pp. 157–68.
196 TNA FO371/11582 637/25/16, 1926. Documents indicate that the assassination plot might have been masterminded by the chief of the royal cabinet, Hasan Nasha'at. The same palace clique may well have been behind an assassination attempt on Zaghlul, TNA FO141/787/27, 1928, 'Political Murders in Egypt'.
197 Tom Stevenson, 'Sisi's Way', *London Review of Books*, 37/4 (2015): 3–7.
198 Muhammad Anwar el-Sadat, *Revolt on the Nile* (New York: John Day Company, 1957).
199 Seth, *Russell Pasha*, p. 159.
200 For example, the assassin of al-Nuqrashi was judged not guilty of the intent to bring about revolution because political circumstances, such as the situation in Palestine and British military occupation, created extenuating circumstances. See Richard P. Mitchell, *The Society of Muslim Brothers* (Oxford: Oxford University Press, 1969), pp. 75–8.
201 Lawrence Durrell, 'Introduction to the New Edition', in E.M. Forster, *Alexandria: A History and a Guide* (London: Anchor Press, 1982), p. xi.

EGYPT

202 Robert Mabro, 'Alexandria 1860–1960: The Cosmopolitan Identity', in Anthony Hirst and Michael Silk (eds), *Alexandria: Real and Imagined* (Aldershot: Ashgate, 2004), pp. 247–62. Mabro refers to the principle of 'coexistence', not cultural mixing, as the key to the community's success in this period. Political and religious issues were never discussed, people therefore conversed on business and leisure pursuits.
203 Michael Haag, *Alexandria: City of Memory* (New Haven: Yale University Press, 2004), p. 130.
204 The phrase was used by Jasper Yeates Brinton, an American resident of Alexandria, as cited by Haag, *Alexandria*, p. 132.
205 Wright and Cartwright, *Twentieth Century*, p. 459.
206 Ibid., p. 429.
207 Will Hanley, 'Foreignness and Localness in Alexandria, 1880–1914' (PhD dissertation, Princeton University, 2007), pp. 60–6.
208 Ibid., p. 300.
209 Wright and Cartwright, *Twentieth Century*, p. 459.
210 Ibid., p. 432.
211 MECA GB 165-0246 35, Frederick Terry Rowlatt, photocopies of minutes of a meeting of British merchants, Alexandria, 1864.
212 Wright and Cartwright, *Twentieth Century*, p. 432.
213 Ibid., p. 433.
214 Robert Ilbert, *Alexandrie 1830–1930, histoire d'une communauté citadine* (Cairo: Institute Français d'Archéologie Orientale, 1996), 2 vols, vol. 2, p. 537.
215 Ibid., vol. 2, pp. 514–19.
216 Ibid., vol. 2, p. 520.
217 Ibid., vol. 2, p. 544.
218 Ibid., vol. 2, p. 524.
219 Ibid., vol. 2, p. 521.
220 Ibid., vol. 2, p. 526.
221 Ibid., vol. 2, p. 514.
222 Forster, *Alexandria* (2004), p. 87.
223 Ibid., pp. 29–30.
224 Ibid., p. 51.
225 Ibid., p. 51.
226 As cited by Lawrence Durrell, *Justine* (London: Faber & Faber, 1961), p. 253. The 'properly' was inserted into the 1938 edition, the original 1922 edition read, 'She never functioned again for over 1,000 years.' See Forster, *Alexandria* (2004), pp. 54–5.
227 A.J. Butler, *The Arab Conquest of Egypt and the Last Thirty Years of Roman Dominion* (Oxford: Clarendon Press, 1902) & Anthony De Cosson, *Mareotis* (London: Country Life, 1933), p. 53.
228 De Cosson, *Mareotis*, p. 51.
229 Oric Bates, *Cairo Scientific Journal* 6 (1912), as cited by De Cosson, *Mareotis*, p. 58.
230 Forster, *Alexandria* (2004), p. 69.
231 Ibid., pp. 55 & 120.
232 De Cosson, *Mareotis*, p. 57.
233 Ibid., pp. 59–60.
234 Ibid., p. 63.
235 Ibid., p. 100 & G. Caton-Thompson, 'Kharga Oasis', *Antiquity* 5 (1931): 221–6.
236 Michael Ondaatje acknowledged A.M. Hassanein Bey, 'Through Kufra to Darfur', *Geographical Journal* 64/4 (1924): 273–91.
237 De Cosson, *Mareotis*, p. 182.
238 Forster, *Alexandria* (1982), p. lxii.
239 Francis Rennell Rodd, *General William Eaton, the Failure of an Idea* (London, 1933), as cited by De Cosson, *Mareotis*, p. 128.
240 Forster, *Alexandria* (2004), pp. 156–7.

PROJECTS

241 Ibid.
242 De Cosson, *Mareotis*, p. 190.
243 E. Breccia, 'Alexandria Museum of Archaeology', in Wright and Cartwright, *Twentieth Century*, p. 138.
244 Forster, *Alexandria* (2004), p. 135.
245 Gladys Peto, *Egypt of the Sojourner* (London & Toronto: J.M. Dent & Sons, 1928), p. 47.
246 Forster, *Alexandria* (2004), p. 276.
247 Haag, *Alexandria*, pp. 120–4. See above, n. 229.

CHAPTER FOUR

Colonial life

Herbert Addison was lecturing on engineering at Leeds University when one of his students, 'Abd al-Majid 'Umar, recruited him to teach at the Egyptian state school of engineering in 1921. He arrived in the midst of a political crisis. The revolt of 1919 had undermined the Protectorate, and the government of Lloyd George was involved in fruitless negotiations with Egyptian nationalists: 'moderates' behind 'Adli Yakan Pasha and 'radicals' led by Sa'd Zaghlul Pasha. Addison checked into the Helwan Hotel, a resort on the desert's edge occupied by retired officials like Sir William Willcocks and officers of the 47th Squadron of the RAF, the latter group in the process of establishing permanent installations nearby. The impression of a besieged colonial enclave could only have been magnified when Addison found lodgings in the new suburb of Ma'adi. In *Oriental Spotlight*, C.S. Jarvis described Ma'adi as bourgeois; its colonial residents wrote poetry and tended their gardens. Yet Addison nostalgically recalled in the 1970s that after three decades this colonial 'oasis' had evolved from exclusivity into a 'multi-racial' community.[1] The theme of multiracialism was Addison's response to historical works appearing in the 1960s and 1970s, like Jacques Berque's portrait of the ruling caste in *Egypt: Imperialism and Revolution* or Peter Mansfield's theory of 'social apartheid' in *The British in Egypt*.[2] Addison's memories were of an entirely different type.[3] According to him, Berque and Mansfield had it wrong. Edward Cecil's *The Leisure of an Egyptian Official* was notorious among British residents for its ridicule of Egyptians. Suburbs like Ma'adi were composed of diverse nationalities, where residents entered into social circles on equal terms. The result was an international society, tolerant of difference.[4] Nostalgia meant that Addison was quite incapable of appreciating, or remembering, that it was exactly that process of elite 'cosmopolitanism' that Berque credited in his study as one of the primary causes of revolution, in so far as the Westernised culture of the elites alienated the mass of the population.[5] Social histories of Egypt have likened Ma'adi to the 'hill stations' of the Raj – in other words, exclusive British reserves designed to provide a refuge that replicated the conditions of metropolitan life.[6] Some nationalists and most Islamists abhorred foreigners and the Westernising trends of the elites, more so that the Egyptian government tolerated these incursions, a sign of the underlying colonial order of things: Jewish, Lebanese, and Syrian firms owned the fashionable department stores of Cicurel, Sednaoui, and Orosdi Back; Greeks monopolised the groceries, such as Lappa, Puchlivano, Vazelak, Macriganni; Italians the art shops; the Armenians the jewellers; British firms included Shell and Imperial Chemical Industries. When Addison arrived in the 1920s, the higher schools of engineering, medicine, and agriculture had British personnel and instruction was in English. Whereas these 'realities' raised the ire of nationalists, Addison's perspective was that Egypt tolerated cultural difference through liberal political principle and a culture of hospitality. Addison made the point by recounting a conversation with an engineering associate from South Africa who:

> suddenly asked one, 'And what do you do about your colour problem in Egypt, Professor Addison?' ... I could only answer, 'But we haven't got a colour problem.' Nor had we ... anyone could go into Shepheard's Hotel if he seemed to be appropriately dressed in a summer suit, in a dark suit, in white tie and tails, in the uniform of an Egyptian or British army officer, or what was then beginning to be described as National dress – cloak and turban, *agal* and *kuffieh*.[7]

Arguably, the diversity of elite society blinded colonials to the mass of those Muslim Egyptians excluded by poverty and cultural difference, that is to say their inability to enter into the multiracial society Addison described. To employ Albert Memmi's scheme of colonial, coloniser, and colonialist, Addison was a 'colonial', a coloniser who 'refuses' to engage in the political project of negating the colonised, but was equally implicated.[8] Also implicated were the Egyptian elites because race was not the primary sign of exclusion: social mobility in colonial Egypt was a reflection less of race than of the attributes of the 'civilised'.[9]

For Addison, coexistence was a reality, threatened only by the political. He was critical of the way the imperialistic mind-set stoked nationalist political fires. As an example, Addison mentioned Churchill's statement in 1935 that Britain would defend Egypt from Italian aggression, which caused a storm in the classroom because it offended Egyptian national pride. The implication was that Egypt was a mere colony under British protection. But Addison asserted that British expatriate, salaried officials in the Egyptian government service, like himself, 'were not directly concerned with the political contests of [Egyptian] PM, [Egyptian] King, and HC [British high commissioner]'.[10] Within the university British staff and Egyptian student isolated political opinion from personal relationships, 'I always regarded my Egyptian colleagues and students as friends and allies, and if they thought differently about me they kept very quiet about it.'[11] These reflections amount to a critique of imperialism and nationalism, concluding that imperial politics ruined a uniquely tolerant, multicultural society. Berque would have argued that the 'secret history' of diplomacy and nationalism was irrelevant to the underlying causes of conflict: colonial society was fundamentally unsustainable because of its class inequalities and cultural contradictions.[12] How can any society succeed that is premised on a future (Westernisation and modernisation) that denies and negates the culture of the society it seeks to lead and transform? Thus, for many critical observers of Western imperialism the idea of cosmopolitanism was but a veil for European supremacy, which attended the exploitation of resources and the servitude of colonised peoples. Colonial society was divided between European and 'native' sectors, establishing the framework for 'social apartheid' or 'ruling caste' ideology. Cosmopolitanism in this sense was employed by Berque to equate elite colonial society with Westernisation and a cultural transformation whereby non-Western cultures followed a trajectory plotted by the dominant Western world. Cosmopolitan, in this definition, posits that one culture or civilisation is supreme.[13] Indeed, the theme of assimilation was a hallmark of colonial ideologies. It is not surprising that theories of nationalism were highly critical of the assimilated or Westernised intellectual or what Frantz Fanon referred to as the 'cosmopolitan mould' of the 'national middle class'.[14]

These interpretations consign colonial society to a very narrow box. In fact, colonials and Egyptian elites stepped out of these confines and found common ground by excluding the political, the religious, and other signs of difference. The Egyptian elites of the era were not 'Westernised', only adopting elements of foreign culture selectively.[15] Likewise, the lived experience of the colonial diverged from the dictums of imperialist and nationalist ideologies, whether those of Cromer and Milner or Fanon and Memmi. In his descriptions of the ordinary regime of everyday chores, office, and leisure, Addison refused to regard race or culture as markers of difference. Penelope Lively recalled her childhood in Egypt through the prism of class, not race. There were no references to the 'fellaheen', whether negatively or positively. On exoticism, Addison had nothing to say. He was a lecturer in the university and his Egyptian associates were culturally much like himself. Thomas Rapp, a consular agent, had something to say on the harem, drugs, and other exotic habits of the Egyptians, yet he and his wife had close social ties with Egyptians of the upper classes – again, culturally similar. Rapp had little to say on empire, in spite of the fact that he was a representative of the British state in Egypt, except to reproach the miscalculations of its agents at critical moments, like reprisals against Egyptians in the Canal Zone in the 1950s. These memoirs, alongside guides, travel books, poetry, and novels, configure the formulaic references of imperial discourses differently and disclose that colonial identity was multiple, not singular. Individual persons did not fit into a single pattern, or necessarily show obeisance to the high rhetoric of imperialism or nationalism. Comparisons tend to suggest a familiar frame of reference: for many the point was that life in Egypt was normal, enjoyable, a 'home' – if one could avoid the politics.

Domesticity

Florence Nightingale found her vocation in Egypt, Gertrude Caton-Thompson reassembled the archaeological record, Vivien Jennings-Bramly collaborated with E.M. Forster on the second edition of the *Guide*; not all women were nurturers in the home. Nevertheless, according to Mabel Caillard, most women respected the hierarchical order of colonial society.[16] Lady Cromer led British women on social visits to the royal palace every fortnight through the 'season'. Women were expected to follow strict decorum in dress and behaviour as representatives of British imperial prestige before the 'gilded settee' of the Vicereine.[17] Violet Cecil, on the other hand, rejected the rigid forms of colonial society after following her husband, Edward, to Egypt in 1901. The Cecils were an attractive and sought-after couple; however, Violet found the social milieu stifling and dull. She observed that British women were required to adopt a demure and restricted social role comparable to Egyptian women. The rationale might have been to avoid upsetting Muslim sentiment by the spectacle of British women mixing freely at public engagements, but the consequence was the seclusion and segregation of British women. Her contacts with Egyptian women were 'formal and banal'.[18] She was unable to make friends outside the British ruling set and it shocked her that marriages between British and Egyptians were practically forbidden, noting the case of a high-ranking officer in the Sudan service who was demoted for marrying a Muslim woman. Not only was British colonial society stifling, but Cairo's development as a capital of international finance and leisure pinched the penurious British official class. Like other colonial women, Violet was confronted by the choice of staying with her husband in an impoverished colonial setting or with her children, who would be sent to boarding school in Britain. Violet left Egypt in 1902. She preferred the openness of London society, as well as the company of Alfred Milner, with whom she had a life-long affair. It is therefore telling to rehearse Edward Cecil's reflections in *The Leisure of an Egyptian Official* on both the trials and virtues of British colonial women:

> Their personal appearance is rarely pleasing – climate and anxiety have seen to that; and their clothes, well, all that can usually be said of them is that in the daytime, at all events, they are amply sufficient for the requirements of decency. Their qualities that matter are on a different plane. For genuine kindness, real warmth of heart, noble uncomplaining devotion to their husbands and children, they are as a rule above criticism. Poor things! many of them, military and civil, have never had a home of their own since they married; the climate, which is unpleasant for the man, means sickness and pain to them. They must leave the delicate child they love at home, and too often must watch those they love with them wither because they are too poor to send them away. Their very bread depends on the often frayed and slender thread of their husband's life, and their daily existence is one long struggle to make the two ends meet.[19]

Cecil honoured what was taken as the norm, those women who accepted the sacrifices and constraints of empire. His wife chose her children, her lover, and London over service. Perhaps this accounts for the acidity of Edward Cecil's memoirs. Another high-ranking official offers a comparative perspective. Sir Alexander Keown-Boyd was a contemporary of Cecil's. Joining the Sudan service in 1907, he rose up the ranks in the Egyptian service to director-general, European Department, Ministry of the Interior from 1923 to 1937. Alexander's son, Henry Keown-Boyd, published a memoir in the form of a historical study, although his private papers provide a more intimate glimpse into domestic relations. One of these papers is simply entitled 'Memoir by Henry Keown-Boyd of his father's orderly Ahmed'. The memoir said that when serving with the Egyptian army in the Sudan, Alexander Keown-Boyd engaged 'Ahmed' as an orderly with the rank of corporal (*ombashi*). The connection with the Keown-Boyd family assured Ahmed's rise in the Egyptian service. He was transferred from the military to the police at the rank of *bash-shawish* (sergeant-major), which according to family 'legend' was entirely the work of Henry's mother, Joan Keown-Boyd, who pressured her husband to win the promotion not out of love of Ahmed but because she had heard that another orderly of a British officer had that rank. Even the rank of servants was a mark of relative privilege in the colonial pecking order. Joan Keown-Boyd ruled the domestic household in a domineering fashion. Her political views on imperial politics were decidedly conservative. Ahmed feared her. In a telling note of the intimacy of the household, Henry Keown-Boyd recalled that 'Ahmed was certainly one of my earliest memories.' He exerted considerable influence over the other domestic staff and despised junior members of the family, including Henry. Ahmed's loyalty was entirely to the 'master' of the household. Ahmed and Henry's father had, recalled Henry, a 'curious relationship as I do not think I ever heard them address a word to each other ... When my father died Ahmed wept ... Was he mourning a beloved master and friend or a meal-ticket? Who knows – perhaps both.' Afterwards, Ahmed transferred his 'grudging' loyalty to Henry, 'appearing every morning on a motorcycle with a side-car and wearing a peculiar looking French beret'. And although he served the family through two generations, 'when things looked bad for the British during the 1956 Suez crisis he disappeared and I never saw or heard of him again'.[20] Known only as 'Ahmed', the man's personal history was unknown to the Keown-Boyds, although he was reputedly from Morocco and had a 'negroid' complexion. The practice of employing Sudanese or Nubians is comparable to the preference for people of African American descent to serve as porters on sleeping cars in the United States (where they are always referred to as 'George'). Other terms denoting African servants across the British Empire were 'John' and 'Caesar', employed generically, not unlike the use of the label 'Sarah' for downstairs female servants in aristocratic houses in England. The point was to strip the person of their identity.[21]

Domestics were employed by many British residents, certainly all those seeking status. Normally, it was said, communications between colonials and servants were made only in 'kitchen Arabic', which consisted of words in the imperative (orders) or stock nouns and adjectives. Tourists and short-term residents typically knew only a few such phrases. The most common Arabic terms were *imshi* and *yalla* – 'Go!' As Gladys Peto reported in 1928, 'In the homes of British residents and Government officials (there are still a few of the latter) the servants are not allowed to speak English.'[22] This was pure ritual, Peto observed, because she said that English was perfectly well understood by Egyptians employed as servants.[23] Commonplace terms in colonial parlance were quickly picked up by visitors: *imshi*, *yalla*, *shufti* (look), *kulu* (everything), *mafish* (nothing), *kuwayis* (good), *mish-kuwayis* (not-good), or *bukra* (tomorrow, a term commonly used by Egyptians to put off the completion of orders indefinitely). These handy phrases mostly betoken a power relationship, typical of employers, tourists, and soldiers. In some cases, the 'master' identity fits a type without a stake in the colonial situation, whose motives for entry into Egypt (from port or barrack) fitted into the conventional pattern of finding a temporary outlet or release from work through shopping, sex, sightseeing, drink, and the freedom of lording it over the supine providers of these services. It was often the case that long-term residents had attitudes unlike visitors' or tourists'.

The latter often displayed extreme xenophobia or racist attitudes, whereas the colonial seldom openly expressed such sentiments.[24]

Wealthy or high-status British normally had a large household of servants. A senior British official might employ a *sufraji* (or 'suffragi', sometimes translated as manservant or butler), normally Nubian; a cook and kitchen boy (*marmitun*); valet or orderly (usually an ex-Egyptian NCO or policeman); a 'lady's maid' (usually Greek, Italian, or Swiss); also chauffeur, gardener, garden boy, *bawwab* (doorman), and *sayes* (groom or car-washer), washer-woman (*ghassala*), ironer (*makwaji*), and nanny or governess (usually English, Scottish, French, or Swiss).[25] The daily life of a colonial household was recorded in the memoirs of Penelope Lively, who was the daughter of a British business executive. Lively claimed the norms of a colonial household were those of Edwardian England, with all its emphasis upon convention and ordered relations between parent and child, master and mistress, mistress and domestic, to the exclusion of warm personal relationships.[26] Lively was born in Cairo in 1933 and left Egypt at the end of the Second World War. Her father was employed in the National Bank of Egypt after the First World War, with a villa near the village of Bulaq Dakhrur, four miles west of Cairo, as well as a summer villa at Sidi Bishr, Alexandria.[27] Lively's household contained a British governess, an Egyptian *sufraji*, cook, gardeners, and a 'garden boy', as well as a British caretaker, known as Nunn, who bullied the other domestic staff with a combination of kitchen Arabic and military invective. A cast-off soldier, who perhaps had served in the Boer War, Nunn's taciturn personality was a sign of his 'frustration and loneliness, his xenophobia an expression of his own insecurity'.[28] Lively's judgement in this case might reflect a more general diagnosis of the colonial identity. The rural location of the residence meant that Lively was relatively secluded from social contact with other British children. Her society consisted mostly of the domestic staff. Her mother made a weekly visit to Cairo, when she would spend the day at the Gezira Sporting Club, the Cairo Zoo, or donkey and camel rides at the pyramids. Her mother's life revolved around villa and garden, modelled on English design, although not entirely 'English'. Each summer a snake charmer was procured to exorcise snakes from house and garden with chants that were supposed to mesmerise the snake into betraying its hiding place (a colonial ritual repeated everywhere from consular residency to suburban home). Other enduring memories were of the kitchen and pantry. Hassan the cook received daily orders from Lively's mother in the pantry. Her mother did not trespass into the kitchen, a forbidden, disorderly territory of laughter, quarrels, and commotion. The back steps and garden resounded with the sounds of spoken Arabic, another preserve of servants, exclusive of the adult world of parents, but privy to a child. As was the norm, many of the male servants were Nubian or Sudanese, including in Lively's case the *sufraji*, Daod, Hassan, the cook, and Mansour, the head gardener. Each had a strong and definite personality. The *sufraji* had status, grave; Hassan was friendly; Mansour grim. Lively's relations with the Egyptians were intimate, but bewildering. She interpreted that world by analogy to the literature of Ivy Compton-Burnett or Lewis Carroll, mirroring an 'Edwardian household in which children and servants exist in a stratum of their own, locked in a relationship rich with ambiguities'. As Lively said, all elite families in Egypt would have had one or two or more servants. 'It seems more like another century than another place.'[29] For Egyptian elite families, the image is similar, although inverted: for instance, the household of 'Ali Ibrahim Pasha included twenty-seven servants, one of these, the governess, was 'English'.[30]

Taking the colonial household as a model of British–Egyptian relations supports the master/servant formula. The colonial patriarch's relationships with Egyptians were those of command and obedience, as well as a ritual cultural distance, as reflected in the taboo against speaking English to servants, or indeed of speaking at all to the servants. However, the model shifts when viewed from the perspective of a colonial child. Lively's most intimate relations were developed with the servants. Familiarity with the servants and exposure to Egyptian culture and Arabic had an impact on Lively's identity. Because of the colonial fear that children would not receive a firm British cultural grounding, British families in Egypt almost always employed a nanny. Lively's governess, Lucy, was of English lower-class origins, but trained to meet upper-class standards. She spoke 'gentrified' English and took on the task of instructing Lively on 'Englishness' – British history and customs.[31] This instruction involved learning to despise things Egyptian, as a necessary cultural directive in the persistent effort to sustain a British identity against alienation, exile, and absorption into 'native' culture. As Lively said, the result was that colonial culture took the form of an 'exclusive club', homogenous and cohesive in its opposition to all things 'Egyptian'. But the 'Englishness' transmitted by Lucy was a constructed thing. When Lively returned to Britain it struck her that her accent was 'inauthentic', her cultural location akin to that of Egyptians who had acquired English and a British education at the Egyptian schools. 'Now I too discovered that English is spoken in many different ways, and that there were apparently mysterious gradations of Englishness which appeared in some perverse way to mirror Lucy's definition of degrees of non-Englishness. It was bewildering. My previous indoctrination was that English was an exclusive club.'[32]

Lively never felt comfortable or secure in her 'Britishness'. Britain was not 'home'. The nearest thing to 'home' was the villa's garden, the back steps, or her cloistered study hours with Lucy. Egyptian elites, particularly young Egyptian women nurtured by foreign governesses, experienced quite similar ambiguities. The daughter of a high-status Egyptian family had a sentimental education in French and English and manners, learnt through intimate association with her governess as 'surrogate mother'. The effect was to instil admiration for the French or British, without, however, failing to be aware of that other 'identity' that belonged to the Egyptian nation. The foreign governesses, mostly French and British, formed an appreciable social category in Egyptian elite society in the first half of the twentieth century; mainly motivated by the opportunities and rewards of employment overseas, the governesses had a significant cultural impact.[33]

These characteristics of the elite colonial household changed according to class situation and cultural trends. Gladys Peto, the wife of a junior officer in the British military, published a practical guide for British residents in 1928, *Egypt of the Sojourner*. As a guide, the book is rich in descriptive detail, with some emphasis upon exotic attractions. On social relationships, her comments suggest that while there were strict rules of racial and imperial decorum for high British officials and the very wealthy, these rules did not necessarily apply to ordinary British in the interwar period. Junior officers' families lived in barracks, flats, huts, bungalows – even tents at bases on Cairo's outskirts, such as the air force base at Heliopolis or army base at Hilmiyya. Peto said that Hilmiyya reminded her of an English village. Egyptian schoolboys played in the streets; there was a milkman; goats and camels wandering in a desert plot substituted for cattle and sheep. There were blocks of modern flats and houses adjacent to the Egyptian village, with its mosque, a distant obelisk, and the little church at the nearby 'Virgin's Tree'.[34] The base at 'Abbasiyya was immense, with buildings neatly laid out, sports grounds, parade, a church, a mosque, and great eucalyptus trees. Adjacent were the Egyptian barracks where, in 1928, ten British officers were employed by the Egyptian army. These types of military housing were self-contained. Yet, some service families lived in the nearby suburbs of Zaitun and Mataria. Only the most senior British officials or officers lived in villas, which were grand, built in the Dutch colonial style, with high rooms opening one from another, flowering trees, climbing plants, parquet floors, furniture of walnut and mahogany against white panel walls. Even modest flats and bungalows normally included a cook and *sufraji*. When writing of the colonial norm never to speak English with servants, Peto said that rather than a hard rule it was simply an aspect of the social dynamics of expatriate life. The custom of seasoned expatriates to order servants in the 'most curt and distant manner' was a 'reaction' against the inclination of the 'newcomer' to make the most 'incredibly familiar and indiscreet conversation'.[35] The commentary gives some sense of the way colonials were schooled in the informal racial line, to which Peto appeared somewhat amused and indifferent. She had an interest in Egyptian culture (she learnt Arabic), but her social relations were motivated largely by a straightforward desire for 'companionship and company'.[36] Writing principally to advise other British residents or visitors, Peto claimed that sociable company was really the most important thing, suggesting that communities separated themselves out only on the positive principle of seeking inclusion in a social group. Social relations from this perspective fitted the pattern of similar types attracting each other, rather than repelling the other. For this reason, Peto preferred Cairo. She said that although junior officers' living conditions were far from luxurious, Cairo was the very best billet for service families west of Suez because the size of the garrison meant that there was the possibility of an ordinary social life.

Partly an aspect of class differences between soldiers and high officials or business executives, Peto's more relaxed analysis also suggests social change from the era of high imperialism to the interwar period. Choices that created social distance were founded not so much on a negation of the other, but as a perceived need to build a normal and secure middle-class life. But cultural threat was also present. Written by a consular official of medium status in the same era, Thomas Rapp's memoirs can be compared to Peto's. As Rapp said, the pleasures of colonial society were offset by the 'heat, squalor, the contrasts of wealth and poverty, the noise and widespread restlessness and deep discontent'.[37] Like Rapp, Peto was conscious of tropical diseases, although her list was more exhaustive: bilharzia, hookworm disease, undulant fever (Malta fever), enteric dysentery, and malaria, as well as 'Gyppy tummy'. There was an equally long list of cures and essentials, including potassium permanganate, cresol, tincture of iodine, boric lotion, chlordane, aspirin, quinine, clinical thermometer, lint, cotton wool, bandages, fly nets and covers.[38] The complications of colonial family life persisted into the twentieth century. Even while living in modern suburban Heliopolis, Rapp and his wife chose to return to Britain for the birth of their first child. Rapp took a short leave in Britain when the baby was born and returned to Egypt alone. His wife and child came out two months later. This was a typical colonial expedient. Another problem that continued to haunt families was children's education. Rapp said that women confronted the difficult choice of parting with children or husband with some anguish.[39] One compromise was to send the boys to Britain and keep the girls in one of the many foreign schools in Cairo or Alexandria, mostly French. That expedient indicated that the desire to wrap children in a British cultural fold was practically impossible. Also Egyptian cultural constraints could determine lifestyle. Peto echoed Violet Cecil's commentary when she noted the way 'old-fashioned' ideas of female decorum crept up on the 'independent' woman living in Egypt, so that it was rare for her to walk out alone after sunset or drive her car without her servant as chaperone.[40] The potential of mingling with Egyptians, with the exception of servants, was slight. Peto recalled train trips that obliged her to take the 'Harem' carriage. While boarding and waiting for departure the 'veiled' women sat quietly and sedate, but when the train lurched away from the station veils were removed and the Egyptian women smiled and engaged her in their conversation. Reserved postures were resumed at the station.[41]

With the exception of the 'loathing' harboured by the 'non-European student' for foreigners, Egyptians treated her with kindness and graciousness on tram, in shops, in cafés, on street corners.[42] Yet, in Cairo, neighbours of different national backgrounds rarely met socially, unlike in Alexandria, where one might, 'very occasionally, actually *meet* a Greek gentleman or even a Coptic lady, and try to get a view of life from their angle'.[43] And although socialising with Egyptians was rare, Peto observed that Muslim women had recently adopted European dress, with a 'compromise' in the form of a black frock and head-covering of a black silk scarf (the style known as, *muhajjabat*).[44] Even in the absence of obvious social interaction, the differing communities could meet, however inadvertently, through shared leisure activities. This was far removed from what Peto referred to as the really 'old fashioned family' where Muslim women 'never, in any circumstances, leaves her husband's house at all'.[45] Her commentary was far removed from the exoticism of popular Orientalist representations: rather than insisting that Egyptians remain different, Peto documented an Egypt-specific adjustment to modernity.

Leisure

The hunt, feast, and drink; that was the way the merchant adventurers of the Levant Company spent their idle hours in the eighteenth century. For British men of some status, nothing much had changed over the following two centuries. These pursuits were institutionalised. Sport was essential to career advancement. Leisure therefore was a very formal social exercise, integral to colonial order because it established the rules of decorum and sociability. The racecourses were built by the British for the recreation of officers and officials; however, horse racing was pre-British and most horses were owned by the Egyptian elites. Polo had been played by the Mamluks. The annual migration of birds offered excellent sport for hunters in the lakes of the Nile Delta and the oases. The Turf Club originated as a gambling club; in 1893 it became an exclusively British club where gambling was banned. Outside these pursuits, officers were primarily occupied with polo and cricket. Many bureaucratic officials began their careers as soldiers, and thus military culture appealed to a large sector.[46] The Sporting Club on the island of Gezira in central Cairo had an exclusive air because it was designed as a resort for the British military; however, Egyptians were allowed admittance. Khedive Taufiq was its founding patron. Its exclusivity was one of class and culture, not race. Indeed, it was one of the most popular of clubs for elite Egyptians. By 1913, elite figures like Muhammad Mahmud had joined and, in spite of racial slurs endured during the First World War, he remained a member into the 1930s. In 1938, recognisably Egyptian names in the membership lists amounted to 10.5 per cent of a membership that also included many 'Levantines'; British membership was in decline until given a boost by the Second World War.[47]

Before the First World War, according to John Young, Cairo was an 'Oriental capital of Turkish Pashas, Harims, Black Eunuchs, and domestic slavery'.[48] At the exclusively male and British Turf Club, conversation turned on projects, promotions, and appointments.[49] British preferential sinecures were reinforced by the comforts of Cairo. The residential quarters in central Cairo were mostly two-storey villas standing in their own gardens. The streets were lined with acacia trees. Donkey and camel shared the streets with leisurely carriages ('arabias') and trams. The most desirable residential district was in the region around the consul general's official residence, known as Qasr al-Dubra, and the Gezira suburb of Zamalek. The Qasr al-Nil bridge joined the two districts, its iconic lions serving as symbolic sentinels and reminders of the imperial stamp. The portrait of colonial society offered in Young's memoirs also reflected pomp. At the dances and balls, which 'took place nearly every night', British officers were required to wear the kit of the British or Egyptian militaries: 'Their bright uniforms gave colour and variety to all meetings whether in clubs, private houses, or the Opera.'[50]

In the same pre-war era, Humphrey Bowman's diaries and letters give the impression that empire allowed young middle-class men to aspire to be gentlemen. Leisure activity was essential to establishing necessary contacts in society. Egypt during the 'season' was 'full of distinguished guests', British royalty and the titled elite of Europe.[51] The gaiety of the 'season' included dances at Gezira Palace Hotel and the Savoy, dining with acquaintances from Britain, tours of Coptic churches and the Roman antiquities of Old Cairo, quail shooting in the desert, snipe in a marsh, and on Friday the races at Gezira. Christmas 1904 included champagne, dinner, dance, singing at the piano, which 'reminded us more of Oxford than of anything ... To make it as thoroughly English as possible, and to end finally at midnight, we made "Punch" and drank it as we sang Auld Lang Syne.'[52] The dinner was managed by his Egyptian cook and other servants. There was also the theatre and variety shows near Azbakiyya, which Bowman found 'amusing, tho' rather vulgar'.[53]

On the one hand, colonial Egypt was a locale to establish an imperial career where social manners were carefully policed; on the other, colonials were notorious for defying conventions. Mabel Caillard recalled that during the First World War the Levantine elites 'wore their clothes with chic and their complexions with charm ... The British Army was at their feet.'[54] In spite of the best attempts of Lady Allenby and other leaders of the British colony, numerous romances required 'Consular benediction'.[55] Many soldiers long away from 'home' began to doubt that they would ever return and thus were 'utterly separated from their old ties and associations, and were indulging in wild flirtations. The Armistice burst like a bombshell on their happiness.'[56] John de Vere Loder was a relatively restrained, and therefore probably typical example of this tendency. From a prominent family in England, his wartime experiences and exposure to Levantine Alexandria and the imperial grandeur of Cairo had an impact on his subsequent career. In 1919 he entered the diplomatic service and took a role at the League of Nations from 1922 to 1924 and wrote a study of the post-war Middle East that demonstrated his rejection of the methods of pre-war imperialism.[57] His internationalist politics seemed to owe something to his professional, or perhaps more importantly, his leisure activities in Alexandria and Cairo. He was only twenty years of age when he served and suffered injury at Gallipoli in 1915. Before transfer to Cairo, Loder spent several months convalescing at Muntaza Palace, turned into a Red Cross hospital during the war; later he recovered at the barracks at Mustafa Pasha. He was initially disappointed with the city: 'It is not really an Egyptian city. The greater peculiarity is the extraordinary mixture of races. Most people speak English of a sort.'[58] His initial impressions also underlined the insularity of colonial society.

> You can have tea at the sports club where there is polo and tennis to watch and a band twice a week. There is also a nine-hole golf course. You can drive along the Mahmoudieh Canal and see the native villagers or go to the public gardens where there is a band, a small zoo and a lake to sail on.[59]

Of a shopkeeper he observed, 'I used to go and argue with him. We argued in French and Arabic sentences learnt beforehand out of my phrase book.'[60] Loder also recorded the concern of colonial society to maintain cultural distance: 'The Colonial [Australian and New Zealand troops] is the last word in indiscipline and I am told has done enormous harm to the white man's prestige among the natives.'[61] With ambitions to enter the diplomatic service, Loder began to take lessons in Arabic in Alexandria and also, it would seem, learnt something of colonial attitudes. Of the 'natives' he observed, 'They are a low, thieving, set of ragamuffins, but most amusing.'[62]

Loder gradually acclimatised and was increasingly engaged by the conventions of colonial society. As he said: the 'English' colony 'got on much better with the Italians than the French. The Italians and the French did nothing but be spiteful to each other. The Greeks are in a class apart and disliked by everybody.'[63] At the same time, he found himself disengaged from the conventions of 'home'. On the 26 March 1916 he recorded that he had forgotten it was Easter and felt the need to exercise to ward of the ennui brought on by the climate. He was increasingly attracted to a Coptic family from Asyut that summered in a villa near the barracks in Ramla. Described as representing branches of the Wisa and Khayyat families, the younger members of the family were educated along British lines and played tennis. 'The girls have been brought up by English governesses. Their manners and customs are naturally a bit odd to our ideas, but are a very tolerable English imitation considering the fact that most of them have never been to England.'[64] Loder wrote that the women's status in the family was ruled by the remit of 'ancient prejudice' that restricted their social movement. Yet, he observed that although somewhat secluded, the girls were educated and allowed 'reasonable freedom'.[65] Egyptian families were, he said, reticent about foreigners for fear of public opinion if the women made the acquaintance of strangers, yet the prohibition was not absolute. Loder was at last invited into the villa's grounds to play tennis. In a letter to his mother, he confessed, 'My only amusement is to know all sorts and kinds of people and to go to tea and have drinks with them. It doesn't sound a very high ideal but then I am getting to be quite a passable Levantine now.'[66] Concerned, his mother gave stern warnings not to return home with a foreign bride.[67]

By 1917 Loder had secured an appointment in Cairo, where General Edmund Allenby had assumed command. Loder's distance from 'home' was apparent in his observations on official society. He said that Lady Allenby 'does not appreciate cosmopolitan society I am afraid'.[68] And that it was believed by the authorities that the very 'mixed nationality' character of Egypt would deter the development of patriotic resolve among troops.[69] Thus, it was all that much more important for leaders of the community to fly the flag, deploy marching bands, and conduct nationalistic balls and parties. In short, stern measures were required to maintain morale. Both of the wartime British high commissioners in Egypt, Henry McMahon and Reginald Wingate, banned the drinking of alcohol at the High Commission or Residency. Loder was entirely indifferent. For him, Cairo was a grand distraction from war and Lady Allenby's jealous guarding of Britishness laughable. She held a weekly *thé dansant* at the Continental Hotel where prominent officers' wives acted as hostesses. Women had to apply to a committee to attend the dances, whereas men purchased tickets from a hall porter. Loder commented, 'Gallant attempt of limited and unattractive English womanhood to pulverize the influence of the fascinating dago girl.'[70] Outside of work, there were restaurants, cinema, and theatre, which he described as 'polyglot', with the dialogue and music delivered mostly in French and Arabic, with some smattering of Turkish, Greek, Italian, as well as English, appealing to an audience that, as Loder said, comprised mostly 'local effendi'.[71] The British enjoyed the same sorts of entertainments as Egyptians of a similar social class. From an aristocratic family in Britain, Loder easily fitted in with the effendis, beys, and pashas, all of which terms signified status, class, and wealth.

Loder is comparable to Rapp, who served in France. In a style typical of post-war memoir writing, Rapp began his reflections with disillusion with 'England'. Paul Fussell has referred to this formula as the 'I Hate It Here opening'.[72] Rapp said nothing of his wartime experiences, only that he was possessed of the feeling that serving one's country as a soldier was a 'handicap on return to civilian life'.[73] He was conscious of not having been fully rehabilitated from the wounds, 'moral, even more than physical, the war had inflicted on the survivors ... The ideals and hopes in which my generation was nurtured had been shattered to leave a vacuum that most of us would never fill.'[74] His mood after the war was 'restless, desultory', and he found the day-to-day life of ephemeral pleasures unfulfilling. And then by 'pure chance' he happened upon an advertisement in *The Times* discussing the importance of consular service in the period of 'post-war reconstruction'.[75] Consular service in the 'Levant' was appealing because it offered a chance to return to Cambridge. After a year's training in Arabic, Rapp was posted to Port Said in February 1920, just as nationalist boycotts of the Milner Mission were strangling the British-led administration in Cairo. Seemingly impervious to these political developments, Rapp set about establishing a most normal and conventional career in Egypt, with his leisure activities punctuating the everyday routine of work. In 1922 Rapp married and moved to the new Cairo suburb of Heliopolis. 'We were never really happy in Cairo. Those who enjoyed it most had money and leisure in abundance, and of these two commodities our supply was scanty.'[76] There was the costly burden of keeping up appearances, the danger of typhoid and dysentery. Meanwhile, those expatriates who could afford it enjoyed a breathless round of sports, dances, and nightclubs, 'for the post-war urge to give vent to pent up feelings was still strong'.[77]

The Rapps preferred Port Said. Thomas Rapp recalled that it was composed of a well laid-out European quarter and 'jerry-built native quarters' – the same was true of Suez and even more so of Isma'iliyya. The dichotomy between European and Egyptian quarters, the one entirely European in character, the other like a temporary camp, struck Rapp as designed, 'as if to emphasize that though the Canal might pass through Egyptian territory the Company itself was not Egyptian owned or administered'.[78] The Company remained a French preserve, 'jealously' guarded by the French colony. British residents normally sent their children to the Lycée Français. Social relations between the British and French at Port Said were 'close and easy'. Rapp recalled, 'We were always welcome visitors at the French Club, which was subsidized by the Company.'[79] The largest sector of the British colony in the Canal Zone (a term originating with the military administration during the First World War) was the staff of the Eastern Telegraph Company, seventy men charged with maintaining the important relay station at Suez. There was also the British staff of the Anglo-Egyptian refinery on Suez Bay. Unlike the telegraph employees, these workers were mostly married men with families, living in suburbs with schools, hospitals, and leisure facilities comparable to those in Britain, not unlike Port Said. Evelyn Waugh's description emphasised its normality, fitting the conventions of middle-class British lifestyles. The banality of Port Said was relayed by a comic application of Forster's *Guide* formula in *Labels: A Mediterranean Journal*, complete with a detailed map to cultural sites. Waugh's map included such 'sites' as the red-light district, 'touts and whores', hotel and club, and a seaside esplanade notable for an emporium of cheap tourist wares known as 'Simon Arzts'.[80] Waugh visited Egypt in 1929. For him, the principal attraction of the British colony in Port Said was the absence of nonsense like 'tropical romance'. There was 'no indomitable jungle, no contact with raw nature ... no malaria, delirium tremens, or mammy-palaver' and 'no one was trying to forget'. There was not the slightest inclination to 'go native'.[81] The British colonial resident was well adjusted and content, which Waugh found refreshing.

> The [British] women seem particularly carefree; they live in manageable modern flats and are served by quiet man-servants, whose response to

all orders, however ill-comprehended, is a deferential inclination of the head and a softly spoken 'All right'. No one is troubled by social aspirations because there is no direction in which to aspire; everyone knows everyone else, and there are no marked disparities of incomes. No one wants to keep a car as there is nowhere to drive ... The men live within five minutes of their work, they have none of that feverish bustling in and out of railway trains and omnibuses which embitters middle class life in London ... They live in a Utopian socialist state untroubled by the ardours and troubles of private enterprise. I think many of them were conscious of the peculiar felicity of their lives. Certainly, those who had lately been home on leave and returned with a slightly dissatisfied air. England was changing, they said; damned Bolshies everywhere. 'You have to come out of England,' one of them told me, 'to meet the best type of Englishman.'[82]

Waugh's portrait rings true because it defied any strict categorisation. Port Said had been labelled a sink pot of iniquity during the war and had since been cleaned up, much to the disappointment of tourists and travellers on overnight stops. Forced to linger for several weeks, Waugh befriended a British solicitor, who purchased vintage First World War pornographic postcards, which he posted to his friends in England in heavily wrapped parcels. Waugh noted that, in doing so, he surely subjected himself and his friends to the risk of criminal prosecution. The strict hierarchy of colonial society (consuls, doctors, lawyers, the chaplain, the British head of police, followed by the heads of the shipping offices) was blurred every Saturday evening, as all shared a propensity to drink too much. Waugh questioned several of the residents about the local red-light district; however, they were 'as vague about it as Londoners are about Limehouse'. Yet, they good humouredly tolerated Waugh's interest and assured him they would be interested to read about it in his book, although content in the meantime to stick to whisky and soda at the club. So Waugh and the solicitor decided one evening to follow the line of local cabs towards the infamous locale on their own. He noted the cabs were filled with tipsy sailors and 'grave, purposeful Egyptians'.[83] En route, Waugh observed the social life of the Egyptian quarter, although quick to remind his readers that his interest was not driven by a desire for the exotic or an interest in the habits and customs of another 'race'. He was nevertheless spellbound by the 'intoxicating sense of vitality and actuality' permeating these quarters and struck by the 'joviality and inquisitiveness' of the Egyptians. Waugh's text therefore recognised the fact of objectification and denigration of the Egyptians through exoticism, pornography, and so on, but he had no interest in the exotic, nor was he a sex tourist (he was on his honeymoon, whilst seeking material for a travel book). Port Said was culturally familiar and Waugh's interest in Egyptian popular culture, including hashish smoking, song, and dance, was of fascination to him for a comparison of the Egyptian variety of these entertainments with the same distractions he was accustomed to in Fez or in London's West End.

Peto's helpful 1928 guide to Cairo also included an inventory of clubs where officers and their wives had drinks and dinner or stretched out across the garden lawns with picnic and magazines at the weekends. Far from cosmopolitan decadence, these interwar snapshots were of modest middle-class entertaining. The 'gaiety' of Cairo's nightlife was, according to Peto, the result of the fact that all the revellers were 'at least slightly, acquainted'.[84] Clique-ism or snobbery was the norm in colonial society. Peto confessed there was resentment among the 'particularly handsome and friendly crowd' when anyone arrived at the Gezira Club whose 'history and business' was unknown.[85] The military clique stood apart, even from other British, and there was little inclination to embrace those outside the social circle. She recalled that whilst engaged in a feverish new fad on the dance floor – pelting other couples with rolls of cotton balls – she caught the disdainful looks of bejewelled Levantine parties sitting stiffly at their tables. Also, at such entertainments, one might find Egyptian couples, men dressed in fez and suit sitting with 'emancipated' women having 'lately, one imagines, left off their veils'.[86] Or country gentlemen, dressed in 'coloured silk' *jallabiyya* and 'gleaming white' *'imma* (turban). Evidently the elite social venues embraced multiple types and the Egyptians were culturally abreast of the British, yet there was a brake upon fully sociable mixing. At these venues the breathless British dominated the scene, including governesses out for the evening, 'for we are a long way from the governess of Victorian fiction'.[87] There were debutantes recently arrived on the 'fishing fleet'. Also, unlike the pre-war ritual, the officers were not required to wear full dress uniform at social engagements. Social constraints were more the product of class differences. Peto was conscious of the way British middle-class culture clashed with the customs of Levantine and Egyptian elites. Besides the disapproving glances at hotel ballrooms, she recalled how bare-legged, with soaking wet frock, she hurried past polished groups taking drinks at the casino club deck. Other venues appealed to middle classes of diverse backgrounds. At the open-air cinemas in Cairo she found British officers in groups or British couples alongside middle-class Egyptian couples in effendi dress and the head-covering (*muhajjabat*), as well as southern European and Greek families. Peto described a middle-class milieu, attractive to various nationalities, sharing similar cultural references, which had a humanising function; Egyptians were shown to differentiate themselves in their adoption of the modern, as in the shift from seclusion and veil to sociability and the head-covering. There was a cultural convergence of 'East' and 'West', Egyptian and British, a shift from old to new cultural models, with Peto observing that the veil and seclusion had been discarded to engage in contemporary conventions in lifestyle and leisure.[88]

Upper- and middle-class British shared a common interest in drinks, dinners, dancing, and sports, although on different social planes, with the new middle classes of the interwar period insisting on a degree of informality. There continued to be distinctions between official and non-official colonial culture. Leisure among official classes, even among the subaltern British soldiers, bespoke hierarchy and an imperial pecking order, whereas among non-conformist British leisure interests heralded the dissolution of that order. The trend had been evident in Forster's writings, but taken to new extremes among the set of poets and dissolute types celebrated in Lawrence Durrell's fiction. For these, leisure was symbolic of a cultural door that opened into a subterranean or 'dream-city'.[89] The point for Durrell was to escape the nationalistic culture of the Second World War – he hated the way it absorbed all aspects of life. Exiled by the war from Greece, where he had worked for the British Council, he was employed in Egypt by the Ministry of Information as a press secretary in Alexandria. Durrell probably met his second wife, Eve Cohen, at one of the parties given at the Ambron Villa on Ma'amun Street, Muharram Bey district. Owned by Aldo and Amelia Ambron, patrons of the arts, the huge villa with grand staircase housed exotic plants, marble antique sculptures, columns, capitals, and a sundial, as well as a great banyan tree in the garden. Subsequently, the villa served as a nostalgic memorial to the 'dream city'. Cohen was from a French-speaking Jewish family that had lived in Egypt for generations. Her life involved a not-unpleasant round of beach, café, and cinema. In the quartet's first book, *Justine*, Darley (Durrell's fictional counterpart) worked at the British Council, its 'parsimony, indigence' served as the opposite to Justine's (Cohen's) Levantine languor. Such descriptions establish the dichotomy of exotic Egypt and drab Britain. But Darley, a young British instructor at the Council, was drawn out of his own cultural restraints and into a milieu that initiated a process of deracination, delineating a specifically colonial space marked by transgressions. As Justine said, 'How is it you are so much one of us and yet ... you are not.' As intellectual 'refugee', Darley departed from his own culture for an alternative landscape.[90]

Durrell carried E.M. Forster's *Guide* with him and used it to construct an imagined Alexandria, not devoid of Orientalist visions, desires and fears. *The Alexandria Quartet* sometimes replicated typical motifs of Orientalist or colonial narratives – tyranny, violence, squalor, discomfort, and sensuality. And although many have denied that Durrell's Alexandria had any resemblance to 'reality', the imagined landscape captured the anxiety of a colonial city in an African setting. Expressed with Orientalist-like allusions to race, Durrell identified the social processes of colonisation – urbanisation, demographic growth, and rural to urban drift:

> The women of the foreign communities here are more beautiful than elsewhere. Fear, insecurity dominates them. They have the illusion of foundering in the ocean of blackness all around them. The city has been built like a dike to hold back the African darkness. But the soft footed blacks have already started leaking into the European quarters: a sort of racial osmosis is going on.[91]

The demographic drift was real, the osmosis imaginary. Nevertheless, the idea of osmosis shattered the colonial dogma of segregation and exclusion and marked his initiation into the world of colonial taboos. Likewise, the ancient sites of Alexandria were symbolic of a palimpsest landscape wherein the European was sure to follow in the footsteps of the pharaonic, the Greco-Roman, and the Arab civilisations. As Durrell said, Alexandria was the 'ash-heap of four cultures'.[92]

These reflections were more hopeful than regretful, just as Forster articulated a doctrine of 'Universal Exhaustion' in a 1942 article published in *Citadel* that called for 'apathy, uninventiveness, and inertia' to replace the destructive exertions of the war.[93] It is instructive that the characteristics that Forster celebrated represented those that the so-called Orientalists claimed distinguished the Eastern mentality from the Western: sloth, languor, degeneracy or decadence. Forster and Durrell inverted the formulaic references of imperial discourses into a positive, rather than negative, characteristic. By doing so, they did not transform the basic effect of Orientalist literature to displace the 'reality' of the colonial location into something symbolic, aesthetic, and ornamental, indicative of Western desires.[94] Whatever the merits of the symbolism, the 'dream-city' inspired those pursuing escape from 'reality'. The idea for *the Alexandria Quartet* may have originated in the garden of the Anglo-Egyptian Union where poets, artists, journalists, and others seeking diversion in their leisure hours, consumed copious drinks under a canopy of enormous trees whilst enjoying plays, readings, and recitals. Durrell mixed with the Personal Landscape and Salamander groups of poets at the Union, as well as war poets like Keith Douglas, who also published in *Citadel*. The latter journal was edited by David Hicks, a lecturer at the Anglo-Egyptian Union.[95] Members of these groups were consciously not the 'Poet in Democracy and in War'.[96] It is debatable to what degree these poets were representative of other British in Egypt, but their art nevertheless expressed the 'anxieties, separations, and travel' that were experienced during the war or indeed as an ordinary consequence of empire.[97] Keith Douglas was one of the more promising poets. He was sent out to Egypt in 1940 and died in Normandy in 1944. In his war memoir, *From Alamein to Zem Zem*, Douglas located typically colonial moments of leisure in his description of Alexandria in the lull before the battle at Alamein: the 'clanging slug-like course of the trams' in narrow wall-like streets.[98] He made his way to the eastern suburbs where 'at Stanley Bay troops on leave and the huge indolent population of smart women hid the sand and dotted the blue half circle of sea'. He spent a love-sick evening at a café on the Corniche, 'the sea growling and stinking like a wildcat'.[99] His war narrative went so far as to imagine a future in the 'world', that is to say, outside Britain.[100] Meanwhile, with the great battle just fifty miles away, Alexandria was more at love than at war, as in his poem, 'Egyptian Sentry, Corniche, Alexandria': 'In the cafes and cabarets seating/gossipers, soldiers, drunkards supple/women of the town, shut out the moon with slats.'[101]

Indeed, colonial life carried on quite impervious to the war or Egypt's enduring political battles with the British. In a letter from late 1945 Thomas Russell remarked that the murders of Lord Moyne and Ahmad Mahir, as well as the attempted murder of Amin 'Uthman (he was later assassinated in 1946), interfered with his customary pursuits: 'I never seem to have luck these days with my duck shooting on Saturdays: both the last days I've been stopped going by these crimes.'[102] On the weather in the winter of 1947 Russell observed, 'Cold for Egypt, as no actual frost I'm glad to say, for my mangos which are out in blossom and which only need a couple of degrees of frost to cut them.'[103] Gardening was a favoured leisure activity. Lively's memoirs were named after the 'oleander, jacaranda', and large roles were played by the eucalyptus and tortoises, as well as snakes. Gardens combined uniquely the domestic and the exotic, an ordered refuge and tropical experimentation – in short, all the best empire had to offer.[104] True to the imperialist spirit, the British made the foreign seem like home. Thus, after a visit to a superior's posting in the provinces, John Young and Humphrey Bowman returned to the train station on foot. They sat down on the way 'under a spreading acacia and almost imagined ourselves in England'.[105] Colonial estates had familiar names, like 'Cloisters'; although a contrary trend was evident in 'Burg El Arab'.

War

In 1897 the British population in Egypt was 19,557.[106] Census records broke down the 'British' population into categories of military (4,909), Maltese (6,463), Indian (614), with the remainder described as 'in-land' *British*.[107] Soldiers were a preponderant social category in colonial society.

The numbers dramatically increased during wartime. In 1914 the Suez Canal Defence Force consisted of sixty thousand troops, including the 42nd Lancashire, the Australian Imperial Force, the Indian Expeditionary Force, and a Flying Corps involved mostly in reconnaissance. By 1917 troop numbers for the Egyptian Expeditionary Force were approximately a hundred and seventy thousand.[108] Over three hundred thousand troops were stationed in the Middle East in late 1941, with half that number from the Dominions or India. Given the strategic importance of Egypt, troop numbers in the interwar period were normally around ten thousand.[109] A small percentage of that number were officers, who served on two-year contracts, renewable for up to ten years or longer, and most had the means to establish semi-permanent homes and families. The military character of the colony was undeniable, at war or peace.[110]

Although Egyptians were not the enemy, they were treated by the army as a conquered, hostile people. Captain T. Valentine was shipped out to Egypt in September 1914 and stationed at Qasr al-Nil barracks in Cairo. As he said, he and his unit were forced to endure the 'tedium of drill and confinement'. An important function of the troops was public display: 'General [John Grenfell Maxwell] in command of the troops in Egypt is very strict and that as he says we should lose our prestige with the natives if they saw any slackness or untidiness.'[111] There were marches through Ezbekiyya Square, into the desert, through the City of the Dead and Gezira, with Egyptian men and women staring, children chasing behind. Nevertheless, Valentine saw very little of ordinary Egyptians, with the exception of the 'native bloke' behind the bar at Qasr al-Nil barracks.[112] The marches failed to overawe the Egyptians. There were demonstrations and revolts. On 2 November 1914, martial law was declared, and British troops were restricted to barracks except when accompanied by an armed, bayonet-drawn escort. Troops took shifts on a constant piquet. Valentine recorded that those posted during the evening reported a punctual flogging of a 'native' at eight o'clock and, he concluded on this evidence that someone was flogged, 'whether they had done anything wrong or not'.[113] Floggings involved a prisoner brought into the yard of the barracks where four policemen held his arms and legs, a fifth held the prisoner's head between his legs, while two policemen wielding large canes 'lay into him with their sticks as hard as they can'. On one occasion a man and boy were flogged. Valentine wrote of his anguish, shared by others, as they watched the boy 'wriggling and screaming with pain ... but of course we could not interfere'.[114]

Locals and foreigners listened to the Qasr al-Nil regimental band play in Ezbekiyya Gardens through the month of December 1914. The infamous rioting of Australians and New Zealanders occurred on the eve of their departure for Gallipoli, April 1915. As the Australians marched to the train terminal in Cairo they sang their favourite song: 'Australia Will be There'. Shortly thereafter Valentine's regiment, also bound for Gallipoli, boarded a train to Suez. Briefly stationed at 'Kantara' (al-Qantara al-Sharqiyya) with the Suez Defence Force, he commented that the village had been 'blown up by the Engineers' and converted into a massive wartime facility. Valentine observed first-hand the modern war machine, including new railways, paved roads, water-pumping systems, hospitals, and massive warehouses.[115] The scale of military construction was immense: 30 million sand bags were required for the trench works that formed the line against the Ottoman advance from Syria and Palestine. Over 1 million tons of stone were quarried by the Egyptian Public Works for road paving after the Ottomans were repulsed in late 1914 and the front was inched forwards into Sinai.[116] At Gallipoli, Valentine was similarly overwhelmed by the host of imperial troops: Egyptian and Sudanese, Gurkhas, Sikhs, Egyptian Camel Corps, and the British Lancers. After two months of active service at Gallipoli he was 'shipped out' to Egypt on a Chinese ship and convalesced at the Red Cross hospitals in the Gezira Preparatory School and the Al-Hayat Hotel, Helwan. He left for Britain shortly afterwards, without, it seems, at least on the basis of his diaries, ever establishing the slightest relationship with anyone outside military ranks, with the exception of his bartender.

The diary of trooper W. Richardson of the Suffolk Yeomanry described mostly drudgery, tedium, and a few exquisite moments in the ordinary life of a soldier in the Egyptian Expeditionary Force. No mention of an Egyptian was made. Days off were dull, unless a football match was played with another unit. On the anniversary of the embarkation for Gallipoli troops were given plum pudding, beer, and apples. During the advance through Sinai to Gaza, he recorded that 'one fellow of the Suffolk Yeomanry shot himself this morning'.[117] Equally terse entries recorded 'the stony hinterland and the terrors of the Judean mountains'.[118]

One trooper that did have contacts with Egyptians was Noel Duncan Braithwaite, who was responsible for organising Egyptian work gangs at a military base hastily constructed near the pyramids. His term of reference for the camel drivers was 'camel-wallah', which had the rough meaning of camel driver. He recounted an occasion when one of these unleashed an 'astonishing flow of language' regarding an excessive camel load. Braithwaite shoved him out of the way and was organising the hoist when the driver railed back at him, 'gabbling as if his indignation would drive him silly'. Braithwaite had a section 'cuff' him and 'pack' him up, which settled the affair. In conclusion Braithwaite said,

'I picked up a good deal of Arabic on this trip.'[119] Largely conscripted by force, the Egyptian Labour Corps were employed for three-month periods; these were illegally increased as the advance across Sinai proceeded. In 1916 the Corps numbered three thousand; in May of 1917 seventeen thousand. The numbers increased to twenty-six thousand in 1918.[120] Seventy-two thousand camels were purchased or requisitioned by the British army during the war; altogether a hundred and seventy thousand Egyptians served in the Corps in Egypt, Palestine, Syria, and Europe. The hardships endured were such that 'fellahin drafted into it gave themselves up as lost men'. Of the camel drivers, two hundred and twenty were killed in action, fourteen hundred wounded, and four thousand died in field hospitals.[121]

British officers fared better than these examples of the British and Egyptian rank and file. John de Vere Loder was able to secure a transfer to an elite unit after being injured at Gallipoli and convalescence at Muntaza in Alexandria. He took a position at the Intelligence Bureau under Brigadier-General Gilbert Clayton operating from the Residency, where High Commissioner Reginald Wingate was in charge. Loder soon aspired to a permanent posting at the Residency or the Egyptian Ministry of Finance, the two key centres of power of the colonial administration. As he noted in his diary, the political scene had been altered with the declaration of a British protectorate under an Egyptian sultan in 1914. Kitchener and Cecil had both been recalled to London and, after McMahon's removal, Wingate assumed power in Egypt. Loder, like others, was drawn to the new avenues of imperial appointments that the war had opened up. While employed at the Residency Loder made contacts with important officials: Maurice Amos, whom Loder described as 'no. 2 at the Ministry of Justice'; Ronald Storrs, who was known for his 'clever conversation'; and Clayton, who held positions as intelligence officer in the British and Egyptian military establishments. He also met Ahmad Bey Hassanein, desert explorer and one of the more important collaborators with the British. Loder recorded that during lunches at the Residency 'pashas and beys' attended and freely associated with British officers.[122] General Sir Edmund Allenby assumed the role of Commander-in-Chief of the Egyptian Expeditionary Force in 1917, replacing Sir Archibald Murray. Under Allenby, the Expeditionary Force finally advanced across the Egyptian frontier into Palestine by the clever use of a feint at Gaza followed by the unexpected massive assault at Beersheba. The enemy was also outmanoeuvred at Megiddo in 1918. Of the soldiers of the Egyptian Expeditionary Force that had followed Allenby through Sinai to Jerusalem and Damascus, T.E. Lawrence and Archibald Percival Wavell were to become the most well known. Each had taken similar lessons from the experience: that Zionists' aspirations would lead to trouble in the Middle East; that mechanised mobility would define future warfare; and that military victories were not accomplished without a political strategy.[123]

Allenby was appointed high commissioner in Egypt by the Lloyd George government under the assumption he would use his military prestige to restore order after the massive revolt in 1919. He did, but chose the path of compromise with the nationalists advocated by the Milner Mission. Wavell rose from captain to brigadier-general during the war and returned briefly to Egypt in 1919, under Allenby. Lawrence went to Versailles and returned to Cairo with Churchill in 1921 to work out the overall political settlement. Fame was followed by obscurity in the RAF, under an assumed name. Wavell's career suffered from the general interwar retrenchment of the military, yet his theoretical and practical work on developing the armoured divisions was a legacy of the wartime experience.

Cairo was the general headquarters of the military in the region, as well as the effective capital of a newly extended imperium inclusive of Palestine, Transjordan, Iraq, briefly Syria, as well as parts of Cilicia and the Taurus Mountains, not to mention the Persian Gulf, Sudan, and East Africa. Thus in an interwar period when the military endured contraction, Egypt's force levels increased and new air force bases were constructed as part of a regional defence system. As a result of the continued presence of the British military in the Cairo and Alexandria bases, the political conflict between the British government and the Egyptian nationalists was not resolved. Nevertheless, the strategic investment seemed to have paid off when Italy invaded Ethiopia in 1935, threatening imperial communications through the Canal to India, Australia, and the Far East. Under these circumstances, the 1936 Anglo-Egyptian Treaty was negotiated to ensure the continued use of the bases. Wavell was made responsible for Palestine in 1937 and Commander-in-Chief Middle East in 1939.

General headquarters during the Second World War was again in Cairo. As Commander-in-Chief Wavell was responsible for Egypt, Sudan, Kenya, Palestine, Transjordan, Cyprus, Iraq, Aden, the Persian Gulf, and British Somaliland; he claimed that as the war progressed he had to handle 'something like a million men'.[124] In 1939, however, British forces in Egypt were ill-prepared for war, even with reinforcements in the form of the 4th Indian Division, total forces stationed in Egypt in 1940 numbered only thirty-six thousand in a total under his command of eighty-six thousand. The army was therefore occupied in avoiding any provocation of the Italians and focusing on administrative considerations, including the expansion of ports and docks, railways, new roads, permanent base camps, training schools, repair shops, and hospitals, all of which infrastructure the Egyptian government was obliged to provide by the terms of the 1936 treaty. When the phoney war ended and the Italians entered the war in June 1940, the lessons of the First World War came into play. On the western frontier of Egypt Wavell's forces engaged in mobile strikes and feints; an entire dummy army was created along the sixty-mile frontier between the sea and the Qattara Depression. Meanwhile small patrols of the 7th Armoured Division crossed the Libyan border and engaged in hit-and-run-type tactics against the much larger Italian formations. Also, Italian counter-offensives in July were reversed. The improvised tactics were a necessity; none of the British formations was complete. Another unorthodox formation, for which Wavell was renowned, was the creation of the Long Range Desert Group, designed to penetrate into the southern Sahara and, through harassment, divert enemy forces from the main front. It was composed of the desert explorers that had been involved in navigating the Western Desert in the 1920s and 1930s. Major R.A. Bagnold organised the group, with ranks drawn from the New Zealand Division, its equipment largely borrowed from the Egyptian army, which was already engaged in desert patrols on the northern end of the battlefront.[125]

Alec Strahan was with the Royal Horse Artillery of the 4th Indian Division that arrived in Egypt in 1940. Born in Hong Kong, where his father had worked as a doctor. After serving in the war he made a career as a schoolteacher in the south of England. A draft of his memoirs and wartime diary entries can be read at the Middle East Centre Archives, Oxford. Strahan had a keen eye for the cultural and social artefacts of empire. Passing through Cairo on his way to Alexandria and the Western Desert front, it struck him that Cairo's Continental Hotel was a 'monument of faded magnificence', Gezira Sporting Club a 'monstrous citadel of sporting imperialism', and Qasr al-Nil an example of crumbling 'nineteenth century splendour'. Of the imperial institutions in Egypt he said, 'The whole place has an air of imminent decay.'[126] In the summer of 1940 he was in Mersa Matruh near the battle front. Barely out of college, twenty-two years old, he said that the 'first surprise was the presence of Indian soldiers everywhere, all very smartly turned out'. The Indian soldiers drove trucks, carried provisions and ammunition. Also, there was a host of un-enlisted hangers-on, including barbers, launderers, tailors (*nappi, dhabi, dursi*), and water carriers (*bhistis*). Several officers had Indian 'bearers' to look after them.[127] The multinational character of the imperial army was not the only surprise – the army also provided him with his first contact with the British working man. He recorded the 'mixture of dialects from Tyneside to Devon, sprinkled with anglicized Urdu and Arabic'. For example, 'Pegdo the fucking subcheese' ('Throw the whole lot away'). On leave in Cairo he

[165]

frequented the haunts of the colonial elites. Of Gezira he said, 'Here we would watch a group of girls, the daughters of the rich Greeks and Egyptians, performing gracefully on the diving boards ... We never tried to speak to them; they seemed quite out of our world.'[128] Little did he know that the war had shaken the social setting to such a degree that Egyptian girls were coming to the Gezira Club for the first time – their encounter with the British was equally breathtaking.[129]

Meanwhile, Wavell was preparing for his first major offensive in the Western Desert, known as 'Compass'. On 7 December 1940 he and his wife and daughters attended the races at Gezira: 'Cairo's cosmopolitan society saw them all strolling through the paddock; the Press photographers approached and were not shooed away.'[130] He feigned normalcy also at a dinner party he gave that evening at the Turf Club for fifteen senior officers of his command. The offensive began on the morning of 9 December. The Italians at Nibeiwa were pounded by artillery from the 4th Indian Division, and then surprised by squadrons of light tanks pressing down from the south-west. The Western Desert forces had their first victory, entering Libya with the capture of Bardia and taking Tobruk in January 1941. Wavell's careful planning was harassed by Churchill's need for dramatic victories and scores, including the invasion of the Balkans through Greece. There were also the German infiltrations into Syria and Iraq, which Wavell hoped to defuse politically and therefore stalled military intervention, to Churchill's extreme irritation. Finally, Wavell diverted forces from North Africa to Greece, and when forced to fall back on Crete against a brilliant German offensive, managed a risky rescue of the remaining British forces. Another source of friction was the British ambassador, Sir Miles Lampson, who did not come under Wavell's authority, communicated independently with Churchill, and was convinced of the necessity of imposing British control over Egyptian domestic politicians and the king. Wavell resisted. These political troubles resulted in Wavell's replacement in the summer of 1941.

Strahan fought at Tobruk, where he caught a shell in the leg, which nearly killed him. He convalesced in Cairo and was, on recovery, stationed at Qasr al-Nil barracks. He was therefore one of those called upon to participate in Lampson's controversial intervention in Egyptian politics on 4 February 1942. Wavell would have disapproved of an act that humiliated the king because of the negative political fallout. The use of British forces to intimidate the king into dismissing his government was a departure from the post-1918 policy of seeking political solutions, rather than demonstrations of imperial power. Strahan commented that 4 February 1942 was 'a bare-faced act of political piracy': 'Doubtless we shall now be at pains to emphasize that our gallant ally is a sovereign state and His Majesty's Government has no wish to interfere with her internal affairs.'[131] These types of reflections on the part of a young captain in the Horse Artillery are notable, although it is impossible to determine to what degree these were generally held. Strahan was clearly sympathetic to nationalist protests against British wartime policies, which became acute after Husayn Sirri Pasha was forced by Lampson to break off diplomatic relations with Vichy France:

> The government of Sirry [Sirri] Pasha fell and none of us quite knew what would follow ... The people were crying out for wheat and flour and were being given a rice substitute ... we were all organized into internal security companies and that night a New Zealand battalion came into Kasr el-Nil barracks ... Feverish consultation took place at the palace ... We were paraded again and again ... And on Wednesday night [4 February] we were called out. The big crisis had arrived ... The Ambassador, accompanied by General Stone, the GOC, their two ADCs and three Majors from the OCTU, Tom Cavenagh (OC RA Wing – my boss), Snapper Martin, and Philip Graves-Morris, entered the Palace, clad in their smartest clothes, their revolvers concealed about their persons ... Six 25 Prs were in action covering the Palace and the barracks of the Royal Bodyguard and the four tanks were nosing gently at the palace gates and railings.[132]

Lampson's account supports the descriptive details, but it is important to note that Lampson 'enjoyed' the affair immensely, entering the royal presence after the king's chamberlain was 'brushed aside', imposing British imperial will upon a monarch whom he considered of suspect loyalty and dubious character, at least according to Lampson's recollections in his diary. As he said, only with 'tongue in my cheek' were assurances made that British interference would henceforth be restrained.[133] While Lampson's actions and private reflections sustain the idea of a resolute imperial will during the war, Strahan's do not. His attitudes rapidly altered over the course of his few years in Egypt. After Alamein, he recorded that he 'felt more and more detached from home'.[134] It was not exceptional that soldiers with battle experience viewed new recruits as alien interlopers; however it is suggestive that 'old desert hands' regarded 'pale-faced reinforcements' as 'bloody Englishmen'.[135] On his 'old rounds' at bars and clubs, in the company of Lulie Abu al-Huda or Tatiana Preston, he frequented Shepheard's, Auberge des Pyramides, and Groppi's. He perfected his French and exhibited his 'fluency' on Egyptian cultural sites. In his memoirs he recorded that his diary was 'full of moans about the stifling atmosphere of the battery mess ... No wonder that my eyes turned constantly to Cairo; no wonder that, for those months, my diary contains scarcely a word of military matters.'[136] By Christmas 1943 Strahan was still in Egypt. The 8th Army had moved on to Italy: 'Four years ago today, I think it was I left England. I have long since ceased to be homesick or to dream of home. It is all too remote.'[137] Strahan was not alone in these sentiments. Penelope Lively described the imperial pomp of wartime Cairo as a 'determination not to face facts'.[138] The photographer Cecil Beaton was sent out to Egypt in April 1942 and attended a reception for the duke of Gloucester at the embassy, where flags were waved and a brass band played 'God Save the King'. Representatives of the colony arrayed themselves in shantung and ducks. As Beaton said, 'This was more what I imagined happened in India than Egypt.' The garden, river, and the country mansion setting of the embassy with its shuttered windows, balcony, and balustrades, 'reduced' Egypt to England. The whole scene seemed so 'removed from this epoch'.[139] War magnified the disorienting qualities of colonial life. In Keith Douglas's poems there are references to the negative Orientalist formula: legless beggars, slumber, hashish, fatalism, endemic dolour, disease, apathy: 'My God the king of this country must be proud.'[140] But in 'Cairo Jag' Douglas concluded that he and his clutch of comrades were not so different from the 'somnambulists and legless beggars:/it is all one, all as you have heard'.[141]

In Cairo Alec Strahan attended the Anglo-Egyptian Union on Friday evenings. In origin an informal group of British and Egyptians supporting the treaty negotiations, after 1938 the Union was organised as an official arm of British cultural policy. It was funded by the British Council to support teaching and provide a forum for other types of cultural performance and dialogue. During the war the Union was chosen as a vehicle for Allied propaganda. At the Union, Strahan met Freya Stark. As he said, his friend 'Lulie [Abu al-Huda], who spoke Arabic, was now involved in the work Freya was doing for the British government in Iraq and Egypt'.[142] Stark, an Arabist and travel writer before the war, served as assistant information officer employed by the British Ministry of the Interior. The director of publicity for the entire Middle East, Walter Monckton, raised funds to endow Stark's 'Brotherhood of Freedom', a society specifically designed for wartime 'propaganda'. Stark made friends with the Abu al-Huda family, neighbours in Zamalek, and hired Lulie Abu al-Huda as a full-time assistant. Through this connection and a contact at the university, Stark found an audience at tea parties attended by Egyptians with an education in British schools.[143] Strahan and other soldiers also attended. With Lampson's guidance, and with the help of several assistants, the 'Brotherhood of Freedom' expanded to include thousands organised into 'democrat' committees in Cairo, Alexandria, and the provinces.[144] Soldiers of all ranks attended the committees to share 'desert news' and inspire, or as she said, 'persuade'. The results were problematic. Egyptian followers were attracted by the largesse provided by state funding and the promise of 'benefits to come'; otherwise, as Stark said, the committees would have never met.[145] Like many others of her generation, Stark believed in the universal benefits of British imperialism, and in a thoughtful discussion she distinguished between 'propaganda' and 'persuasion', claiming that only persuasion was effective because it was founded on shared values, not 'influence and payment' or 'bribery'. Stark believed the war offered a real opportunity to build 'harmony and friendship' in Egypt and across the region, and that the democrat committees and other cultural institutions, particularly educational, like the British Council, would continue to do so when British military forces withdrew.[146] Indeed, sectors of the Egyptian elite drew closer to the British during the war or were made aware of their connections and affinities with the international community.[147] But Stark's campaign for brotherhood and freedom also struck at the roots of Britain's accommodation with the Egyptian elites. Reginald Davies of the Alexandria municipality doubted the value of propaganda premised on the assumption that Egyptians were 'disinterested' and open to persuasion. A self-proclaimed imperialist, Stark was, however, confident in 'universal persuasion'. As it turned out, it was difficult to control the conversation in the committees and, as it was feared, the 'nationalists' profited from example and subverted committee propaganda to their own ends.[148] The elites, and colonials that stayed on after the war, were left only to contemplate the hollowness of the British 'gospel of peace'.[149]

Egypt was a vital imperial base, particularly evident during the two world wars – wars fought explicitly for the cause of 'universal' freedom. Yet, these wars were waged over a reluctant subject Egyptian population and divided elites. Heightened wartime insecurities stressed the fragile political partnership; there were contradictory responses on British and Egyptian sides, more or less typical of the colonial experience. Imperial triumphalism was characteristic of each war. Yet, the constitutional innovations, political interventions, and the conversion of social events and cultural institutions, including Victoria College and the British Council, to British propaganda purposes were problematic in the broader game of empire.[150] The erosion of individual or institutional autonomy alienated E.M. Forster (during both wars), as well as members of the Personal Landscape group and students at Victoria College during the Second World War. The wars created disillusion, even cynicism, among members of the British rank and file, as reflected in the memoirs of Loder, Strahan, and Douglas. The stress and arduousness of a soldiering life led to excessive outbursts, racism, and alienation. For soldiers and intelligence officers reflecting on these issues, the British experience in Egypt was defined by contradiction between freedom and imperialism, British liberty and national power. Even Churchill had to skirt these issues in his discussions with his American allies during the Second World War.[151] There was the perception that as a result of the sacrifices of the troops during the wars, imperial reform was necessary and new methods needed to be adopted to ensure more effective international relations. The new imperialism was evident in the policies of Allenby, Churchill, and Lawrence after the First World War, as well as the strategic thinking of Wavell and diplomatic and cultural initiatives in the subsequent period. However, as a result of expediencies driven by the war, there was little capacity within Egyptian national sentiment, nor among the British, to restore good relations after 1945. 'Ash-heap of four cultures', the Egyptians could recognise imperial decline when they saw it.

Notes

1 MECA GB 165-0002, Herbert Addison (hereafter 'MECA Addison'), unpublished typescript, 'Oases Waxing and Waning', pp. 1–5.
2 MECA Addison, memoir, 'The Pleasures of Anglo-Egyptian Cooperation', ch. 3, 'Egypt and its Universities', p. 6 & letter, Addison to Roger Owen, St Antony's College, Oxford, 1973, with critique of Jacques Berque's *Egypt: Imperialism and Revolution* (London: Faber & Faber, 1972). The letter also makes reference to Peter Mansfield's *The British in Egypt* (New York: Holt, Rinehart and Winston, 1971).
3 MECA Addison, letter, Addison to Roger Owen, 1973.
4 MECA Addison, 'Egypt and its Universities', p. 4.
5 Berque, *Egypt*, p. 290.
6 Magda Baraka, *The Egyptian Upper Class between Revolutions 1919–1952* (Reading: Ithaca, 1998), p. 106.
7 MECA Addison, 'Egypt and its Universities', p. 5.
8 Albert Memmi, *Colonizer and the Colonized* (Boston: Beacon Press, 1967), pp. 19–44.
9 Michael Ezekiel Gasper, *The Power of Representation: Publics, Peasants, and Islam in Egypt* (Stanford: Stanford University Press, 2009), pp. 40–1, 51–4 & 123–4.
10 MECA Addison, 'Egypt and its Universities', p. 9.
11 Ibid.
12 Berque, *Egypt*, p. 673.
13 Ibid., p. 290.
14 Frantz Fanon, *The Wretched of the Earth* (New York: Grove Press, 1963), p. 149.
15 Baraka, *Upper Class*, p. 153.
16 Mabel Caillard, *A Lifetime in Egypt, 1876–1935* (London: Grant Richards, 1935), pp. 106–7.
17 Ibid., p. 107 & Roger Owen, *Lord Cromer: Victorian Imperialist, Edwardian Proconsul* (Oxford: Oxford University Press, 2004), p. 254 & Huda Shaarawi, *Harem Years: The Memoirs of an Egyptian Feminist*, trans. Margot Badran (New York: City University of New York, 1986), pp. 12 & 50, in this account the ritual was not purely functional or ornamental, the 'Vicerine', Amina Hanim Afandi, bestowed patronage and 'compassion' on her subjects. Nevertheless, the memoirs of Huda Shaarawi support the idea of women's critique of the 'harem', p. 56, where – after her subsequent exposure to feminist ideas – Shaarawi recalls the 'sympathy' that European women must have felt towards her, a child bride.

18 Hugh and Mirabel Cecil, *Imperial Marriage: An Edwardian War and Peace* (London: John Murray, 2002), p. 188.
19 Lord Edward Cecil, *The Leisure of an Egyptian Official* (London: Hodder and Stoughton, 1921), p. 92.
20 MECA GB 165-0167 Alexander Keown-Boyd, Box 1, Folder 3, 'TS Memoir by Henry Keown-Boyd of his Father's Orderly Ahmed'.
21 Catherine Hall, 'Culture and Identity in Imperial Britain', in Sarah Stockwell (ed.), *The British Empire: Themes and Perspectives* (Oxford: Blackwell, 2008), p. 209.
22 Gladys Peto, *Egypt of the Sojourner* (London & Toronto: J.M. Dent & Sons, 1928), p. 7.
23 Henry Keown Boyd, *Lion and Sphinx: The Rise and Fall of the British in Egypt* (Durham: Memoir Club, 2002), p. 54.
24 Penelope Lively, *Oleander, Jacaranda: A Childhood Perceived* (London: Viking, 1994), p. 54.
25 Keown-Boyd, *Lion and Sphinx*, p. 33.
26 Lively, *Oleander, Jacaranda*, p. 37.
27 The National Bank of Egypt was created in 1898, largely to finance the Aswan Dam, a private company run by London financiers, notably Sir Ernest Cassel.
28 Lively, *Oleander, Jacaranda*, pp. 33–4.
29 Ibid., p. 37.
30 Baraka, *Upper Class*, p. 182.
31 Lively, *Oleander, Jacaranda*, pp. 18–25.
32 Ibid., pp. 33–4.
33 Chafika Soliman Hamamsy, *Zamalek: The Changing Life of a Cairo Elite, 1850–1945* (Cairo: American University Press in Cairo, 2005), pp. 141–2.
34 Peto, *Egypt of the Sojourner*, pp. 138–41.
35 Ibid., pp. 84–5.
36 Ibid., p. 52.
37 MECA GB 165-0234, Sir Thomas Rapp, memoirs, p. 40.
38 Peto, *Egypt of the Sojourner*, p. 13.
39 MECA GB 165-0234, Sir Thomas Rapp, memoirs, p. 31.
40 Peto, *Egypt of the Sojourner*, p. 186.
41 Ibid., p. 138.
42 Ibid., pp. 186–7.
43 Ibid., p. 189.
44 Ibid., p. 195.
45 Ibid., p. 195.
46 Mansfield, *British in Egypt*, p. 87.
47 Baraka, *Upper Class*, p. 193.
48 MECA GB 165-0310, John Young, unpublished manuscript, 'A Little to the East: Experiences of an Anglo-Egyptian Official 1899–1925', ch. 1, 'Introduction', pp. 3–4.
49 Ibid., p. 8.
50 Ibid., p. 10.
51 MECA GB 165-0034, Humphrey Bowman, Box 3, diary, 15 Jan. 1905.
52 Ibid., 1 Jan. 1905.
53 Ibid., 15 Jan. 1905.
54 Ibid.
55 Ibid.
56 Caillard, *Lifetime*, p. 201.
57 John de Vere Loder, *The Truth about Mesopotamia, Palestine and Syria* (London: Allen and Unwin, 1923).
58 MECA GB 165-0184, John de Vere Loder, 'Memoirs', 28 July 1915.
59 Ibid., 10 Dec. 1915.
60 Ibid., 10 Dec. 1915.
61 Ibid., 20 Dec. 1915.
62 Ibid., 21 Feb. 1916.
63 Ibid., 17 June 1917.

64 Ibid., 24 July 1916.
65 Ibid., 24 July 1916.
66 Ibid., 1 July 1917.
67 Ibid., 20 Aug. 1917 & Oct. 14 1917.
68 Ibid., Feb. 1918.
69 Ibid., 1 Jan. 1917.
70 Ibid., 17 Jan. 1918.
71 Ibid., 23 Dec. 1917.
72 Paul Fussell, *Abroad: British Literary Traveling between the Wars* (Oxford: Oxford University Press, 1980), pp. 15–23.
73 MECA GB 165-0234, Sir Thomas Rapp, memoirs, p. 5.
74 Ibid., p. 7.
75 Ibid., pp. 2–3.
76 Ibid., p. 40.
77 Ibid., p. 30.
78 Ibid., p. 10.
79 Ibid., p. 40.
80 Fussell, *Abroad*, p. 181.
81 Evelyn Waugh, *Labels: A Mediterranean Journal* (New York: Penguin, 1985), p. 60.
82 Ibid., p. 62.
83 Ibid., p. 69.
84 Peto, *Egypt of the Sojourner*, p. 114.
85 Ibid., p. 106.
86 Ibid., p. 116.
87 Ibid., p. 115.
88 Social and cultural histories of modern Egypt have documented this cultural convergence, without the loss of signs of cultural difference as adapted to modern lifestyles: Kenneth M. Cuno, *Modernizing Marriage: Family, Ideology, and Law in Nineteenth- and Early Twentieth-Century Egypt* (Syracuse: Syracuse University Press, 2015) & Mona L. Russell, *Creating the New Egyptian Woman: Consumerism, Education, and the National Identity* (New York: Palgrave, 2004).
89 Michael Haag, *Alexandria: City of Memory* (New Haven: Yale University Press, 2004), p. 303.
90 Lawrence Durrell, *Justine* (London: Faber and Faber, 1961), p. 39.
91 Ibid., p. 66.
92 Roger Bowen, *'Many Histories Deep': The Personal Landscape Poets in Egypt 1940–45* (New Jersey: Associated University Presses, 1995), p. 148.
93 E.M. Forster, 'The New Disorder', as cited by Artemis Cooper, *Cairo in the War 1939–1945* (London: Hamish Hamilton, 1989), p. 156. See also Bowen, *Many Histories Deep*, p. 145.
94 Nicholas Thomas, *Colonialism's Culture: Anthropology, Travel and Government* (Princeton: Princeton University Press, 1994), p. 53.
95 Desmond Graham, *Keith Douglas: A Biography* (London: Oxford University Press, 1974), p. 148.
96 Mursi Saad el-Din and John Cromer, *Under Egypt's Spell: The Influence of Egypt on Writers in English from the 18th Century* (London: Bellew Publishing, 1991), pp. 75–6.
97 Keith Douglas, *Keith Douglas: The Complete Poems*, ed. Desmond Graham (London: Faber & Faber, 3rd edn, 1998), p. v.
98 Keith Douglas, *From Alamein to Zem Zem* (London: Editions Poetry, 1946), p. 78.
99 Ibid., p. 80.
100 Graham, *Keith Douglas*, p. 153.
101 Douglas, *Poems*, p. 90.
102 MECA GB 165-0247, Thomas Wentworth Russell, letter, Russell to Francis Moore, 1945.
103 Ibid., Russell to Moore, 1947.

COLONIAL LIFE

104 John Lonsdale, 'Kenya, Home County and African Frontier', in Robert Bickers (ed.), *Settlers and Expatriates: Britons over the Seas* (Oxford: Oxford University Press, 2010), p. 85.
105 MECA GB 165-0034, Humphrey Bowman, Box 3, diary, 8 June 1905.
106 British Parliamentary Papers, Accounts and Papers, vol. cvii, Egypt, no. 1 (1898): Reports on the finances, administration, and condition of Egypt and the progress of reforms (London, 1898),p. 651.
107 Ibid.
108 Imperial War Museum (hereafter IWM) 7180 79/48/4, Sir Archibald Murray, 'Papers Prepared for the War Cabinet by General Sir Archibald Murray', CIGS, Oct.–Dec. 1915.
109 Over fifty thousand Australian, Indian, and New Zealander troops were stationed in Egypt, alongside the 42nd Lancaster division upon the outbreak of the war in 1914. The figures for the interwar period are given in TNA FO371/20125, 'Strength of the British Garrison in Egypt', Lampson, 14 Aug, 1936.
110 Keown-Boyd, *Lion and Sphinx*, p. 29, noted the difficulty that members of the military had to establish normal domestic lives, resulting in prostitution, mistresses, even harems; for the period between 1882 and 1925, eleven hundred British officers served in Egypt.
111 IWM 4069 84/52/1, Valentine, diary, 5 Oct. 1914.
112 Ibid., 27 Oct. 1914.
113 Ibid., 11 Nov. 1914.
114 Ibid.
115 Ibid., 16 April 1915 & IWM 7180 79/48/4, Sir Archibald Murray, Campaign in Egypt, 1916, 'Reports of Engineers Works'.
116 IWM 7180 79/48/4, Sir Archibald Murray, 'Reports of Engineers' & P.G. Elgood, *Egypt and the Army* (Oxford: Oxford University Press, 1924), p. 235.
117 IWM 14918 06/33/1, W. Richardson, diary, 6 Aug. 1917.
118 Ibid., 13 Dec. 1917.
119 IWM 15596 07/26/1, N.D. Braithwaite, diary, 25 Nov. 1914.
120 Elgood, *Egypt and the Army*, p. 317.
121 Ibid., pp. 243–4.
122 MECA GB 165-0184, John de Vere Loder, 'Memoirs', 28 Nov. 1917.
123 Elgood, *Egypt and the Army*, pp. 305–6 & John Connell, *Wavell: Scholar and Soldier* (London: Collins, 1964), pp. 159–69.
124 Ibid., p. 210.
125 Ibid., pp. 222–45 & Robert Woollcombe, *The Campaigns of Wavell 1939–1943* (London: Cassell, 1959), pp. 17–18.
126 MECA GB 165-0273, Alec Strahan, 'Memoirs', ch. 9, 'Overseas', pp. 1–5 & ch. 12, 'Cairo', pp. 1–2.
127 Ibid., 'Overseas', p. 2.
128 Ibid., p. 6.
129 Hamamsy, *Zamalek*, p. 7, who said that these changes in social habits indicated a case of 'global emulation' brought on by the war, suggesting, that the war was a lost opportunity to bring Egyptians and British closer together.
130 Connell, *Wavell*, p. 289.
131 MECA GB 165-0273, Alec Strahan, 'Cairo'. p. 10.
132 Ibid., 'Extract from the Diary of Captain A.J. Strahan, RA, Kasr al-Nil Barracks'.
133 MECA GB 165-0176, Sir Miles Wedderburn Lampson, 1st Baron Killearn, Diaries, 4 Feb. 1942. TNA FO921/1852, Middle East Office, 1942, File 44, Egypt Political, where there were references to the palace clique as 'Quislings' in correspondence between Antony Eden and Lampson.
134 MECA GB 165-0273, Alec Strahan, 'Cairo and Alamein', p. 1.
135 Ibid., p. 2.
136 Ibid.
137 Ibid.

138 Lively, *Oleander, Jacaranda*, p. 59.
139 Cecil Beaton, *Near East* (London: Batsford, 1943), p. 37.
140 Douglas, *Poems*, p. 93.
141 Ibid., p. 102.
142 MECA GB 165-0273, Alec Strahan, 'Cairo and Alamein', p. 2.
143 Cooper, *Cairo*, p. 97 & Freya Stark, *Dust in the Lion's Paw: Autobiography 1939–1946* (London: John Murray, 1961), pp. 62–4 & 71.
144 TNA FO371/24619, Lampson, 'British Propaganda in Egypt', 26 June 1940, where Lampson supported a campaign involving social engagements to counteract German propaganda.
145 Stark, *Lion's Paw*, p. 70.
146 Ibid., pp. 64–7 & 139–40.
147 Hamamsy, *Zamalek*, pp. 291 & 296.
148 Stark, *Lion's Paw*, pp. 68–9.
149 Waguih Ghali, *Beer in the Snooker Hall* (New York: New Amsterdam, 1987, originally published, 1964), p. 76.
150 Sahar Hamouda and Colin Clement (eds.), *Victoria College: A History Revealed* (Cairo: American University Press, 2002), pp. 142–5.
151 Lawrence James, *Churchill and Empire: Portrait of an Imperialist* (London: Phoenix, 2014), pp. 318–21.

CHAPTER FIVE

Imperialists and colonials

As has been said, it is difficult to recall an authentic historical voice. Lower-class experience was mediated through elite discourses. Likewise, the colonial and colonised identities were not isolated, but interrelated by the nature of the cultural 'dialogue' that colonialism created.[1] Egyptian elites and British colonials collaborated before the First World War, often in projects designed to uplift, if not emancipate, the lower classes; however, the British had difficulty transferring from the patrician culture of the pre-war era into the democratic, nationalist era. Certainly many colonials were wedded to the conservative idea of British supremacy and Egyptian servitude; however, others envisaged a future built on coexistence and parity in international relations. Which was the more representative position within the colony? Like the authentic voice, the representative is just as difficult to survey. Moreover, both conservative and liberal positions were premised on continued British imperial power. After the First World War, there was adjustment, but the empire continued.[2] Even decolonisation was a plan designed to sustain the British Empire indefinitely.[3] Arguably, ideas like commonwealth, dominion status, or 'treaty states' in alliance with Britain were only a cover for 'covert empire' or 'undeclared empire'.[4] Yet, new policy ideas and critiques of the old were advanced by Leo Amery, Lionel Curtis, J.A. Spender, and T.E. Lawrence, among others after the First World War. In the Foreign Office, the newly organised Egyptian Department questioned the old idea of imperial rule grounded in aristocratic relations between lords and tenants, princes and their peasants, while documenting the changing nature of Egyptian national opinion.[5] These liberal views were informed by an appreciation for the agency and autonomy of the Egyptians. On the other hand, conservative imperialistic critics of these polices felt that the liberals or internationalists (a term used by the conservatives in a pejorative sense) were sacrificing national security and the welfare of colonised peoples for a pipe dream.

Colonial opinion in Egypt on these debates centred around the policy shift marked by the Milner Report of 1920 and the course that treaty negotiations took thereafter, ultimately leading to the Anglo-Egyptian Treaty of 1936. While the treaty offered a new and more equitable basis for international relations, the Second World War and heightened security concerns resulted in the British government transgressing the stipulations of the treaty. At least, that was the opinion of some colonials and many Egyptians. The publication in the 1970s of selections from the diaries of the ambassador of that era, Sir Miles Lampson, occasioned retrospective debates on these issues. Some colonials took exception to the suggestion in the introduction to the diaries that criticisms of Lampson were merely 'fashionable', that the diaries demonstrated that Lampson's treatment of the Egyptians was fair-minded. The editor of Lampson's diaries, Trevor Evans (Lampson's private secretary in Cairo) rebutted criticisms that Lampson was guilty of undue interference in Egypt's domestic affairs or of antagonising the Egyptian king.[6] The conventional view on Lampson had been voiced by John Marlowe in 1954 when he said that Lampson had checked the power of the pro-Axis Egyptians and brought to power a Wafd government in 1942 that 'stood firm' during the war in the Allied cause.[7] Malcolm Yapp, a specialist on modern Middle Eastern history, characterised Lampson as a 'supple' diplomat in a later edition of the diaries.[8] Likewise, Walter Reid characterised Lampson as one of the 'good' high commissioners, whereas others, like Sir Percy Loraine, were 'bad'.[9] Gordon Waterfield (a commando in the Middle Eastern theatre during the Second World War) took the opposite point of view because, as he said, while Loraine tolerated royal autocracy he did not treat Egyptians as pawns in an imperial game, as would Lampson. Waterfield's position was shared by many in military and journalistic circles, including the Reuters correspondent, Gerald Delany.[10] Alongside these colonial voices, revisionist historians in the 1970s argued that Lampson's interventions in Egyptian domestic affairs were an example of the domination school of imperialists and contravened the 1936 Anglo-Egyptian Treaty. Lampson's interference was misguided and fateful, impacting negatively across the region.[11]

On the other hand, Lampson's reputation rests in part on his negotiating the 1936 treaty: it established Egyptian independence and secured the British base by providing the conditions for mutual defence and accommodation of British military facilities. By intervening in Egyptian politics after the treaty was signed, however, Lampson contravened the stipulations guaranteeing Egyptian autonomy in its internal affairs. Therefore, revisionists argued that Lampson's interventions in Egyptian domestic politics marked a momentous turning point in imperial history by spurring extremist nationalism. Most conspicuously, the 1942 ultimatum forced the Egyptian king to form a government of Lampson's choosing. Charles D. Smith concluded on that evidence that the 1936 treaty was not designed to put British–Egyptian relations on an equal footing, but was simply a convenient way to legitimise a perpetual British military presence in Egypt. In other words, the 1936 treaty was a cover for empire by enabling British interference in Egyptian politics. Academic opinion remains divided on this point. Martin Kolinsky has said in his study of the period that the British stood by the principle of non-intervention except in emergency: only in necessity did Lampson and the Foreign Office manipulate Egyptian politics.[12] This interpretation suggests a kind of unwritten method of operations. Wm. Roger Louis, however, has not offered any such conclusion (it would be hard to substantiate such an unwritten mode of operations as offered by Kolinsky), but rather suggests that Lampson's forceful displays of imperial determination indicated a lack of energy on his part in the game of Egyptian politics.[13] Manipulation or intervention was thus a lapse of British diplomatic expertise, not a typical demonstration of it. These revisionist conclusions echo the contemporary judgements of colonials, including Gerald Delany and Gordon Waterfield, as well as many soldiers who served in Egypt during the Second World War.[14]

Yet, imperial sentiment was, and possibly remains, the more dominant discourse. Winston Churchill, an icon of nation and empire, was a 'die-hard' on issues that affected imperial prestige.[15] Churchill's 'geo-political' or security-oriented approach to policymaking meant that there was little room for compromise with nationalists, particularly on vital imperial assets like Egypt and India.[16] Motivated as much by imperial sentiment as he was by security issues, Churchill was an implacable opponent of any policy that constituted, to his mind, imperial retreat. This was the defining feature of the die-hards, a group that emerged in 1919 in opposition to the policies of the Lloyd George government and again in the 1930s against reforms in India.[17] According to the die-hards, Indians and Egyptians were incapable of serving as responsible partners in any treaty settlement and only a policy founded on force would keep these 'Orientals' in line.[18] Wm. Roger Louis argues that characterising Churchill's attitudes as racist is justified by the evidence. Even near the end of empire, by 1953, when Churchill had accepted the logic of troop withdrawal, disengagement, and reconciliation between Egyptians and British, the change of heart was grudging and came only when the British military command had come to believe that the Suez base was strategically obsolete.[19] In public statements in the Commons, Churchill supported the conditions of troop withdrawal negotiated by Anthony Eden in 1954, yet his concern that the 1954 treaty would be interpreted as imperial retreat meant that he gave unofficial encouragement to the die-hard 'Suez Group' of backbenchers that opposed the treaty and ultimately pushed for a military confrontation with Jamal 'Abd al-Nasir in 1956.[20]

These debates on British–Egyptian relations began after the First World War when conservative imperialists regarded the changing nature of Egyptian politics as a threat, particularly forms of ethnic and religious nationalism that challenged the liberal nationalism of the pre-war nationalist parties. This is also an important issue in the historiography, with conservative academics like Elie Kedourie blaming the British government for capitulating to intolerant nationalist governments, beginning in Egypt immediately after the First World War with the Milner Proposals, and subsequently in Iraq and India. Kedourie longed for a past imperial order and its supposed promise of a liberal political culture.[21] For conservative imperialists and academics, like Kedourie, Sir Miles Lampson stood firm against fascism and extreme nationalism, defending the European colonies and British security interests. This was Britain's 'finest hour'. The alternative point of view held by colonial liberals and Egyptian nationals was that Lampson was a British proconsul in the image of Cromer and Kitchener, arrogant and overbearing. That opinion is documented, for instance, in the memoirs of Chafika Soliman Hamamsy.[22] Following that logic, the categories of 'liberal' and 'conservative' used in this context are defined by policy towards Egypt and not identical to political party orientation in Britain: For instance, Cromer, a Liberal, was a conservative imperialist; Wilfrid Blunt, a Conservative, was a colonial liberal. The liberals accepted Egyptian autonomy and agency within an imperial framework, whereas for conservatives like Churchill and Lampson, the Egyptians had no choice but to assent to the imperial will.

Colonial liberals and the Egyptians

Conservative opinion in the post-First World War era mourned the loss of British 'prestige', which began, it was said, with the wartime administration 'over-ruling the powers of the man on the spot'. These opinions were expressed by the leaders of the British Union, a colonial organisation founded in 1904.[23] In its capacity as self-declared representative of the 'non-official' British community, the Union demanded an end to uncertainty and the re-establishment of 'trust' after the tumult of 1919.[24] By doing so, the Union protested the vacillating policy of the British administration in Egypt.[25] One spokesperson, W.E. Kingsford, imagined a restoration of the pre-war status quo founded on collaboration between British officials and Egyptian elites. Famed engineer William Willcocks was more forthright in his opinion; he argued that 'trust' was only possible when the British officials were the 'intellectual and social superiors' of the Egyptians: 'politeness and good breeding are considered as the very highest of all the virtues a man can possess'. Elitist, paternalistic, and conservative, the commentary also pointed to the ruinous consequences of introducing massive numbers of British soldiers and military administrators into Egypt. These opinions were directed at the Milner Mission, an official inquiry into the causes of the 1919 revolt. Recommendations from senior missionaries heard by the mission included the restoration of the 'Oriental, paternal' policies of Kitchener, which meant establishing 'intimate' connections with local magnates: 'The patriarchal is, and for a very long time will continue to be, the method of government which the masses of Egypt will understand and to which they will rally, with enthusiasm.' In conclusion, the missionary testimony recorded that the old paternalistic style of colonial rule had been destroyed by recent developments. Particular exception was taken to the practice of British officers racing over the countryside by motor car. The disapproving tone was a conservative yearning for the status quo ante bellum, including a pastoral landscape of lords and peasants, an order of things associated with Cromer and Kitchener, who had the 'trust' of Egyptian princes and notables.[26] The passing of a golden age of colonial rule was already mourned in conservative language evoking paternalism, hierarchy, obeisance, and respect for the authority of the ruling 'race'.[27]

More liberal opinion can be found in the letters of E.M. Forster. He was an insightful observer of wartime culture, capturing the voice of the colonised within his letters and professional journalism. Forster chose to spend the war in Alexandria because of his pacifist tendencies; employed as a 'hospital seeker' for the Red Cross in Alexandria, he engaged in the standard tours of the sites: Abu Qir, Rosetta, and the Western Desert. He bathed on the beaches and attended the parties of the 'rich Levantine' elite.[28] As Forster remarked in a letter to Florence Barger, 'There is plenty of interest and of tolerance in the mixed communities out here but nothing remotely resembling what Cambridge knew as thought.'[29] He met Robert (Robin) Furness and George Antonius, both employed as censors and, like Forster, Cambridge graduates.[30] Furness was a classicist and introduced Forster to Alexandria's literary society.[31] Forster met the Alexandrian poet Constantine Cavafy, who impressed Forster with his knowledge of early Christian history, of which Alexandria was so important a setting.[32] The version of 'The Gods Abandon Antony' in Forster's *Alexandria: A History and a Guide* (1922) was the first published translation of Cavafy's work in English. These interests absorbed most of Forster attention. Yet, in journal articles he offered several vignettes of colonial Alexandria that sometimes played on Orientalist images ('accredited oriental ingredients, such as camels, a mirage, and Bedouins'), yet developed a perspective on colonials not unlike that in *A Passage to India*.[33] Indeed, Forster's experiences in Alexandria read like a rehearsal for the drama played out in that novel: the sudden collision of worlds supposedly hermetically closed off from each other. Typical of many, Forster was initially repulsed by the Egyptians. Unlike some, however, he was troubled by that sentiment, because, as he said, it had been 'exactly the emotion that I censured in the Anglo-Indian toward the native there'.[34] Diagnosing the problem, he found that he had initially conformed to a colonial 'theory' of segregation based on racial difference. 'Natives, especially of the lower city class, are dirty in body and mind, incapable of fineness, and only out for what they can get. That is the theory to which, after some reluctance, I had fully subscribed, and like all theories it has broken down.'[35] Forster was conscious of the ease with which individuals were drawn into a colonial 'theory' that negated and segregated Egyptians. By referring to that tendency as a 'theory', he showed that he understood that the dominant imperial doctrine was a constructed thing. This was an issue explored in his fiction and journalistic writing: that each and every individual is constrained by imposed cultural norms, but not imprisoned by them. Colonials alternately denigrated and validated the 'other' depending on circumstances. Indicating the power of the official culture of imperialism, magnified by war, Forster easily fitted into the stereotypes of the colonial. He was conscious of this himself. 'I better understand the Anglo-Indian irritation though I'm glad to say I'm as far as ever from respecting it!! It's damnable and disgraceful, and it's in me.'[36]

Forster, however, embraced the Alexandrian lethargic indifference to the war, enjoying its cultural eclecticism as much preferable to the conformism and jingoism of wartime Britain. For him, exile in Alexandria represented a 'conscious shirking'.[37] It was a protest against the wartime culture of the 'respective governments' of Europe that crushed individuality.[38] The theme was worked out in his writings for the *Egyptian Mail*, published between 1917 and 1919. One article described the distinction between 'Gippo English' and 'Army English'. A kind of pidgin English, 'Gippo English' was celebrated by Forster because it represented a cross-cultural leap, indicating willingness on the part of Egyptians and British to 'move', to adjust to new cultural influences and to interact. He pointed as an example to one sign targeting Britons: 'Whose for a feed at the old Angleterre.'[39] 'Gippo English' contrasted with 'Army English', with the latter anonymous by its claim to an ultimate authority, the 'Immanent Will' of the nation-state. By killing 'direct speech' the nationalistic culture of wartime effaced human relationships.[40] 'Gippo

English' was, on the other hand pure, irrepressible human expression. But 'Gippo English' died, Forster implied, with the derisive laughter of service people for its grammatical oddity and hybrid absurdity.

Forster made a cultural leap through his meeting with Muhammad al-'Adl in the winter of 1917. Al-'Adl was a conductor on the Ramla tramline, which Forster took daily to the hospital at Muntaza. The two shared 'Gippo English'. Their first date was at the Municipal Gardens. Without curing Forster of his propensity for making categorically negative remarks about Egyptians, emotional intimacy with al-'Adl 'broke down' the barriers. 'The practical difficulties – there is a big racial and social gulf – are great: but when you are offered affection, honesty, and intelligence with all that you can possibly want externals thrown in (including a delightful sense of humour), you surely have to take it or die spiritually.'[41] The relationship came with a social cost. It challenged the accepted norms and conventions of British officialdom. Furness, who had professional ambitions (he was employed at the high commission in Cairo from 1917), was nervous given the 'general conditions, onlookers, etc'.[42] He advised Forster not to pursue the relationship. However, Forster accepted the social costs and, eventually, celebrated a personal transformation from the voyeurism of the tourist to the intimacy of the resident. Forster was explicit about his cultural conversion, remarking in a letter to Virginia Woolf that civilisation was already dead in Cairo where there reigned 'war correspondents and 119 Generals and clubs of perturbed and earnest men. But in Alexandria it seems still possible to read books and bathe.'[43] In letters to Siegfried Sassoon, he made it clear that he preferred Alexandria's indulgence of luxury to the austerity of wartime Britain, all too obvious in the military ranks in Egypt. For him, the Levantine way of life was a protest against the war and the dull conformism of public life. By 1918 Forster looked forward to a future of 'general apathy' in public life and an international order governed by a 'league of nations'.[44] These feelings were compounded by his relationship with Muhammad al-'Adl, who had complained of the racism of British soldiers even before his beating at their hands.[45] Forster's barrage against the British regime in Egypt was occasioned by al-'Adl's mistreatment and the subsequent illness that led to his death.

Simultaneously, the Egyptian revolt against the British Protectorate erupted in the spring of 1919. In the *Manchester Guardian*, 29 March 1919, Forster said that the Egyptian fellahin had suffered forced conscription, brutal working conditions, and appalling disorders in the hospitals in recompense for their contribution to the Allied victories. He therefore called for compassion and understanding for Egyptian grievances.[46] He was not alone in this opinion. Articles appeared in *The Times* arguing for Egyptian self-government; a letter appeared in that broadsheet from Andreas Cameron, the British consul at Alexandria, arguing that S'ad Zaghlul Pasha, leader of the Wafd or Delegation, should be appointed to the premiership, not exiled. Forster also contributed, at Leonard Woolf's request, to the 'Labour Research Department' pamphlet on 'The Government of Egypt' in 1920, which made an informed argument on Egypt's constitutional history.[47]

From deep within the colony voices such as Forster's spoke about the need to respect the essential humanity of the colonised and the legitimacy of their 'grievances'. These voices countered the previously dominant imperial discourses that emphasised the interests of lords over fiefdoms of peasants, of pashas, princes, and kings manipulated on the wide board of empire. The new line of argument was apparent in the letters of journalists and writers, as well as officials, active during the Milner Mission and afterwards as treaty negotiations were set afoot. The letters of Reuters correspondent Gerald Delany reveal not only his own political engagement, but the manner in which he worked with Egyptian agents, including the great nationalist leader, Zaghlul. The case of Zaghlul is interesting because whereas through late 1918 to early 1924 he was irreconcilable to the British, demanding immediate Egyptian independence from the British Empire, his position moderated after the first elections were enabled by a liberal policy of concessions to nationalists. In his letters, Delany revealed Zaghlul's close associations and dialogues with colonials through contemporary letters and retrospective sketches of these dialogues from the 1920s through to the 1960s and 1970s. Overall, these letters evoke a strong sense of regret. Delany did not blame nationalists like Zaghlul for the violence and catastrophic ruin of the colony by the mid-century, rather he faulted British leaders incapable of seeing the Egyptians as anything more than pawns in the imperial game. He therefore stood at odds with a group that held British 'prestige' above all else. It would be going too far to say that Delany went over to the side of the nationalists because he was certainly interested in maintaining British influence in the region. But he was opposed to the misuse of the Egyptians, the cynical manipulation of pashas and party divisions, as represented by the recommendations of Winston Churchill or his agents.[48] Delany and his associates underlined the complexity of Egyptian political society and the legitimacy of its constitutional autonomy. Not blinded by the 'trail of imperial glory', Delany was capable of an insight withheld from others: Egyptians were not immobilised, nor manipulated, by imperial power.[49] This observation might be taken to imply that Delany was unconventional, but the opposite is true. He was a conventional colonial, as the following brief biography suggests.

Delany was born into a family of first-generation Irish immigrants to England, middle class, yet the early death of his father meant that his schooling was limited and that he went to work at a young age. He was employed by the Walter Savill shipping firm in London, where he worked as a clerk in accounts. Taking advantage of opportunities for the aspiring middle classes unavailable in Britain, his brothers emigrated to Egypt. Delany joined them in 1907. Just as he arrived, the renowned British diplomatic agent and proconsul in Egypt, Lord Cromer, was forced to resign from his post as a result of the combination of nationalist demonstrations in Egypt and Liberal opposition in Britain. Sir Eldon Gorst succeeded Cromer and introduced a policy of concessions to the nationalists.

In Edward Said's *Orientalism* Cromer appears as a straightforward proponent of Western imperial power that left little agency to the Egyptians. A Liberal who found it easier to work with Conservative governments in Britain while acting as the British agent and consul general in Egypt, Cromer nevertheless always worked within a framework of informal empire, in accordance with Egypt's status as hereditary monarchy, autonomous, within the Ottoman Empire. This was the international framework before 1914. The Egyptian pashas and effendis operated the Egyptian administration with British advisers, but within an increasingly diminishing sphere of real authority. Notably, after Cromer solved political and financial issues that involved the other European powers by 1904, there was a push to bring Egypt into the imperial system in a more formal manner. As a result, the more radical nationalists gained ground against those Egyptians who had accepted on face value the British pledge to withdraw from Egypt after its financial and political administration was reformed. Gorst came to Egypt with the purpose of restoring more of the responsibilities of the administration over to the Egyptians and strictly respecting its status as a hereditary monarchic state. This was resented by some in the colony and when Kitchener succeeded Gorst there was a restoration of the imperialistic trend evident in Cromer's last years. Kitchener identified the British-run administration with the fellahin against Egypt's ruling classes, a typical feature of Cromer's thought as expressed in *Modern Egypt*. Kitchener adopted a paternalistic attitude, with his legacy remembered by colonials in terms of the myth of the 'native'. As Delany recalled, the 'fellah' in the 'golden era' of Cromer or Kitchener not uncommonly appeared at the doors of the British consular agency on donkey or camel to plead to the 'Lord', Cromer or Kitchener, with the expectation of justice dispensed by dictate. As in most colonial narratives, Delany regarded the war as the turning point. It was at this time, 1914, that Baron Herbert de Reuter made Delany the offer of the position in the Alexandria press office, after which he served as chief correspondent from 1915 to 1940. Egypt was transformed by the First World War and Delany was a first-hand observer of the political battles that followed.[50]

Delany credited his political beliefs to the influence of J.A. Spender, who had been appointed to the Milner Mission in 1919.[51] In letters written in the 1960s and 1970s to Gordon Waterfield, by then a journalist in the BBC, Delany claimed that Spender contributed to the realisation of an 'Anglo-Egyptian settlement' through his influence over public opinion in the press in Britain and Egypt. It is important to underline, as Delany did, the criss-cross nature of this process. British journalists in Egypt could influence editorials in London, just as Egyptian journalists in Britain read these same editorials and relayed them back to Egypt, with the necessary party spin. Spender had been the editor of the Liberal *Westminster Gazette* and was well known to the Egyptians. After the war he devoted his time to writing books. In *The Changing East*, published in London in 1926, Spender described his work with the Milner Mission, which included being smuggled in the back seats of cars to secret meetings with Egyptian nationalists while officially the Milner Mission endured a boycott. Spender had greater freedom to act as interlocutor between Milner and the nationalist politicians because, as a journalist, he did not officially represent the British government. He was regarded as a 'liberal-minded' person and therefore he was selected by the Egyptians as intermediary. Meetings were secret because of intimidation of 'collaborators' by the more uncompromising nationalists and as a result conversations took place in private apartments, in back rooms of small shops, often in the 'native' quarters of Cairo and usually under the cover of darkness. Spender's activities involved considerable risk: during a demonstration in Tanta he was abandoned by his Egyptian guard and escaped an angry crowd only with the assistance of an Egyptian boy. This story underlines the basic humanity of the Egyptian populace, which was of course demonised by some sectors of the British press during the period of nationalist demonstrations.[52] Delany assisted Spender during this series of interviews, arranging a meeting between Spender and 'Ali Mahir at Shepheard's Hotel in early 1920. Mahir was instrumental in convincing Zaghlul to abandon his boycott of Milner and meet him for discussions in London in the summer of 1920.[53] This was an important political breakthrough.[54] As a result, Spender and Delany doubled their efforts in the press to make the 'realities of the situation as widely known as possible'.[55] Alongside this effort to inform the British public, Delany and Spender tried to moderate the Egyptian position, advising the Wafd politicians that their demands had to be made with an understanding of British public opinion and wider international relations.[56] They reminded the Egyptians that if Britain pulled out of Egypt, another power would step in. Egypt's independence would always be limited by its strategic location in the world international system.[57] For Delany and Spender, the Milner Proposals offered a middle way between Egyptian nationalists and the imperialists in the British cabinet.[58] However, Spender noted in *The Changing East* that it was virtually impossible to convince some members of the British cabinet that Egypt was not an integral part of the empire. 'One of the most distinguished of them, to whom I had introduced certain of the Egyptian leaders, opened the conversation by addressing them as citizens of the British Empire and politely expressing the hope that Egypt would soon be the most contented of the Dominions.'[59] While Spender did not identify the author of this statement, it has been shown that Churchill used nearly identical language in similar situations.[60]

According to Delany, the British cabinet had been determined to annex Egypt in 1914 and to maintain the Protectorate in 1919. Milner called for concessions that would appease nationalists and bring Egypt into the imperial system as an autonomous nation, limited only by Britain's control of defence and imperial communications. The justification for these reforms was made on Egyptian constitutional grounds and the new spirit of internationalism that emerged after the world war. These themes were reflected in Delany's correspondence with Waterfield, where Delany faithfully reproduced the position taken by Lord Milner and, subsequently, by Field Marshal Viscount Allenby and his staff at the high commission in Cairo. Delany argued, like others at the time, that Egypt had its own autonomous constitutional history, which the Protectorate regime (1914–22) had disrupted but not abrogated. This, he said, was obvious to Milner, who was an 'old hand' in Egyptian affairs. The same point was made by Spender, who said that some members of cabinet mistakenly held that negotiating with Egyptian nationalists was akin to 'parleying with rebels'.[61] The position that Egypt was constitutionally autonomous was also ultimately accepted by the Foreign Office, with Austen Chamberlain accepting the arguments of the chancellor of the Egyptian Department at the Foreign Office that the methods of Lord Cromer had died with his escort from Egypt along a line of British bayonets.[62] Nevertheless, talk of concessions to nationalists stirred up imperial sentiment because any concession was construed as a sign of imperial weakness that encouraged, or even fomented, the 'rebels'. Thus, in the late summer of 1920 Milner's recommendations were leaked to the press, provoking a public outcry in British political circles and the press, led by Winston Churchill.[63] Delany wrote that the imperialists in the British cabinet (Churchill, who swayed Lord Balfour and Lloyd George, while Lord Curzon wavered) capitalised on the resulting controversy. Churchill was the first to argue that concessions to nationalists in Egypt would encourage agitation in India and Ireland, while Milner's recommendation that British troops be withdrawn from Egyptian cities would weaken the overall imperial system of defence. According to Delany the cabinet then 'unwisely' published the Milner Report.[64]

The publication of the report spoiled the negotiations for Milner, giving Zaghlul the ammunition to demand maximum concessions whilst denouncing the set of 'reservations' on Egyptian independence outlined in the report. The report also undermined the Egyptian 'moderates' in the Wafd, resulting in a rupture in Egyptian political society, which was subsequently divided between the Wafd and the Ahrar Dusturiyin or Liberal Constitutionalists.[65] Zaghlul's intransigence played into the hands of the imperialists, who, Delany claimed, 'were only too anxious to shelve the report'.[66] In a familiar imperial game, the progress of reform was deadlocked by 1921. Delany's notes on this affair are retrospective; he blames Churchill. But it is not clear where he stood at that historical moment, except that the letters suggest that he had a part in forming the Liberal Constitutional Party, where his closest Egyptian political allies formed an opposition to the Wafd. His moderate position meant that although 'liberal' in political orientation, he was hardly beyond the pale of what was acceptable in colonial society. The forwarding of the moderate or liberal Egyptians as treaty negotiators resulted in waves of demonstrations in the spring of 1921 that made it clear that Egyptian opinion would not accept a political outcome managed by the British government and its colonial agents. These events created the conditions for Allenby's unilateral declaration of Egyptian independence in 1922.

The 1922 declaration was entirely the initiative of British personnel in Cairo, led by Allenby, including the most prominent British officials: judicial adviser Maurice Amos, financial adviser Reginald Patterson, and the 'Oriental secretary' Robert Furness. The declaration was a unilateral statement of Milner's recommendations and bound the British government to the Milner Proposals. Egypt was declared an independent nation with four 'reservations' left to future negotiations: security of imperial communications, defence of Egypt against foreign aggression, protection of foreign interests and minorities, and the final status of Sudan. Opinion on the declaration was divided. Arch-imperialists like Churchill and Lord Lloyd opposed the 1922 declaration on principle. It was regarded as a betrayal of empire because it 'sold the pass' (Suez Canal).[67] From a tactical point of view it was criticised for conceding independence without gaining anything in return, whereas, in Delany's view, the declaration was 'a great step forward' because it checked the annexationist camp led by Churchill.[68] It established the conditions for a negotiated settlement by securing the political breakthrough made by Milner. It set the stage for successful negotiations in 1936. It also of course led to the writing of an Egyptian constitution and elections in 1923. As Delany said, relations between the British agents and the Egyptian political leadership were revolutionised by the successful implementation of Milner's recommendations. After Zaghlul's election in 1923, Allenby broke with colonial protocol by calling on Zaghlul at his residence. The act signified a normalisation of relations between the leader of the British colony in Egypt and the leader of the national government. It also marked a break with the imperial style of authority established by Lord Cromer and maintained by successive consuls general, which is to say standing on British prestige at all costs. Delany recalled that Zaghlul was impressed by Allenby's gesture, saying privately to Delany: 'Did Lord Allenby lose any prestige by calling on me first? On the contrary, Egypt knew that he was big enough to do it.'[69]

These recollections indicate the intimacy of colonial relationships and the possibility of reconciliation; preliminary discussions on treaty negotiations followed. Various initiatives were discussed, including the withdrawal of British troops to the Canal Zone.[70] The talks were perilous. Zaghlul was himself the target of an assassination attempt on the eve of treaty negotiations with the Labour government of Ramsay MacDonald in the summer of 1924. Afterwards, Delany censured Zaghlul for allowing the 'extremists' in his party to hold him hostage: 'Zaghlul now appeared to be running after the crowd which he was supposed to be leading.'[71] Nevertheless, Delany observed that prior to the assassination of Sir Lee Stack in November 1924, relations between Allenby and Zaghlul had been 'developing favourably'.[72] Recording the substance of conversations with Zaghlul, Delany noted that Zaghlul had moderated his position as a consequence of the opportunity for meaningful negotiations created by Allenby's initiative. Another factor was the emergence of the monarchists as rivals to the Wafd. As Delany wrote in a 1973 letter to Gordon Waterfield:

> I think the King's attitude would have drawn Zaghlul closer to Allenby. Indeed, he [Zaghlul] did say to me after one audience he had had with [King] Fuad that the latter was roving so unfriendly that he would need the help of a 'strong arm' to deal with him. He was aware of course of the struggle that Allenby had had in London to persuade the British Government to grant independence to Egypt, and then only with those four reservations; they had been thrust upon him.[73]

The commentary suggests that there was a large measure of mutual support between the leaders of colonial and nationalist camps, working in concert to build a new framework for international relations to foster coexistence between nationalists and colonials. The purpose of 1922 was to withdraw the British army from the scene and leave domestic politics to the Egyptians, albeit within an overarching imperial framework. As Delany observed, Zaghlul would certainly have continued to press for the withdrawal of the reservations after 1922 and the British government would not have agreed to troop withdrawal unless some new 'pact of relationship' was forthcoming. Each party to the discussions sought some formula that would remove its apprehensions. Delany asked, 'In the circumstances of the time would this have been possible?' Delany thus posed the central question of colonial history. Could the two communities be reconciled? From the perspective of the 1970s, the answer was pure conjecture but, as Delany said, the 'portents did seem favourable for private and friendly talks between Allenby and Zaghlul'. Delany concluded by drawing on the opinion of Field Marshal Archibald Wavell, who, Delany said, agreed that 'some form of treaty might have been forthcoming if Allenby and Zaghlul had remained on the scene'.[74]

The assassination of Sir Lee Stack, the governor general of the Sudan and sirdar of the Egyptian army, had 'far-reaching' repercussions.[75] The assassination 'stirred' British public opinion. The opportunity of a treaty was lost, which served the purposes of extreme nationalists and conservative imperialists. Zaghlul described the assassination as a 'deathblow' to his political career.[76] The assassination also led 'indirectly' to Allenby's resignation. Stanley Baldwin's government had formed only fifteen days before the assassination. It included Austen Chamberlain as foreign secretary and Winston Churchill as the chancellor of the Exchequer. Delany's most severe criticism falls upon those, like Churchill, who used the assassination of Stack to 'set the clock back'.[77] Ultimately Lord Lloyd was chosen as Allenby's successor, with 'the backing of Winston Churchill'.[78] Foreign Office agents in favour of treaty negotiations, like Amos and Furness, resigned. And although the Foreign Office advised Lloyd to follow British policy according to the letter of the 1922 declaration, the Baldwin government ensured Lloyd stayed in Egypt in spite of his obstructionist policy.[79] Thus, the 1922 declaration was converted from an instrument to facilitate treaty negotiations into one of imperial control. The sequence of events might suggest that colonial agents like Delany and his strategies were ultimately tools in the hands of conservative imperialists, but Delany's correspondence indicates that he had envisaged an entirely different scenario and subsequently stubbornly opposed the status quo that emerged after 1924.

The conservative turn in 1924 drove Delany further away from the middle ground and pointed towards his future disillusion with the policies of the British government. Nevertheless, the liberal policy of Milner transformed colonial politics. Even the spokesperson of the British Union, Kingsford, conceded the idea that Egypt was constitutionally a 'self-governing country in close and friendly alliance with the British Empire' by December 1921. The Union only opposed plans that would have made British nationals subject to the criminal jurisdiction of the Egyptian government if the Capitulations were abolished, as had been proposed in preliminary talks on treaty negotiations. The Union defended the 'rights' of Britons existing under consular jurisdiction.[80] This was Kingsford's response to Allenby's proposal for the unilateral declaration of Egyptian independence based on the judicial adviser's legalistic arguments for Egypt's independent constitutional history, submitted as a preliminary to the unilateral declaration.[81] A reluctant, but bewildered, cabinet gave way to Allenby in December 1921 and the declaration was made in February 1922, but the British Union kept up a rearguard action that ultimately provided the rationale for critiques of Allenby, his resignation, and the appointment of Lord Lloyd in 1925. The language of paternalism was far from dead. The Union argued: 'It is obvious there is a lack of the deeper knowledge of the problem, ability to see through the manoeuvres of Orientals, and above all strength of purpose.'[82] The election of a Wafd government was regarded as a threat. In 1923 the Union declared that even a constitutionally elected Wafd government must be blocked from office unless it accepted the 'reserved points' of the 1922 declaration. That Allenby and his 'misguided' advisers (Furness, Amos, and Patterson) did not interfere to rig the elections meant that the Union desperately called for the creation of an advisory committee to the high commissioner composed of members of the non-official community, which amounted to a declaration of non-confidence in the Allenby administration.[83] The Union triumphed in 1925 with Lloyd's appointment, probably at Churchill's bidding.[84] As Delany said, 'Lloyd came to establish a modern Cromer regime.'[85]

There is a certain ambivalence in the colonial liberal position after Stack's assassination. Lloyd was opposed and Allenby's advisers, mostly removed from Egypt, continued to defend the Milner Proposals. Amos, who retired in 1925, spoke on the issue in Britain; for instance, he gave a public lecture on Egypt's constitutional history in 1929.[86] Furness left the high commissioner's residence for a position at the Egyptian university in 1926 and lobbied for treaty negotiations in press campaigns.[87] Yet, in a 1926 memorandum Furness said of the situation: 'We [the high commission] were considering, not without perplexity, how to re-establish ourselves, when the murder of Sir Lee Stack provided a fortunate opportunity.'[88] The assassination enabled the British government to restore something like the pre-war status quo by using the new Egyptian monarch as an instrument of British influence, which was Churchill's design.[89] To implement the new policy, Allenby resigned and many of the officials at the Residency were transferred to other postings. Others quit. In correspondence with Furness on these events, Archibald Kerr (one of those officials transferred from Egypt in 1925) commented on Churchill's 'playacting'. The commentary suggests that British officials loyal to Allenby were quite cognisant of the imperial game afoot and the way Churchill, and others, manipulated events to serve their policy preferences. Furness and Kerr, for instance, knew that Allenby was forced out because he regarded the strategic value of the military base as dependent upon the working out of a political settlement with the Egyptian nationalists, a course rejected by conservative imperialists, including the British Union. Kerr asked Furness to keep his comments from the staff at the high commission, now a redoubt of conservatism, although he said that he could confide in Delany at Reuters.[90] The final note underlines Delany's central role in colonial politics and delineates two fairly powerful colonial lobbies, as represented by colonial liberals like Delany and conservative imperialists in the British Union. The former had political patrons in Milner and Allenby, the latter in Churchill and Lloyd. The contest was more than a bureaucratic squabble; it included members of the colony of diverse sorts and public figures with their various constituencies. However, Furness's correspondence also suggests that after November 1924 Lord Lloyd ensured that negotiations were little more than a 'game' and thus brought about a restoration of something resembling the pre-war 'Cromerian' regime.

Delany was alienated from the British administration in Cairo; yet, his instinctive faith in the Egyptians was not shaken. Given a historical narrative that has often been represented in terms of British power manipulations against a powerless, beaten or craven political leadership in Egypt, Delany's letters suggest a balance of power between Egyptian and British camps, with much mediation carried out between the two. A telling episode was the events surrounding the first elections after the appointment of Lloyd. The new high commissioner claimed that the British response to the assassination of Stack had 'chastened' Zaghlul and that less than subtle threats ensured Zaghlul did not head the ministry of a coalition government in 1926.[91] The prominent Egyptian historian Afaf Lutfi al-Sayyid Marsot similarly argued that Lloyd bullied Zaghlul into declining the premiership, with power passing to the more collaborative Liberal Constitutionals.[92] Indeed, Lloyd had done all in his power to forestall the formation of a Wafd-Liberal Constitutional alliance in 1926. Lloyd warned Delany about involving himself in the 'tea party' meetings between the party heads in early 1926. Delany ignored him. As for Zaghlul's refusal to become the prime minister, Delany said that rather than being pressured by Lloyd, Zaghlul judged that national politics was better served if he took the role of 'peacemaker' and left the premiership to the Liberal Constitutionals.[93]

Whereas Lloyd played up the titanic struggle between imperial power and irresponsible nationalists, Delany's narrative underlined the way Zaghlul worked within the constraints imposed on him to ensure that Lloyd would not have the excuse to intervene.[94] The Liberal Constitutional government, led by 'Abd al-Khaliq Tharwat, entered into talks on treaty proposals with the Foreign Secretary Austen Chamberlain in the summer of 1927. Zaghlul died that summer, however, and talks stalled. A new Labour government in 1929 changed the political landscape, resulting in talks between the Liberal Constitutional government of Muhammad Mahmud and the Labour foreign secretary, Arthur Henderson. As it was reported in *The Times*, the election of a Labour government opened the door to imperial reform, described as an evolution from 'empire to commonwealth'.[95] The colonial liberals in Cairo were certainly swift to capitalise on the opportunity, using their influence within Egyptian political circles to initiate informal discussions in London between Mahmud and Cecil Campbell, who was then the secretary to the financial adviser in the Egyptian government. Mahmud and Campbell met at Little Bardfield Hall, where, 'for the first time an Egyptian Prime Minister expressed his consent to British troops remaining on Egyptian soil ... When Campbell reported the results of this meeting to the FO [Foreign Office], the latter was encouraged to go ahead with "talks".'[96] The Foreign Office kept Lord Lloyd in the dark about the talks because of his obstructionist policy, but of course there were leaks. As a result, Lloyd resigned in June 1929. In one letter to Furness, Delany reported that Lloyd went to Mahmud at his London hotel on 28 August and said that 'he had warned him [Mahmud] of his friend Delany and now you see what has happened. It is due to his intrigue that I have been removed from Egypt!' Then Lloyd questioned Mahmud about negotiations and Mahmud replied: 'I can tell you nothing,' to which Lloyd replied: 'Well I shall oppose what is offered to you!'[97]

Conservative opinion rallied, ironically, with the arrival in London of the Wafd politician Makram 'Ubayd, who alerted interested parties that Mahmud had suspended constitutional life in Egypt and thus represented an unpopular tyranny.[98] Articles were published in the *Manchester Guardian* along these lines. That line of argument was combated by Furness, who sometimes acted as correspondent to the

Manchester Guardian and therefore used his influence to modify its tone.[99] Delany's position, as stated in a letter to Furness, was that: 'It is immaterial who negotiates a treaty so long as it is a good treaty and one that Egypt as a whole can accept through a restored parliament.'[100] The observation indicates the awkward stance of the colonial liberals: Delany relied on a prime minister governing in the absence of parliament, subject to nationalist resistance, while holding in theory to the principle of Egyptian constitutional government. That position was also typical of the Egyptian liberals, like Mahmud, who placed more emphasis upon constitutional checks on the monarch than universal franchise. Arguably, such commentary indicates the degree to which Delany was immersed in the Egyptian political milieu. There was considerable cultural overlap. Liberals in Egypt were grounded in the evolutionary thinking of colonial doctrine, wherein the liberals viewed themselves as uniquely endowed to guide Egypt 'forward', because, according to Egyptian liberals, the extreme nationalists and the masses generally were not yet properly schooled in 'civilised' politics.[101] In another cross-cultural alignment, the Labour government was agreeable to the logic of Egyptian nationalists that the Wafd Party had a unique claim to legitimacy because of its mass base, as demonstrated in past electoral successes. On these grounds, Wafd nationalists worked to frustrate treaty negotiations through the summer of 1929. In Egypt, the Wafd Party leader, Mustafa Nahhas, organised a committee to boycott the purchase of British goods, which undermined Labour arguments that British–Egyptian relations would develop along the friendly lines of commercial cooperation in the future.[102] Ultimately the Labour government communicated to the Egyptian king, who had also taken up residence in London, that Britain was committed to the restoration of a constitutionally elected parliament.[103]

Treaty negotiations collapsed and the status quo was maintained. Delany was consoled by his part in toppling Lloyd. Also, in retrospect, he claimed that Mahmud's negotiations were an important stepping stone to the 1936 treaty.[104] As he said in his correspondence with Gordon Waterfield, the negotiations had established the principle that Egyptians could accept a military alliance and British military bases in the Canal Zone, as well as provisions for the increase in troop numbers and the necessary infrastructure in the event of war (the signal features of the 1936 treaty). The British government had likewise accepted that the strategic value of the bases depended upon a viable political accord with the Egyptians, recognising Egypt's constitutional autonomy. Even Austen Chamberlain, the Conservative foreign secretary under Baldwin, had come to view Lloyd's policies as obstructionist.[105] Yet, Churchill strongly protested Lloyd's resignation, claiming that the resignation was 'forced' by a 'socialist' government that had abandoned the 'Reserved Points' policy.[106] An editorial in *The Times* pointed to the error of conducting negotiations in secret and the folly of the MacDonald government making a breach with Lloyd, which was obviously the result of long-standing disagreements between the high commissioner and the Foreign Office. The editorial rejected the idea that there were fundamental constitutional principles involved.[107] The council of the 'British Community in Alexandria' and the British Chamber of Commerce voiced their support for Lloyd, expressing regret for his resignation while recognising gratefully his efforts to support business interests in Egypt. Lloyd was described as the first high commissioner to make British trade a keynote of his policy, with many British business contracts solely the result of his efforts. Letters to the editor in *The Times* also pointed to his service to the British colony more generally, such as his work in building schools. In this way the conservative voice of the British Union was heard. Commentary and letters in *The Times* also suggested that Henderson's policy threatened Britain's status in other colonies, which were now 'gasping' at the 'ultra-sympathetic attitude' of the Labour government towards Egypt.[108] Whereas Henderson claimed that Lloyd had failed to carry through the 1922 policy, his critics said the 1922 policy meant abandoning 'the protection of that vital Imperial link, the Suez Canal'.[109] These debates between the British left and right obscured the subtle interplay of colonials and colonised. There was meaningful and substantive identification between the Liberal Constitutionals and the liberal colonials, but more complex was the criss-cross pattern of interchange between London and Cairo, journalists and party hacks, effecting some strange alignments, ideological and tactical. Labour, Conservative, and the Egyptian Nationalist Wafd lined up against the liberal colonials and their Egyptian allies to kill treaty talks.

Conservative imperialists and the war

Lord Lloyd's *Egypt since Cromer* (1934) entered into the imperial debates of the interwar era. Liberal and conservative camps were divided over the degree and type of British control in Egypt, and specifically whether negotiations would abrogate the Capitulations and draw down the British military establishment in Egypt – in other words, bring down the pillars of the colonial establishment. Ultimately, the Capitulations were traded for the continuance of the military occupation in the 1936 treaty. Lloyd's *Egypt since Cromer* was highly critical of the liberal position of conciliation. In it, Lloyd made the case for Allenby's 'weakness' or appeasement of nationalism. T.E. Lawrence's private review of the book was polite, in deference to their friendship (Lloyd and Lawrence had served together during the First World War, under Allenby). However, Lawrence was clearly critical of Lloyd's policy of re-establishing a vice-regal British presence in Egypt, complete with marching bands, parades, and guards of honour. Lawrence's review indicated that he believed that Egyptians, like the 'Arabs', should govern themselves. Lawrence confided to Lloyd that he would have dismantled the top-heavy diplomatic staff at the Residency and conducted British foreign relations in Egypt from the seat of his motorcycle.[110] Likewise, Delany, Amos, and Furness were quick to respond to Lloyd's assessment of British relations with Egypt. They ensured that critical reviews of Lloyd's book appeared in the British and colonial press. Amos published a review in the *Manchester Guardian* referring to Lloyd's book as 'a political pamphlet on a large scale on the policy of annexation'.[111] The mouthpiece of the British colony in Egypt, the *Egyptian Gazette*, also published a review identifying Lloyd's book with an 'expansionist' imperialism counter to Britain's liberal politics.[112]

Reviews in *The Times* broadcast the conservative imperialist arguments, particularly the critique of 'conciliation' as represented by the 1922 declaration, which, as Lloyd said, was unworkable. Lloyd said that the greatest threat to British power was a type of post-war internationalism that sapped the British imperial will and allowed the British government to neglect its obligations overseas. Talks on treaties only led to Britain abandoning its 'great heritage'. Sniping at colonial liberals and the Labour Party, Lloyd said that Britain's strength was not founded on constitutional theory, but sound colonial administration. This heritage had been obscured by colonial politics. Allenby's policy, said Lloyd, was premised on establishing a sound body of Egyptian political opinion. But, according to Lloyd, that was a non-sequitur: politics in Egypt was based purely on personal power, whether that of the king or the leaders of political parties. He said that Arthur Henderson's policy had been to negotiate a treaty favourable to the Egyptians, which would be ratified by a restored Egyptian parliament friendly to Britain. The policy failed because, Lloyd claimed, a sound body of Egyptian political opinion could not be built. Lloyd thus invoked a familiar colonial doctrine: wherever parliamentary government had been tried in the 'East' it had failed. Self-government, he said, led to corrupt government. It was Britain's duty to instil the principles of liberty, but there was not any obligation to institute it in a specific time frame or in a particular form.[113] These were Lloyd's concluding observations in *Egypt since Cromer*. In the year of its publication he made public speeches along similar lines: He asked if the youth of England could be kindled into enthusiasm by a 'drab internationalism preached in terms of increasing national enfeeblement at home and disintegration overseas'.[114] In one speech he referred to the long list of government policy papers ('White Papers') countenanced by the Stanley Baldwin government. Lloyd said that neither Baldwin nor Ramsay MacDonald had a mandate to dispense with empire. In a standard conservative imperialist argument, he reminded his listeners that empire had provided employment at home and order overseas. If the Conservative Party, he said, could not protect the interests of the British public, it should not wonder why the public chose the 'Black Shirts' over another 'White Paper'.[115]

Lloyd could count on the support of the military chiefs of staff, committed to a military presence in Cairo and therefore opposed to the 1929 negotiations and 1930 draft treaty, as well as the opening of new treaty negotiations afterwards. Delany made reference to this in a letter to high commissioner Sir Percy Loraine in 1933.[116] A chiefs of staff paper of February 1936 said that the defence of Egypt 'can be safeguarded only by the domination of Cairo, which will be the source of all plots against our interests'.[117] These strategic interests were the natural ally of the British Union, which, as Delany said, represented a social category that 'enjoyed special privileges under the Capitulations'.[118] The British Union position was described by staff at the Egyptian Department in the Foreign Office as typical of the most reactionary 'Turf Club opinion', representative of only a small section of the British community in Cairo. Similarly, the *Egyptian Gazette* wrote in an editorial that while Lloyd had been energetic in pushing British trade, even Lloyd and the Union could not 'put the clock back ten years'.[119] The Foreign Office made the case that concessions were inevitable, citing, for example, that in 1919 when there were sixty thousand troops in Egypt, the government of the day chose conciliation; with ten thousand troops in 1934 concessions were a necessity. Indeed, the diplomats at the Foreign Office adopted the logic of the Milner Proposals, making the case that concession had been the basis of policy since 1904.[120]

Lloyd's *Egypt since Cromer* provoked debate, with the colonial liberals leading the charge against the book. However, it was the international crisis that followed the Italian invasion of Ethiopia that brought British and Egyptian governments into negotiations that led to the Anglo-Egyptian Treaty of 1936. The treaty seemed to have realised liberal colonial objectives. In a 1936 article by Spender in *Round Table*, a journal disseminating the thought of imperial reformers, the treaty was described as creating a new form of international relations that involved two spheres of authority, an 'inner sphere of self-government' controlled exclusively by Egyptians, and an 'outer sphere of external policy' that required cooperation with the British. The boundary between these two spheres had to be established by 'custom and usage', but of course with Britain dominating the latter sphere. Delany observed in his commentary on Spender's analysis, 'A proper spirit of accommodation would be required to make these institutions workable.' For liberal colonial opinion the 1936 treaty embodied the recommendations of the Milner Report of 1921. The treaty promised Britain's influence and good relations in the long term in exchange for Egyptian self-government. It marked a triumph of the 'liberal' policy of concessions over the imperialists, if the new 'accommodation' was strictly respected.[121]

Delany bitterly reflected on the squandering of the liberal legacy that the treaty represented. Imperial sentiment, the emergency occasioned by the Second World War, and the sacrifices of the troops, meant that this was not a conventional interpretation. The dominant narrative highlighted the legitimate security requirements that led to necessary interventions. Delany, however, was determined to fix this misperception in his correspondences. In a 1953 letter to Lord ('Archie' John) Wavell, Field Marshal Wavell's son, Delany said Lampson undermined the 1936 treaty by his overbearing attitude towards the Egyptian king and governments. Lampson's actions were irrational, driven by a desire to dominate and impose his will. Delany made his case against Lampson by connecting him with authoritarian colonial cultures: 'When Farouk [Faruq] took the throne many British people at the time expressed the hope that we would not repeat the blunder of alienating the youthful king as we had done with a previous ruler ... But this is precisely what did happen.'[122] Delany compared Lampson to Cromer, who had felt it necessary to slap down the young Khedive 'Abbas in 1894 – a straightforward case of colonial paternalism.[123] Lampson referred to King Faruq as 'the boy'. He kept him 'at arm's length'.[124] During treaty negotiations in 1935 and 1936 the British government chose to dispense with the palace clique and turned to the Wafd, an organisation that had lost much of its political support and was desperate for a means to re-establish itself. The treaty had the effect of converting the Wafd into an instrument of British influence, which checked the palace clique. This in turn meant a political contest between Lampson and the monarchists, which began when the king's political agent, 'Ali Mahir, confided to Reuters correspondent Kenneth Anderson that the king intended to dismiss Nahhas in December 1937. Anderson relayed the news to Lampson at the race track of the Gezira Sporting Club. 'The Ambassador had only one comment to make. "This," he said, "may be the end of Farouk."' Delany commented in his letter to Wavell that the Foreign Office had not permitted Lampson 'to go to the lengths he desired' in 1937 because Lampson had a 'poor case': Nahhas was known for his 'anarchic administration', his 'Blue shirt' organisation on the fascist principle, and usurping the functions of the police, all of which contributed to his own downfall. The issue resurfaced when war was declared in 1939 and the royalist prime minister, 'Ali Mahir, decided on a state of non-belligerency rather than a declaration of war against Germany. This 'displeased the British Ambassador'. After Italy entered the war in 1940 and began the offensive against Egypt, Delany consulted with the head of the Egyptian Department at the Foreign Office in London concerning Lampson's desire to bring Nahhas back to power. 'I said that the British government some years back had recognized the principle that the Government of Egypt was a matter for the King and his people, and past experience had shown that we could not successfully impose a particular government on the king.'[125]

Lord Wavell's subsequent correspondence with Delany showed he shared these views. Perhaps he was influenced by his father, Field Marshal Wavell, but in a letter of 1953 he said that the principle of non-intervention had also been the position of many military figures with experience in Egypt (he mentioned Field Marshal Bernard Montgomery and Field Marshal Alan Brooke). 'Die-hards' like Lampson, Lord Wavell said, had always opposed the 1936 settlement with Egypt, whereas in his opinion, shared by other officers, the military bases in Egypt were 'valueless without the goodwill of the people'.[126] Field Marshal Wavell, in a 1946 letter to Delany, said that he never agreed with Lampson's policy of the 'Big Stick and the High Hand, certainly not as instruments of almost daily use'.[127] From the perspective of these non-interventionists, the uncertainty surrounding Egyptian politics was a result of the whims of Lampson, rather than Egyptian provocations. Field Marshal Wavell took the view that maintaining good relations with Egyptians was primary to British interests, contrary to the conservative tendency to impose policy upon the Egyptians based on security concerns, regardless of the political costs. It is difficult to determine how widely held was the non-interventionist point of view. The political influence of the business community waned after 1936, which weakened the British Union sector of opinion.[128] Among British officials, two of the most prominent, Alexander Keown-Boyd and Thomas Russell, both disagreed with Lampson's methods. Keown-Boyd and Russell were responsible for the security of the British colony. Russell was the chief of the Cairo police and Keown-Boyd inspector-general of the European Department at the Ministry of the Interior. Each had long-term relationships with Egyptian politicians. Thomas Russell was well-known for having the trust of Egyptian officials and politicians.[129] Although he arrested and imprisoned Egyptians regularly, he seemed 'immune' from assault by agents of political 'terror'.[130] Lampson resented Russell's attempts to offer advice on the political situation and insinuated that Russell was guilty of 'cowardice' during the war because of his non-interventionism.[131] Keown-Boyd and Hasan Rafaat, director-general of the Ministry of the Interior, were 'firm friends' tied together by a shared antipathy towards 'Wafdist extremism'.[132] Each opposed Lampson's treatment of the king, although Keown-Boyd's wife, Joan, thought Lampson 'too soft'.[133]

Field Marshal Wavell and his wife, Eugénie, three daughters and a nanny lived in Gezira, while his son Archie (later Lord Wavell) was based in Scotland. The family shared a large villa on the edge of the Gezira racecourse with Lieutenant General Maitland ('Jumbo') Wilson. When the news of the French armistice with Germany reached Cairo in June 1940, Wavell was playing golf on the Gezira course. 'I played the two remaining holes, doing them in three and four, I remember. I then went back to my office and wrote out a short Order of the Day.'[134] The image is apt. There is the sense of a leisurely Cairo somewhat removed from the urgency of the European theatre. However, Wavell was under no illusions. By 1940 his 'worst case' scenarios included an occupied Britain, with the war effort continuing from imperial and Commonwealth bases in Australia, Canada, and South Africa. The Middle Eastern Command engendered a wide perspective on imperial strategy, wherein the Iranian oil fields were the first strategic consideration. Wavell's immediate concern was building an effective fighting force from bases in Africa and Asia, which put him on collision course with Churchill, as already observed. The principal difference between the two men appeared to be Wavell's caution against Churchill's urgency. According to his biographer, John Connell, Wavell viewed war as a 'wasteful, boring, muddled affair', whereas Churchill revelled in the glory of it. There were also deep differences of attitude towards empire. The key difference during the war was Wavell's concern to keep a 'delicately poised peace' in Africa and Asia, whereas Churchill's views on empire, according to Wavell's biographer, had not much changed since the era of high imperialism in the late nineteenth century.[135] The empire existed to serve British metropolitan interests, regardless. Lampson's errant 'elephant' approach to things suited Churchill's need to overawe the Egyptians. Derision of the weakling Egyptians resurfaced as an imperial cultural trait during the war. Lieutenant General Cyril Joly recalled, 'To us all it seemed natural that a race [Egyptians] who would not move in self-defence even when the enemy had actually crossed their borders should be reviled in word and deed whenever need or the opportunity arose.'[136] This type of racist disdain for Egyptians was attributed to the British generally; however, Wavell, Delany, and others with a better grounding in the colonial setting resisted the systematic negating of Egyptians characteristic of many.[137]

IMPERIALISTS AND COLONIALS

Wavell had been with Allenby in Syria. Like Lawrence, he was immediately struck by Allenby's military tactics, based on mobility, feint, and a comprehensive reading of the terrain. As noted, Wavell pushed forward these ideas in British military thinking, developing concepts fitted to mechanised armoured units deployed in small, mobile forces, rather than large set pieces. He spoke and published on these ideas widely, so that even Rommel carried a copy of his lectures during the North African campaign. He took over the Palestine command in 1937 in the midst of the 'great revolt' against the British Mandate. Wavell viewed the British situation in Palestine as contrary to conventional British imperial strategy: Britain was compelled by the situation in Palestine to suppress the population, rather than conciliate and collaborate. Moreover, Palestinian opposition turned the population of the entire Middle Eastern region against Britain.[138] The situation was counter-intuitive to Wavell's basic philosophy on British tactics and strategy. He disagreed in principle with the tactics forced upon his command by the circumstances, which included a wire fence on the perimeter of the Mandate and heavy concrete fortifications situated in strategic areas across Palestine. It was in this period that the intelligence officer Orde Charles Wingate developed the Zionist Night Squads. Wavell accepted the need for such tactics militarily, but recognised their negative political consequences. While his command adopted these various counter-insurgency methods, none appealed to him. What was clear from his analysis was that a policy of large-scale military occupation and repression was bound to fail.[139]

These lessons were applied to his thinking on Egypt from 1939. The drama of the North African campaign in military histories deals with the contrary tactics and temperaments of Churchill and his generals. Whereas more attention is given towards relations with Egyptians in regional political histories, with the spotlight of course on Lampson's policy towards the Egyptian politicians and king, the narrative in Delany's letters suggests that the fundamental differences on imperial policy in the interwar period were played out during the Second World War, with Wavell standing in for the Milner tradition of conciliation rather than domination. In Delany's correspondence, the wartime narrative begins with a meeting between him and Wavell at British military headquarters in the Semiramis Hotel, Cairo, in June 1940. Delany informed Wavell that Lampson had offered him a position in the Ministry of Information, but that he had declined because he preferred to be Wavell's political liaison officer. Quitting Reuters, Delany became Wavell's 'de facto' political adviser, whereas Lampson, as the British diplomat in Egypt, was Wavell's 'de jure' adviser. Delany's advice to Wavell followed the pattern of conciliation and collaboration, as already outlined, to which Wavell agreed. Political peace in Egypt was a primary tactical consideration, which could not be achieved through British intervention in the domestic government. Lampson took a contrary view. He was in direct communication with Churchill. It was Churchill's preference that the military command be free of any political distractions, which meant he relied upon Lampson to remove any threat, real or imagined. According to Delany, this went against the spirit of the 1936 treaty.[140]

In the 1953 correspondence with Lord Wavell, Delany discussed the negative consequences of Lampson's policy. Lampson was, according to Delany, quite irrationally convinced that the security situation in Egypt was unstable and he was determined to impose his will upon the Egyptians with the replacement of the government of 'Ali Mahir to secure an Egyptian declaration of war against Italy and Germany from a Wafd government (the Wafd did not oblige, as it turned out). On the other hand, Delany and Wavell regarded the political situation as secure and that the Egyptians had honoured the 1936 treaty's wartime requirements. Delany noted that the Egyptians cooperated in spite of the fact that the treaty put very heavy financial obligations on Egypt in terms of the construction of bases and communication networks. Wavell was content with Egyptian non-belligerency during the war and he respected the treaty, with full confidence that the Egyptian government supported the British war effort.[141] According to Delany, Wavell had no quarrel with 'Ali Mahir in 1940 because he responded to the demands of the British military and 'carried out the letter of the treaty'. In a conversation with Delany in September 1940, 'Ali Mahir said that the Egyptian government had come to an understanding with the government of Italy that the Egyptians would not respond militarily if Italy invaded Egypt; in exchange Italy promised not to engage the Egyptians. This explained Egyptian non-belligerence. There was no government plot (there were of course underground groups) actively to assist the Italians. Delany recalled that Wavell declared that this suited his requirements, as it meant his centres of command and supply in Cairo did not come under direct bombing. When Mahir was replaced by Hassan Sabri Pasha, and shortly thereafter Husayn Sirri Pasha, Wavell's demeanour towards Egyptian non-belligerency was unchanged. Lampson, however, continued to press for a Wafd government led by Nahhas.[142]

During the days immediately preceding Wavell's 1940 'Compass' offensive against the Italians, Wavell stuck to routine. His plans for 'Compass' were well guarded, details only revealed to the General Staff, not Lampson.[143] When on the early morning of 9 December British forces engaged the Italians in the Western Desert, Wavell interrupted his early morning ritual to call on the Egyptian prime minister, Sirri

Pasha, and as a mark of confidence informed him of the military plans. On that same day Delany lunched with Wavell at the Muhammad 'Ali Club, the beating heart of Egyptian political life, with Chief of Staff General Sir Arthur Smith and Brigadier Eric (John) Shearer, director of military intelligence. Nothing of the campaign was mentioned during lunch as Delany briefed Wavell on the political situation, including pledges from all heads of the political parties that 'they would give full regard to his position as Commander-in-Chief in all their political decisions'.[144] Wavell thus carefully monitored the political situation, ensured military security, while at the same time respecting the autonomy of Egypt's political leadership. A letter of Wavell to Delany dated 6 March 1943 remarked, 'I think that taking it all round Egypt and the Egyptians have put up a very good show in this war and done us well, and they have been remarkably steady at the critical times.'[145]

As a necessary preliminary to his indictment of Lampson, Delany recorded Wavell's policies and surveyed the political situation. He underlined that Egypt was a secure military base and there was no need to undermine the existing agreements with the Egyptian government. Delany recognised that the Muslim Brotherhood was 'dangerous', but it was kept in check by the Wafd and other political parties fundamentally hostile to it. Its leader, Hassan al-Banna, had been interred by the Egyptian government as a precaution. The Wafd was disgruntled by its removal from office, but at the king, not at the British. There was a fifth column friendly to the Axis powers, mostly 'sycophants', but they did not represent any political party or group and were marginal. The only political uncertainty troubling the military in 1941 was the rift between the king and ambassador, according to Delany. On Lampson's proposal to remove the king from the throne in 1940, Wavell said that such a British initiative would unite all of Egypt against the British; even the beneficiary of such an act, like Nahhas, would be forced to condemn the British. Delany observed that Wavell's transfer from Egypt in July 1941 removed the only effective check on Lampson's actions. Delany argued that if Wavell had remained, the trend towards increasing nationalist resistance and violence might have been avoided. It was unlikely that Wavell would have agreed to be a party to the use of force on 4 February 1942 when Lampson brought the Wafd back to power. Delany argued that there were alternative methods to induce the king to form a government under Nahhas. Indeed, 'Ali Shamsi, the president of the National Bank of Egypt, informed Delany that King Faruq was working to create a coalition government led by Nahhas. But Lampson was intent upon humiliating Faruq. Lampson's acts, rather than tactical, fitted a pattern of 'bullying' akin to the systematic 'reviling' of Egyptians, as testified to by Cyril Joly.[146]

'It was Lampson's action in surrounding Abdin Palace with armed forces that was to start the cry for the complete evacuation of Egypt, with the sorry results that we all know.'[147] Delany was not alone in this assessment. Wavell had consulted with Delany on the risks as early as 1940 when Lampson first made the proposal. Delany prepared a note dealing with the risks. General Frank Theron, head of the South African troops, was also disconcerted by the proposal and asked for information on Egyptian politics. Walter Smart at the British embassy referred him to Brigadier Sir Iltyd Clayton of the Middle East Intelligence Centre.[148] Clayton advised the minister of state in the Middle East, Oliver Lyttleton.[149] He was totally opposed to Lampson's proposal. On Clayton, Delany said: 'It was he I assume that induced Oliver Lyttelton to advise Lampson not to go to the full length of deportation [in 1942] if Farouk agreed to reinstate Nahas.'[150] Ahmad Hassanein, who succeeded 'Ali Mahir as the king's political adviser, claimed that the three service chiefs in Cairo opposed the use of force in 1942.[151] The commander of the British Army of Occupation, General Robert Stone, with substantial colonial military experience and close contacts in Egyptian political circles, disagreed with Lampson's policy. When Lampson contemplated the further use of force in 1944, the three service chiefs again disapproved. Churchill, however, supported Lampson in 1942 and instructed the military heads to have sufficient troops at the disposal of the ambassador if it was necessary to use force to induce the 'Oriental despot' (King Faruq) to conform to British policy.[152]

The other crucial issue was troop withdrawal from Cairo and Alexandria to the Canal Zone after the North African campaign was won in 1943. According to Delany, Lampson stalled.[153] In notes gathered during a conversation with Delany in 1971, Waterfield recorded Delany's recollections of a conversation in Thomas Russell's garden with General Sir Bernard Paget, Commander-in-Chief in the Middle East from 1944 to 1946.[154] Paget said that British troops must be moved at least thirty miles away from the cities so that Egyptians did not see them in Cairo and Alexandria. That was his recommendation to the War Office. Lampson blocked these redeployments because it would take away his 'bargaining counter' in future negotiations with the Egyptians.[155] A supporting piece of evidence is a letter of Field Marshal Wavell to Delany of 29 October 1945 when he said, 'I agree with Paget that we might move out of Cairo, but it will be a great blow to the amenities in Egypt.'[156] Wavell made a more explicit statement in a letter to Delany on 19 March 1946:

> Trouble need not have occurred and is of our own making. For some reason the Foreign Office have never been able to handle Egyptian affairs

with sympathy or tact ... I could never quite understand why we could not have withdrawn our troops from Cairo and Alexandria soon after the end of the war.[157]

Lampson's policies had the support of Viscount Halifax and Anthony Eden at the Foreign Office. The Foreign Office viewed the political situation as 'uncertain'. The Egyptian government's attitude towards its alliance with Britain was defined by 'ambiguity', which 'affected the security of the base and the lines of communication'.[158] However, that the calculations were more political than security oriented is one conclusion that can be drawn from a reading of Lampson's diaries. In May 1940, Lampson wrote, 'in my own mind I have for many years often thought that the best form of permanent relationship with Egypt lay with her incorporation, in some shape or form, into the British Empire'.[159] In April 1944 Lampson was writing to the secretary of state, Antony Eden, that he wondered 'whether we might not have to take a firmer line and assume more direct control over Egypt'.[160] The belief that the British military was a necessary political instrument was not new. In short it was the imperial mentality that would not trust self-government to the Egyptians and, according to Delany, the fatal inability of Lampson, Eden, and 'no doubt' Churchill, to adapt to the spirit of the 1936 treaty.[161] Lampson's diaries do not confirm that he intentionally delayed the withdrawal of forces from Cairo and Alexandria, but that troops were regarded as an 'asset' in negotiations with Egyptians.[162] This contrasts with those officers and officials who viewed the troop presence as politically counter-productive.[163] In a 1953 letter to Delany, Lord Wavell bemoaned the fact that 'those like yourself who have given so many years of your life to establish good relations with the Egyptians' had lived 'to see so much good will frustrated'. Indeed, the strident tone in Delany's correspondence was of a colonial liberal bitterly reflecting on the ruin of a world that might, in his opinion, have been avoided. Lord Wavell attributed this kind of anguish to many Egyptians also. He noted that the Egyptian foreign minister said that 'appeasement' of the Egyptians by withdrawal after the war would at worst have caused a revolt among Conservative backbenchers ('die-hards'), perhaps the fall of a Labour government. But for the Egyptians it was the spectre of complete political collapse – 'anarchy'.[164] The liberal vision – the effort to establish durable political collaboration between British agents and Egyptian elites – was, according to Delany, Field Marshal Wavell, and his son, Lord Wavell, squandered. Their letters express a similar regret.

The Labour government rejected Lampson's idea that the troops stationed in Egypt represented a 'decisive card' in negotiations. Rather,

Lord Stangate, who led negotiations with the Egyptians, recognised that the troops were in violation of the existing treaty and therefore a stumbling block.[165] By 1951 Labour had reduced troop numbers in Egypt from a quarter of a million to thirty-eight thousand, whereas the 1936 treaty allowed only 10,400.[166] But in negotiations, the Egyptians demanded complete troop withdrawal and Egyptian sovereignty over Sudan. From 1946, these demands were attended by bomb attacks on British civilians and troops and massive demonstrations under the banner of 'Evacuation'. Press releases current with these debates spoke of attacks on British army barracks, social clubs, and churches, as well as synagogues. The Egyptian police were unmoved, thus only the British military stood between the violent protesters and the British colony.[167] Delany left Egypt shortly after the war.

The Egypt of the English

Vivien Jennings-Bramly used the expression 'Egypt of the English' during the war to distinguish the 'English' from the colonial. The flag-waving, marching bands and tea parties for the troops of wartime Egypt reflected imperial sentiment, not colonial sentiment. The vast majority of British in Egypt during the war were short-term residents. However, among the long-term residents there was an awareness of the threat posed by the war to the colony's attachment to place or colonial sentiment. The life of the colony went on as usual during and after the war, evident in Vivien Jennings-Bramly's letters to her parents in England. She commented on days spent riding, a dinner party at Farnall's, which included the Sidonis, Bournettes, Carters, and Mrs Willcox. Letters included the usual chatter: 'Mrs Russell is not at all well.' But Jennings-Bramly was dumbstruck at the spectacle of the 'Egypt of the English' at the Gezira Sporting Club. While her support for the war was obvious in her entertainment of troops with tea and sports, at the same time she referred to being 'lost in wonderment' at the spectacle of British society at the Gezira races. In letters to her mother, Phyllis Jennings-Bramly, she confided sentiments that would hardly have been included in any welcome address to soldiers at such teas: 'One begins to be disgusted with the name of English,' she observed. There is in this colonial self-identification against the 'English' a sense that the colony was far removed from imperial culture and even the culture of the 'home' country: 'The gap increases between our Egypt and the Egypt of the English. The state of the latter is appalling, simply terrifying to look into. Yet here everyone is ready as before to go to any inconvenience at one's slightest wish. – Politicians – Vive Commonsense! But that is not to be.' Referring to the rising tide of discontent with the British in a letter on the 'Evacuation' demonstrations of 1946, she said, 'One of the people who was kicked about in the railway strike was here yesterday and gives the most fearful account of the way in which the ringleaders have been practically encouraged to go and prosper by the Native Authorities. No backing up for the English officials of any sort.'[168]

For liberal-minded colonials, the war ruined any chance of rebuilding international relations as represented by the 1936 treaty. This fact is probably best represented by the collapse of the Anglo-Egyptian Union. Originally designed to sustain and expand cultural and social relations between Egyptians and British, a common perception of the Union was that it was principally the haunt of British literary types.[169] This legend was begun perhaps by Olivia Manning in her description of the Union as a somewhat dissolute refuge for British 'just above the poverty line', mostly teachers in the British schools. In her series of novels of wartime Egypt and Syria, *The Levant Trilogy*, the Union was the setting where a British news correspondent taunted a dignified group of Egyptian officers in the adjoining garden: 'King Farouk, King Farouk/Hang your bollocks on a hook'.[170] In fact, this taunt was regularly sung to the tune of the Egyptian national anthem by British in uniform, with the following refrain, 'Queen Farida/Queen of all the Wogs'.[171] Manning without a doubt provided an accurate reflection of the kind of ridicule systematically directed at king and Egyptians. However, given that the Anglo-Egyptian Union was the unofficial headquarters of literary groups like Personal Landscape, the Union was probably the least likely locale for this type of racist insult. Indeed, Samir Rafaat's online history of the Union also noted the proximity of the Egyptian Officers' Club to the Union and the irony that the Union inhabited the former headquarters of the British military, known as the Sirdaria, a grand palace comparable to Qasr al-Nil. The actual Anglo-Egyptian official records show that membership was restricted to men, although wives of members were freely admitted. Membership was gained by reference from an existing member. In 1945 there were seven hundred Egyptian and five hundred British members. Herbert Addison's collection of memorabilia also indicated that the Union's activities involved teas, films, concerts, and lectures. Its resolutions and notices were given in English and Arabic. Egyptian and British scholars gave lectures. Audiences as large as five hundred attended weekly film showings. Concerts were given by Egyptian and European groups, roughly in equal measure. In a 1947 gala the legendary Egyptian singer and national icon, Umm Kulthum, sang at the Union, at a moment when she was transforming her identity from decorated royalist to leftist-religious populist. Elitism peaked during the war and was then eclipsed.[172]

Indicating the purposefulness of Egyptian nationalism, the Union's collapse was synchronised with political events: massive demonstrations and strikes burst out under the banner of 'Evacuation' in February 1946. There were clashes with British troops outside the gates of Qasr al-Nil. Subsequent demonstrations were organised for the 'martyrs' of that confrontation. The Anglican cathedral was targeted by saboteurs. At a meeting of the Union on 4 April, 1946, the Egyptian membership showed solidarity with the demonstrators by a motion to disband the Union. With the withdrawal of the Egyptian membership, the Union lost its purpose, reflecting a larger trend of alienation in social relations. The Union dissolved in 1949.[173]

Throughout the history of the colony Egyptians hid their close associations with British authorities, if not individuals, to avoid the stigma of 'collaboration'.[174] Conversely, Thomas Rapp recalled that as far as most British were concerned, at no time had 'political divergences or passions' prevented 'friendly relations with the Egyptian authorities or many individual Egyptians'.[175] Marking thirty years of consular service, he said that Cairo in 1951 was still relatively pleasant. He worked at the Middle East Office, a colonial bureaucracy designed to replace the huge bureaucratic infrastructure of the service chiefs and the minister of state in the Middle East. The work of the Middle East Office was carried out in a villa in Zamalek, with leisure hours spent at the Gezira Sporting Club. Rapp recalled the annual dinner of Oxford and Cambridge 'old boys' at the Muhammad 'Ali Club, which, in spite of the political differences between Britain and Egypt, exhibited that 'between us as individuals there was a great fund of good will'.[176] Rapp noted that Egypt's administrative and business elites, as well as minorities (Copts, Syrians, and Turks) were bound to the British by 'self-interest', not love or compulsion. However, the troubled post-war treaty revisions intervened in these everyday social relations. With the future of the British uncertain, the elites 'rallied to the nationalists, at least publicly, while privately hoping that our departure would be delayed because of the economic and social changes likely to follow in its train'. In this tense political environment, Rapp recalled the story of an Egyptian friend, an Oxford graduate married to a British national, who worked in the British intelligence service. After the war, when the British had no more use for his services, he found that association with the British had entirely compromised his future: he was disowned by his family and disqualified for employment with the Egyptian government.[177] According to Rapp, self-interest and institutional connections that had previously cemented collaboration, evaporated after the war. 'And the more the British were driven back upon themselves, the greater the alienation appeared.'[178] Egyptian elites and colonials experienced a similar crisis – as observed by Chafika Hamamsy – that involved a conflict of allegiances, a dichotomy between the 'official self', as defined by nationality, and the other self, shaped by a colonial culture that bred hybrid identities.[179]

From this perspective, the critical turn in colonial relations was the alienation of the Egyptian elites from the British, a point underlined in Edward Said's memoirs. Rather than a revolutionary mass overthrowing the 'cosmopolitan' elites, the masses and the Egyptian elites united and abandoned the 'foreigner' (khawaga). The causes were primarily political, beginning in 1942. Colonial society unravelled during and after the Second World War when Egyptian and Levantine elites began to withdraw from the English schools and other integrative social relations with the British colony. The trend was evident in the student composition at Victoria College, where 'Christian' and 'Jewish' categories rapidly declined after 1945.[180] Edward Said recalled that his family abandoned the Gezira Sporting Club for the Tawfiqiyya Club in 1949.[181] He observed that the cosmopolitan world of *shawam* (referring to people from larger Syria, such as himself) wherein Arabic, English, and French cultures had intermingled, was already undermined through assassinations and disappearances in the late 1940s. Travelling on trams or buses and going out after dark were dangerous. The militancy of the *fedayin* (paramilitary) attacks meant that 'working relationships' in Cairo with British 'doctors, nurses, teachers, bureaucrats' were tense. By the end of the 1940s the Levantine elites – Christian, Jewish, and Muslim – had been marked out as 'foreigners', as 'colonials'.[182] In conclusion, he said that 'slowly members of these communities began to disappear – some to Israel, to Europe, and a tiny number to the United States ... Some left in anticipation of what was to come; later others were forced to leave penniless because of Suez and 1967 wars.'[183]

The dominant voice was the British security interest; no surprise that the state monopolised imperial policy. It muted British liberal principle, the Church and its urge to convert and proselytise, merchant enterprise seeking long-term-ventures, individuals in the military, police, bureaucracy, schools, and other cultural institutions, including the press, all were left gasping at the gambles made in the name of national security.

The theme is apparent in the imperial debates of late empire, with figures like Delany and Waterfield openly questioning the strategic imperatives voiced by conservative imperialists.[184] But did the liberal voice serve only as an apology and/or nostalgia for empire? Was the liberal narrative ultimately powerless and, given that it cloaked the reality of relentless imperial power, meaningless? Is the liberal account of history therefore a distortion of 'real' historical forces? While debatable, the muted liberal voice clarifies the diversity of British opinion. In an unexpected turn of events, the Second World War magnified the British presence and embittered British–Egyptian relations. This was not inevitable. It was not immediately obvious that the proximity of British military forces would no longer safeguard the British colony. Only the prolonged military occupation provoked violent attacks on British soldiers and civilians. Equally severe reprisals sped the cycle of violence. Ultimately, the war demonstrated that the British colony in Egypt was not a major consideration for the British government. The colony did not determine policy; nor could it escape the consequent narrowing of colonial options. Britons engaged in business, cultural, or professional pursuits were keenly aware of their powerlessness before the forces of nationalism and imperialism. But for many of them, Egypt had represented a kind of refuge, whether in its multilayered past or in the vivacity of its contemporaneity. Therefore, the loss of the colony was mourned. When the last troops evacuated Egypt on 24 March 1956, some residents remained, of these most would be expelled and their properties confiscated after the invasion in October. The disaster at Suez terminated many of the multiple cultural, social, and economic institutions founded by the British, but not all. As the stories of Michael Barker and Gerald Delany attest, positive engagement with Egypt remained. For each a final act was to seek a resting place outside of England. Before the end, Delany relocated to Ireland, former British colony, where he wrote some of his most pointed criticisms of the imperialists. Barker's remains were 'repatriated' to Egypt. Those final acts memorialised colonial lives at odds with the ascendant narratives on nation and empire.

Notes

1 David Washbrook, 'Orients and Occidents: Colonial Discourse Theory and the Historiography of the British Empire', in Robin W. Winks (ed.), *The Oxford History of the British Empire, Volume V, Historiography* (Oxford: Oxford University Press, 1999), pp. 596–611, in particular, p. 609 & Jon E. Wilson, 'Agency, Narrative, and Resistance', in Sarah Stockwell (ed.), *The British Empire: Themes and Perspectives* (Oxford: Blackwell, 2008), p. 255.
2 John Darwin, *Britain, Egypt, and the Middle East* (London: Palgrave Macmillan, 1981).
3 Wm. Roger Louis, *Ends of British Imperialism: The Scramble for Empire, Suez, and Decolonization* (London: I.B. Tauris, 2006).
4 Darwin, *Britain*, p. 128 & Priya Satia, *Spies in Arabia: The Great War and the Cultural Foundations of Britain's Covert Empire in the Middle East* (Oxford: Oxford University Press, 2008) & John Darwin, 'An Undeclared Empire: The British in the Middle East, 1918–1939', in Robert O. King and Robin Kilson (eds), *The Statecraft of British Imperialism: Essays in Honour of Wm. Roger Louis* (London: Frank Cass, 1999).

IMPERIALISTS AND COLONIALS

5 TNA FO371/6295 4919/260/16, 16 April 1921, 'Alternative Proposals for Future Government in Egypt', memorandum by Maurice Amos and Reginald Patterson.
6 Trefor E. Evans (ed.), *The Killearn Diaries 1934–1946* (London: Sidgwick & Jackson, 1972), pp. 11–13. Evans said that the diaries demonstrated that Lampson's treatment of king and politicians in Egypt was fair. Gerald Delany's reading of the same selections led him to contrary conclusions; that this was his opinion, among many others, from the 1930s. Detailed references to these critiques of Lampson and Lloyd from the papers of Delany and Waterfield can be found below.
7 John Marlowe, *A History of Modern Egypt and Anglo-Egyptian Relations 1800–1953* (New York: Praeger, 1954), p. 319.
8 Malcolm Yapp (ed.), *Politics and Diplomacy in Egypt: The Diaries of Sir Miles Lampson 1935–1937* (Oxford: Oxford University Press, 1997), p. 6.
9 Walter Reid, *Empire of Sand: How Britain Made the Middle East* (Edinburgh: Birlinn, 2013), p. 272.
10 Gordon Waterfield, *Professional Diplomat: Sir Percy Loraine of Kirkhale* (London: John Murray, 1973), p. 197.
11 Gabriel Warburg, 'Lampson's Ultimatum to Faruq, 4 February 1942', *Middle Eastern Studies* 11/1 (1975): 24–32 & Charles D. Smith, '4 February 1942: Its Causes and its Influence on Egyptian Politics and on the Future of Anglo-Egyptian Relations, 1937–1945', *International Journal of Middle Eastern Studies* 10/4 (1979): 468–74.
12 Martin Kolinsky, *Britain's War in the Middle East* (New York: Palgrave, 1999), p. 15. See also Charles D. Smith's argument that 'the British considered the treaty to be for their convenience to legitimize their intended presence, not as a promise of future concessions leading to British withdrawal and total independence, Egyptian expectations to the contrary', Smith, '4 February 1942', p. 456. Satia, *Spies in Arabia* & Darwin, 'An Undeclared Empire'.
13 Louis, *Ends of British Imperialism*, p. 396.
14 A list of these soldiers can be found on pages 200–1; see also Lord Allanbrooke, *Triumph in the West* (London: Collins, 1959) & Field Marshall Wilson of Libya, *Eight Years Overseas 1937–1945* (London: Hutchinson, 1950) & Lord Douglas of Kirkside, *Years of Command* (London: Collins, 1966).
15 Richard Toye, *Churchill's Empire: The World that Made him and the World he Made* (London: Pan Books, 2011), p. 119.
16 Wm. Roger Louis, *In the Name of God Go! Leo Amery and the British Empire in the Age of Churchill* (New York: Norton, 1992). The term 'geo-political' is used by Louis to describe primarily imperial strategic interests.
17 Andrew S. Thompson, *Imperial Britain: The Empire in British Politics, c. 1880–1932* (Harlow: Longman, 2000), where he says that fundamental to the 'die-hards' was the idea of imperial weakness, 'the feeling that the British Empire might be living on borrowed time', p. 164.
18 Louis, *Ends of British Imperialism*, pp. 609–26.
19 Ibid., p. 616.
20 Toye, *Churchill's Empire*, p. 288 & Louis, *Ends of British Imperialism*, p. 622.
21 Elie Kedourie, *The Chatham House Version and Other Middle Eastern Studies* (London: Weidenfeld and Nicolson, 1970), pp. 262 & 286–316.
22 Chafika Soliman Hamamsy, *Zamalek: The Changing Life of a Cairo Elite, 1850–1945* (Cairo: American University in Cairo Press, 2005), pp. 141 & 221.
23 TNA FO141/581, 'Report of the Council of Cairo Non-Official British Community to the British Mission of Enquiry'.
24 TNA FO141/1398, 'British Influence in Egypt', 12 Dec. 1920.
25 TNA FO141/581, Allenby to Curzon, 19 April 1919, 'British Union in Egypt: Cairo Non-Official British Community: Views on Egyptian Political Situation'. Union members included W.E. Kingsford, J.W Eady, C.R. Beasley, William Willcocks, W.B. Delaney, F.N. Walton, J.P. Foster, F.H. Russell, Roberts, Hart, Mifsud, Beddos.
26 Ibid.

EGYPT

27 TNA FO141/581, 'Copy of Memorandum sent on 2 February by British Union in Egypt' & 'Minutes of First Meeting of the British Union Advisory Committee held at the Residency on Wed the 7th March, 1923'.
28 E.M. Forster, *Selected Letters of E.M. Forster*, ed. Mary Lago and P.N. Burbank (London: Harper, 1983), Forster to Malcolm Darling, 6 Aug. 1916, p. 234.
29 Ibid., Forster to Florence Barger, 8 Nov. 1916, p. 245.
30 Michael Haag, *Alexandria: City of Memory* (New Haven: Yale University Press, 2004), p. 22.
31 Robert Liddell, *Cavafy: A Critical Biography* (London: Duckworth, 1974), p. 191.
32 Mirriam Allot, 'Introduction', in E.M. Forster, *Alexandria: A History and Guide and Pharos and Pharillon* (London: André Deutsch, 2004), p. xv.
33 Forster, *Alexandria*, pp. 240–2 & Anthony Hirst and Michael Silk (eds), *Alexandria, Real and Imagined* (Aldershot: Ashgate, 2004), in particular, David Roessel, 'A Passage through Alexandria', p. 331.
34 Forster, *Letters*, Forster to Virginia Woolf, 15 April 1916, p. 238.
35 Ibid., Forster to Barger, 25 Aug. 1917, p. 268.
36 Ibid., Forster to Darling, 6 Aug. 1916, p. 239.
37 Ibid., Forster to Siegfried Sassoon, 2 May 1918, p. 289.
38 Ibid., Forster to Sassoon, 3 Aug. 1918, p. 292.
39 Pharos (Forster's pseudonym), 'Gippo English', *Egyptian Mail* (16 Dec. 1917), p. 2.
40 Pharos, 'Army English', *Egyptian Mail* (12 Jan. 1919), p. 2.
41 Forster, *Letters*, Forster to Barger, 29 May 1917, pp. 257–8.
42 Haag, *Alexandria*, pp. 21–2 & 36.
43 Ibid., p. 27, Haag citing a letter, 15 April 1916.
44 Ibid., p. 71, Haag citing letters, 2 May 1918 & 3 Aug. 1918.
45 Ibid., p. 36.
46 Ibid., p. 95.
47 Ibid., p. 101.
48 Roger Adelson, 'The British and U.S. Use and Misuse of the Term "Middle East"', in Michael E. Bonine, Abbas Amanat, and Michael Ezekiel Gasper (eds), *Is There a Middle East? The Evolution of a Geopolitical Concept* (Stanford: Stanford University Press, 2012), p. 42 & TNA FO371/6301 8245/260/16, 'Imperial Conference', where Churchill recorded his opposition to the content of the Milner Report & TNA FO371/10889 143/32/16, a file that includes discussion of Churchill's proposal to restore the principles of 'Cromerism', which he interpreted as Crown Colony status with the Egyptian king an ally of British imperial power as the representative of traditional authority. Commentary by the Foreign Office counsellor and head of the Egyptian Department John Murray dissented from this view in a memorandum to the foreign secretary, Austin Chamberlain.
49 'Gerald Delany', Obituary, *The Times* (15 June 1974).
50 MECA GB 165-0084, Gerald Delany, File 2 (hereafter 'MECA Delany 2'), 'Delany MS, Nationalism and the Peasantry in Egypt'.
51 On Spender's thinking on reformed empire, see Thompson, *Imperial Britain*, pp. 26 & 104–5. At the *Westminster Gazette* Spender was known for his moderate position in the Liberal Party and as a proponent for liberal imperialism. He became personally involved in the pre-war campaigns on imperial issues, such as tariff reform and naval supremacy, pp. 74–7, and subsequently 'Eastern' issues.
52 J.A. Spender, *The Changing East* (London: Cassell, 1926).
53 MECA GB 165-0295, Gordon Waterfield, Box 5, File 1 (hereafter MECA Waterfield 5/1), Laurence Grafftey-Smith to Waterfield, 3 Nov. 1974.
54 TNA FO371/6301 8245/260/16, 'Imperial Conference'; where Churchill recorded his opposition to the content of the Milner Report. See also Yapp, *Politics and Diplomacy*, p. 19.
55 MECA Waterfield 5/1, Grafftey-Smith to Waterfield, 3 Nov. 1974.
56 Ibid.
57 Ibid.
58 For a discussion of these views see Darwin, *Britain*, pp. 109–37.

IMPERIALISTS AND COLONIALS

59 Spender, *Changing East*, p. 75.
60 Toye, *Churchill's Empire*, p. 149.
61 Spender, *Changing East*, p. 75.
62 TNA FO371/10889 143/32/16.
63 Darwin, *Britain*, p. 109.
64 MECA Waterfield 5/1, 'Spender and Egypt'.
65 Darwin, *Britain*, pp. 93 & 115-25 & Kedourie, *Chatham House*, p. 138.
66 MECA Waterfield 5/1, 'Spender and Egypt'. See also Darwin, *Britain*, pp. 108-10.
67 MECA Delany 1, 'Lord Lloyd of Dolobren'.
68 Ibid.
69 MECA Waterfield 5/1, Delany to Waterfield, 11 Oct. 1973.
70 TNA FO371/10040 3563/368/16, Minutes of Murray to Oliphant and Ingram, 24 April 1924, which refer also to these discussions, and, 3785/368/16, Cabinet, 16 April 1924, which show that the government was planning on increasing the military bases in the vicinity of Cairo and Alexandria.
71 MECA Waterfield 5/1, Delany to Waterfield 19 June 1964.
72 Ibid., Delany to Waterfield, 11 Oct. 1973.
73 Ibid.
74 Ibid.
75 MECA Delany 1, 'Lord Lloyd of Dolobren'.
76 MECA Waterfield 5/1, Delany to Waterfield, 11 Oct. 1973.
77 Ibid.
78 Ibid. See Evans, *Killearn*, p. 149, for Lampson's account of Churchill's steadfast defence of Lloyd in House of Commons debates against criticisms from members of the 'Government at home'.
79 Churchill College, Cambridge, GLLD 13/3, letter, Sir Austen Chamberlain to Lord Lloyd, 19 Mar. 1928.
80 TNA FO141/581, letter, Kingsford to Allenby, 18 Dec. 1921.
81 TNA FO371/7730 652/1/16, 16 Jan. 1922, 'The Egyptian Question'.
82 TNA FO141/581, 'Copy of Memorandum sent on 2nd of February 1922 by the British Union in Egypt'.
83 TNA FO141/581, 'Minutes of First Meeting of the British Union Advisory Committee held at the Residency on Wed the 7th March, 1923'. Austen Chamberlain appointed a councillor to the high commissioner in December 1924, which might have been a response to the Union's demands. See also Lanver Mak, *The British in Egypt* (London: I.B. Tauris, 2012), pp. 214–39.
84 MECA Waterfield 5/1, Delany to Waterfield . 11 Oct. 1973.
85 Ibid., Delany to Waterfield, 21 Oct. 1964, with attached document: 'This record of my relations with Lord Lloyd, High Commissioner of Egypt from 1925 to 1929'.
86 Amos's lectures in England included the Cust Foundation Lecture and 'The Constitutional History of Egypt', *Publications of the Grotius Society* 14 (1929).
87 MECA GB165-0115, Sir Robert Allason Furness, Box 3, Folder 1 (hereafter 'MECA Furness 3/1'), document entitled 'HE', 1926.
88 Ibid.
89 TNA FO371/10889 143/32/16. Churchill declared that after the fall of the Wafd government Britain was again confronted by the choice between evacuation and annexation, which was a dramatic flourish given that neither was seriously contemplated by the Foreign Office; but it did give him the opportunity to advance the idea of making Egypt a 'Crown Colony'.
90 MECA Furness 3/1, Archibald Kerr to Furness, 8 Dec. 1925.
91 George A.L. Lloyd, *Egypt since Cromer* (London: Macmillan, 1934), pp. 155 & 165-7.
92 Afaf Lutfi al-Sayyid Marsot, *Egypt's Liberal Experiment* (Berkeley: University of California Press, 1977), p. 92.
93 MECA Waterfield 5/1, Delany to Waterfield, 21 Nov. 1964.
94 Waterfield, *Loraine*, p. 197.
95 *The Times* (19 July 1929).
96 MECA Furness 3/1, Delany to Furness, 1 Aug. 1929.

EGYPT

97 Ibid.
98 *The Times* (23 July 1929). 'Ubayd described Mahmud's government as a dictatorship supported by British troops, whereas, he said, Italy's had the support of the people.
99 MECA Furness 3/1, Delany to Furness, 29 July 1929. Delany wrote to Furness to communicate Mahmud's concern regarding 'Ubayd's articles in the *Manchester Guardian*. MECA Furness 3/1, draft of letter to the editor, 1928.
100 MECA Furness 3/1, Delany to Furness, 29 July 1929.
101 MECA Waterfield 3/1, Delany to Loraine, 30 May 1933. Delany discussed Mahmud's attitude towards the Egyptian constitution, showing an appreciation of the liberals much like that found in academic analysis, including cultural distance from the Egyptian mass electorate. See Charles D. Smith, *Islam and the Search for Social Order in Modern Egypt* (Albany: New York University Press, 1983).
102 *The Times* (14 June 1929).
103 MECA Furness 3/1, Delany to Furness 18 Aug. 1929.
104 MECA Waterfield 5/1, Delany to Waterfield 2 Nov. 1971.
105 Churchill College, GLLD 13/3, letter, 28 Mar. 1928, Sir Austen Chamberlain to Lord Lloyd, commenting on press allegations that Lloyd said: 'I am for force both here and India'. Chamberlain's commentary, letter 25 April 1928, suggests that Chamberlain disapproved of Lloyd's obstructionist policy.
106 *The Times* (14 July 1929) & Waterfield, *Loraine*, pp. 147–56.
107 *The Times* (27 July 1929).
108 *The Times* (29 July 1929).
109 *The Times* (1 Aug. 1929).
110 T.E. Lawrence, *The Letters of T.E. Lawrence*, ed. David Garnet (London: Jonathan Cape, 1938), Lawrence to Lord Lloyd, 30 Sept. 1934, p. 820.
111 MECA Furness 3/1, *Manchester Guardian* (24 Jan. 1935).
112 MECA Furness 3/1, *Egyptian Gazette* (29 June 1935).
113 Review of Lord Lloyd, *Egypt since Cromer*, vol. 2, *The Times* (8 June 1934).
114 Lord Lloyd, 'Security at Home and Abroad', *The Times* (2 April 1934).
115 Report on Lloyd's speech on India, 'Black Shirt and White Paper', *The Times* (2 May 1934).
116 MECA Waterfield 5/2, Delany to Loraine, 30 May 1933.
117 Kolinsky, *Britain's War*, p. 29.
118 MECA Delany 1, 'Lord Lloyd'.
119 TNA FO141/626/6, memorandum, Egyptian Department, Foreign Office, British Union in Egypt, 3 July 1930 & *Egyptian Gazette* (17 July 1930).
120 TNA FO141/626/6, note by A. Campbell.
121 MECA Waterfield 5/1, 'Spender and Egypt'.
122 MECA Delany 2, Delany to Lord ('Archie John') Wavell, 27 July 1953. Yapp, *Politics and Diplomacy*, which deals with events in the 1930s, contains one reference to Delany in the diary selections, none in the 'Introduction'.
123 Roger Owen, *Lord Cromer: Victorian Imperialist, Edwardian Proconsul* (Oxford: Oxford University Press, 2004), pp. 264–72.
124 MECA Delany 2, Delany to Lord Wavell, 27 July 1953.
125 Ibid.
126 Ibid., Lord Wavell to Delany, 21 Oct. 1953.
127 Ibid., Wavell to Delany, 19 Mar. 1946.
128 TNA FO141/1398, 'British Influence in Egypt'.
129 Keown-Boyd, *Lion and Sphinx*, p. 111.
130 MECA GB165-0024, Sir Thomas Cecil Rapp, memoirs, p. 30.
131 Keown-Boyd, *Lion and Sphinx*, p. 109.
132 Ibid., pp. 110–11.
133 Ibid., pp. 139–42.
134 John Connell, *Wavell: Scholar and Soldier* (London: Collins, 1964), pp. 239–40.
135 Ibid., pp. 255–6.
136 Cyril Joly, *Take these Men* (London: Buchan & Enright, 1985), p. 174.

137 MECA Delany 2, Delany to Lord Wavell, 27 July 1953, where Delany recalled that Lampson often used most 'undiplomatic' language when referring to King Faruq.
138 Connell, *Wavell*, p. 190.
139 Ibid., pp. 195–6.
140 MECA Delany 2, Delany to Lord Wavell, 27 July 1953 and MECA Waterfield 5/1, Delany to Waterfield, 7 Sept. 1972.
141 Hamamsy, *Zamalek*, pp. 291–9, recalled that Egyptian political society was polarised, but that the political crisis was created by Lampson's interventions.
142 MECA Delany 2, Delany to Lord Wavell, 27 July 1953. See Evans, *Killearn*, pp. 89–90 for Lampson's threat to the throne and Faruq's resentment for his treatment as schoolboy.
143 Connell, *Wavell*, pp. 281–90. See also Artemis Cooper, *Cairo in the War 1939–1945* (London: Hamish Hamilton, 1989), pp. 125–6, where Lampson complained that the Egyptian prime minister was often better informed of British military intelligence than was the British embassy.
144 MECA Delany 2, Delany to Lord Wavell, 27 July 1953. See Evans, *Killearn*, pp. 122–35, for the differing views of Lampson and Wavell on political issues.
145 MECA Delany 2, Wavell to Delany, 6 Mar. 1943.
146 MECA Waterfield 5/1, Delany to Waterfield, 20 Jan. 1964. The long-standing British collaborator, Ahmad Hassanein, used the phrase 'bullied' to describe Lampson's actions towards the Egyptian king. It was Lampson's pressure on Sirri Pasha to break diplomatic relations with Vichy France that occasioned the crisis of 1942. Faruq took the bait and forced Sirri from office for bowing to Lampson, after which Lampson insisted on the appointment of Nahhas.
147 MECA Delany 2, Delany to Lord Wavell, 27 July 1953.
148 MECA Waterfield 5/1, Delany to Waterfield, 20 Jan. 1964.
149 Initially proposed by Churchill in 1941, after discussions with Wavell and Lampson, the minister of state in the Middle East was a cabinet rank appointment designed to coordinate military and political acts in the region. The minister was the highest British authority in the Middle East.
150 MECA Waterfield 5/1, Delany to Waterfield, 26 Mar. 1973.
151 Evans, *Killearn*, p. 301 and MECA Waterfield 5/1, Delany to Waterfield, 23 July 1973. See also Cooper, *Cairo*, p. 168, where Lampson described the service chiefs as 'wobbly'. Foreign Office files indicate that Lampson had support from the office of the foreign secretary, both Viscount Halifax and Antony Eden: TNA FO371/24626.
152 MECA Waterfield 5/1, Delany to Waterfield, 27 Jan. 1974. See also Cooper, *Cairo*, pp. 296–7.
153 MECA Waterfield 5/1, Delany to Waterfield, 23 July 1973.
154 MECA Waterfield 5/2, 'Delany' & 5/1, Delany to Waterfield, 14 Mar. 1973. The conversation took place in late 1944 or early 1945 when the military situation in Egypt was secure.
155 MECA Waterfield 5/1, Delany to Waterfield, 14 Mar. 1973 & 26 Mar. 1973 & 23 July 1973.
156 MECA Delany 2, Wavell to Delany, 29 Oct. 1945.
157 Ibid., Wavell to Delany, 19 Mar. 1946.
158 Kolinsky, *Britain's War*, p. 122. While Kolinsky regards British decision-making as largely driven by strategic interest, he does note that Lampson's judgement was affected by his 'personal involvement' and commitment to 'certain outcomes', p. 38, by which he might suggest his personal domination over Egyptian statesmen.
159 Evans, *Killearn*, 30 May 1940.
160 MECA Waterfield 5/1, Delany to Waterfield 26 Mar. 1973, citing Evans, *Killearn*.
161 MECA Waterfield 5/1, Delany to Waterfield 23 July 1973.
162 Evans, *Killearn*, pp. 289–90, 339 & 358.
163 MECA Waterfield 5/1, Trefor E. Evans to Waterfield 15 May 1973. The letters have excerpts from the diaries attached. Evans defended Lampson's 'progressive' political attitudes in the letters, but the diaries certainly can be read to contrary conclusions.

EGYPT

164 MECA Delany 2, Lord Wavell to Delany, 21 Oct. 1953.
165 Louis, *British Empire*, p. 237 & MECA Waterfield 5/2, 'Delany'.
166 Royal Institute of International Affairs, *Great Britain and Egypt 1914–1951* (Westport: Greenwood, 1978), pp. 82–92.
167 *The Times* (22 Feb. 1946).
168 MECA GB 165-0160, Wilfred Jennings-Bramly, Box 1, Folder 3. Three undated letters, context suggests 1946, with letterhead indicating composed in Mataria, Cairo, all signed 'V', almost certainly Vivien.
169 Samir Rafaat, 'The Sirdaria' *Cairo Times* (15 Feb. 2001), www.egy.com/zamalek/01-02-15.php (accessed 16 Nov. 2016).
170 Olivia Manning, *The Levant Trilogy* (London: Phoenix, 2003), pp. 68 & 188.
171 Mansfield, *British in Egypt*, p. 279.
172 MECA GB 165-0160, Herbert Addison, 'Anglo-Egyptian Union, 1942–49'.
173 'Liquidation of the Anglo-Egyptian Union', *Egyptian Gazette* (10 April 1949).
174 Laurence Grafftey-Smith, *Bright Levant* (London: John Murray, 1970), pp. 92–5 & 113.
175 MECA GB 165-0234 Sir Thomas Cecil Rapp, memoirs, p. 30.
176 Ibid., p. 376.
177 Ibid., p. 41.
178 Ibid., p. 40.
179 Hamamsy, *Zamalek*, p. 265.
180 Sahar Hamouda and Colin Clement (eds), *Victoria College: A History Revealed* (Cairo: American University in Cairo Press, 2002), p. 165.
181 Edward Said, *Out of Place: A Memoir* (New York: Vintage, 1999), p. 198.
182 Ibid., pp. 128, 180 & 199. See also p. 123 where Said described himself as an upper-bourgeois colonial.
183 Ibid., p. 201.
184 Gordon Waterfield, *Morning Will Come* (London: John Murray, 1944).

CONCLUSION

On 26 January 1952, the residents of Ma'adi, the 'English suburb', watched a pall of smoke rising in the air as colonial Cairo burnt. 'The Maadi British were shuddering.'[1] By October 1956 only a few British remained to ponder with equal dismay the possibility that British troops might shortly invade their neighbourhood.[2] Antony Eden's decision to ally Britain with France and Israel against Egypt meant that most British passport-holders were expelled from Egypt after the failed invasion. Some of the exceptions were those married to Egyptians. Samir Rafaat identified eight such British women living in Ma'adi in 1956, mostly recent arrivals who had met their spouses while studying in Britain.[3] Others were performing jobs that Egyptians could not fill. The British poet John Heath-Stubbs returned to his job at Alexandria University in October 1956 in spite of Foreign Office warnings to the contrary. Like the British brides, Heath-Stubbs found that most Egyptians were indifferent to his presence. As he said, 'The general opinion seemed to be that if this man has been allowed to stay by our authorities he must be all right.'[4] The rupture of 1956 can be over-emphasised. Decolonisation was as incomplete in its processes as colonisation. Victoria College and the other 'English' schools sponsored by the British Council were taken over by the Egyptian state and the contracts of British staff terminated; however, Samir Rafaat noted that the repatriation of the British was disorienting for students of diverse nationalities accustomed to a British type of education. The 'revolutionary' regime wanted continuity, rather than disorder, therefore the new regime did not entirely break links with the colonial past. At Victoria College, the Egyptian 'Old Victorians' on the newly nationalised staff were 'more British than the British'.[5] Likewise, American residents replaced the British colony in schools and churches in neighbourhoods like Ma'adi and Zamalek. With the 'opening up' of the Egyptian economy to international finance in the 1970s foreign nationals employed in multinational corporations were shielded from Egyptian law in a manner not unlike the Capitulations.[6] In this way, colonialism was renewed by the government of Anwar al-Sadat.

These continuities suggest that the British colonial experience was not necessarily so exceptional, however rogue the empire might have appeared after the Suez debacle. Colonialism involved the movement of British people to Egypt, often spontaneously in the pursuit of commercial or social interests, not political or strategic. Gerald Delany went out to Egypt only to join his brothers and work as a clerk; his involvement in high politics was accidental. He was typical. His contemporaries from similar social backgrounds started their colonial careers in much the same way. Guy Osborne Lion emigrated to Egypt in 1908, employed as a clerk. Like Delany he came to Egypt because his brother had found employment there. Lion resided at the Anglo-German Pension in Alexandria, working eight hours a day, six days a week – that is, until he became ill with fever, was unable to work, and was sued by his employer after being found not in bed but watching tennis and racket at the Railway Institute. That is all the court proceedings record of this colonial life, and that he was awarded forty pounds in damages (four months' wages), which it might be assumed was used to find a ship home.[7] A similar story also enshrined in court documents was of a foreman carpenter, Sidney Chubb, hired to help in the construction of the 'Abassiyya barracks in 1910. He lost a finger in the machinery and claimed during a suit filed by his employer that the working conditions were harsh; the employer won the case. Chubb admitted he had gone for a camel ride in the desert, rather than work, complaining of the harsh living conditions in a desert cottage of two rooms, shared with another, and the difficulties he faced affording the transit and support of his family.[8] That colonial career might also have been short. Ordinary people migrated from Britain to Egypt because the colony held opportunities unknown in Britain, as Delany's career might suggest, or the story of Richard Warbrick, who was employed by the firm, Mashal Brothers of Manchester, during the First World War. Whilst the British army was waging war, Mashal Brothers was selling cotton fabrics and purchasing carpets and other local manufactures, including gems, through his agents in Iraq and Iran. Warbrick was the company agent in Basra and Aqaba. When he returned to Egypt the company had him arrested for theft, claiming he had profited from goods stolen from the company stores. Warbrick denied this, saying that the cash he had accumulated was from selling carpets independently. Defending his character, he said he had been employed by Mashal Brothers in Manchester as a result of his brilliance in school, which was known to the company because his sister worked as a governess for the family

CONCLUSION

of one of the directors of the firm. He won the case and secured his profits.[9] In each case, the defendants were from lower- or middle-class backgrounds, had migrated because of family connections and employment opportunities, and seemed to suffer from various forms of exploitation at the hands of their employers, as well as uncomfortable living conditions. Much of the colony was transitory and left few records. Loneliness and boredom haunted the colonial, as it had the common soldier, and therefore much of the consular court records deal with very ordinary cases of business deals, inheritance, and marriages and their disputes, including addictions, prostitution, and suicide. These tales, probably as representative as the 'elite' discourses, suggest that empire involved a colonial world of spontaneous migration, from mostly social motivations, at least in this generational 'survey' from these consular reports.

The accounts in this study have been various, including official reports, histories, novels, as well as the memoirists. The British colony comprised diverse types; these colonials pursued ordinary careers in government and business, military and labour. Like the ordinary soldier, it was possible for them to enter the colony and never meet an Egyptian, except perhaps a barman at the barracks or other Egyptians in service industries. Even for longer-term residences, like the wife of a subaltern officer, Egyptians were encountered but interactions were guarded and usually polite. Coexistence was the norm, not acculturation or cosmopolitanism. Of course, many of the memoirs accentuate harmonious coexistence with associates, or even manservant, gardener, and chauffeur. The retrospective glance is nostalgic. Yet, there were various forms of cultural absorption in the Egyptian locale by colonials, including intermarriage, not always involving the 'marginal' British and 'marginal' Egyptians (as the consular officers often had to contend with), but even among the upper classes, official and non-official.[10] The case of Forster and al-'Adl was not exceptional; people of different class and culture formed relationships. The point of these reflections is not to deny that the British in Egypt tried to construct a distinctive British colonial identity, based on theories of race and civilisation or a common set of interests. Even late imperial constructs, like the new English schools directed by the British Council, as well as the new Victoria College campus in Cairo, memorialised and celebrated empire.[11] But for many a colonial – Heath-Stubbs and others – these memorials were as meaningless as they were to the Egyptian or other non-British students. Also, the impulse to impose imperial symbols was contradictory, it countered trends from the 1920s to diminish and mute the colonial profile by integration in the Egyptian elite and withdrawal from administrative roles. To some degree these changes were an attempt to restore colonial relationships damaged by the war or efforts to return to an idyll; however, they also represented a step forwards.

Yet, a toxic combination of racism and security priorities meant that the British government failed to commit itself to the new policy of cultural diplomacy, social integration, and bilateral relations. The undying idea of a British imperial race compromised collaboration; the imperial narrative weakened the position of the Egyptian elites whose bargain with British power had been strategic, founded on the idea of Egyptian national autonomy. In an unexpected turn of events, the Second World War magnified these trends. Consequently, the proximity of British military forces was no longer a safeguard to the British community, but a threat. The presence of British forces in the cities and the Canal Zone provoked violent clashes during and after the war, culminating in British forces attacking Egyptian police at Isma'iliyya, leaving forty dead. Egyptians burnt European Cairo in response. At least thirteen Britons died in that conflagration. And although negotiations with Nasir after the revolution of 1952 resulted in an expeditious withdrawal of British forces from the Canal Zone by 1954, Eden's bid to retain strategic control of the Canal in 1956 squandered the remaining – and not inconsiderable – interests of the British colony in Egypt. Ultimately, the wars demonstrated that the British colony in Egypt was not a major consideration for the British government. The colony did not determine policy. On the contrary, colonials engaged in business, cultural, or professional pursuits were often keenly aware of their powerlessness before the forces of nationalism and imperialism.

It is perhaps not surprising that many colonials, particularly the non-official, remember the colony differently from the dominant representations in official narratives: The recollection of a society tolerant of difference, of a colony deeply rooted in the colonial location, so that the 'British' identity was muted by the 'spirit of place'.[12] That was colonial life as remembered by some recalling a childhood or youth in Egypt. But that memory, so at odds with the official narrative of racial exclusions, is also supported to some degree by the institutional history of hospital, schools, municipality, leisure, as well as official reports of ordinary people in conflicted social situations. The British colony was international, without a clear definition of 'British', given that it included such a diverse range of 'ethnicity' or 'race' or nationality (only this last was ever concretely defined, in due course). The rules of membership in the colony were not clearly drawn, even on legal grounds, and certainly not cultural or political. The elasticity of colonial society was a function of the pragmatism or instrumentality of colonial relationships, founded largely to facilitate business, finance, research, and the development of the necessary infrastructure. The attempts to

CONCLUSION

construct a distinctive 'British' colonial identity met with little success. The English schools directed by the British Council, as well as the new Victoria College campus in Cairo, were designed to foster and continue cultural relations between the British and Egyptians. The cultural model was British, but the emphasis was upon inclusion, which had an impact and stood against the racially driven exclusivity of the English School, promoted by Lord Lloyd. Within the elite structure of society, as well as among the lower-caste soldiers and sailors, the destitute and deviant, there was cultural mixing. Hence the nostalgia for the 'liberal age', a sentiment expressed in colonial memoirs, even those produced by the consular officials responsible for the 'marginal' British.

The liberal era was the colony's golden years. It included a period of imperial policy adjustment after the First World War when there was a genuine social and cultural shift, marked by less confidence in the imperial mission and an easing of colonial rituals of cultural differentiation. The interwar time of uncertainty witnessed a see-sawing of the imperialistic and the liberal or internationalist impulses. Milner's proposals shocked the imperialists just as much as the ferocity of Egyptian revolts and demonstrations. The resultant policy adjustments saw the reduction of the size of the official colony and a high degree of civilian, cultural and social intersection with Egyptian middle and upper classes in the interwar period. The military bases also increased, which meant common soldiers and those in the service sectors sometimes married locally. The memoirists of this colonial cadre did not always consider 'race' a factor and remarked on Egyptian tolerance and hospitality; their critiques were aimed at the colonial old guard and the manner in which certain attitudes perpetuated negative perceptions of the Egyptians. When entertaining the themes of the bovine fellah or romantic Bedouin, these residents viewed such ideas as cultural relics, although such representation remained the bedrock of popular perceptions in postcards and tourist brochures. Certain institutions, like the Church and the military, found it difficult to shed racial or cultural stereotypes.

Not all colonials despised the Egyptians, nor did they necessarily typecast these 'others' in reassuringly nostalgic terms. There was an awareness of Egyptian national sentiment and of a society evolving in conformity with modern habits and lifestyles. Egyptian national culture in this period was one where inclusion and tolerance of others remained the dominant voice. In their observations, colonial memoirists suggest that the colonial modern, like the Egyptian, prioritised the mundane, pragmatic concerns of career, household, schools, and leisure. For each, these sometimes took 'British' forms, although as a consequence of relocation and cross-cultural dialogue, these traits had lost a fixed

EGYPT

belonging to the 'British'. In other words, the colony, from 'elite' to 'marginal', resembled the old world of the Levantine.

Notes

1 Samir Rafaat, *Maadi 1904–1962: Society and History in a Cairo Suburb* (Cairo: Palm Press, 1994), p. 214.
2 TNA FO371/369/5024, Jan. 30, 1954, 'Inspector's Report on the British Community in Cairo', where it is recorded that between 1946 and 1954, the number of 'in-land' British in Cairo had declined from 5,309 to 1,909.
3 Rafaat, *Maadi*, p. 240.
4 Hala Halim, 'Victoria into Victory', in Sahar Hamouda and Colin Clement (eds), *Victoria College: A History Revealed* (Cairo: American University in Cairo Press, 2002), p. 193.
5 Ibid., p. 195.
6 Andrew Metcalf, 'Reshaping Egypt's Legal Landscape: The Growing Role of Arbitration in Egypt', Middle East Studies Association Annual Meeting, Rhode Island, 1996.
7 TNA FO/841/102, File 3, 1908, 'Guy Osborne vs. James Francis Waterlow'.
8 TNA FO/841/115, Dossier 116, 'Consular Court'.
9 TNA FO/841/172, File 81, 1918.
10 TNA FO/141/463/1, 'Marriages in Egypt' & FO/141/463/1411, British Consulate, 10 June 1924, 'Report of the Committee of the British Charitable Fund' & 'Memo Headquarters of Cairo & Alexandria Brigades, Cavalry Brigade, Canal Area', shows 'presence in Egypt of a number of wives of various original nationalities of British soldiers with children'.
11 Rafaat, *Maadi*, p. 241.
12 Lawrence Durrell, *Spirit of Place: Letters and Essays on Travel* (New York: E.P. Dutton, 1971).

SELECT BIBLIOGRAPHY

Archives

British Library, London (BL)
Bodleian Library, Oxford
Churchill College, Cambridge
Egyptian National Archives, Cairo
Exeter University Library, Exeter: Exeter University Special Collections (EUSC)
Imperial War Museum, London (IWM)
Lambeth Palace Library, London (LPL)
Middle East Centre Archives, St Antony's College, Oxford (MECA)
Rhodes House, Oxford (RH)
The National Archives, Kew, London (TNA)

Secondary Sources

Adelson, Roger, *London and the Invention of the Middle East: Money, Power, and War 1902–1922* (New Haven: Yale University Press, 1995).
Ahmed, Leila, *Edward William Lane: A Study of his Life and Works and of British Ideas of the Middle East in the Nineteenth Century* (London: Longman, 1978).
Amos, Sir Maurice, *England and Egypt: Cust Foundation Lecture* (Nottingham: University College, 1929).
Atiyah, Edward, *An Arab Tells his Story: A Study in Loyalties* (London: John Murray, 1947).
Baraka, Magda, *The Egyptian Upper Class between Revolutions 1919–1952* (Reading: Ithaca, 1998).
Barrell, John, 'Death on the Nile: Fantasy and the Literature of Tourism, 1840–60', in Catherine Hall (ed.), *Cultures of Empire: Colonizers in Britain and the Empire in the Nineteenth and Twentieth Centuries* (Manchester: Manchester University Press, 2000).
Berdine, Michael D., *The Accidental Tourist, Wilfrid Scawen Blunt, and the British Invasion of Egypt in 1882* (London: Routledge, 2005).
Berque, Jacques, *Egypt: Imperialism and Revolution*, trans. Jean Stewart (London: Faber & Faber, 1972).
Bickers, Robert (ed.), *Settlers and Expatriates: Britons over the Seas* (Oxford: Oxford University Press, 2010).
Blunt, Wilfrid Scawen, *The Future of Islam* (London: Kegan Paul, 1882).
Blunt, Wilfrid Scawen, *Atrocities of British Justice under British Rule in Egypt* (London: T. Fisher Unwin, 1906).

SELECT BIBLIOGRAPHY

Blunt, Wilfrid Scawen, *My Diaries: Being a Personal Narrative of Events 1888–1914* (London: Eyre Methuen, 1913).
Blunt, Wilfrid Scawen, *The Secret History of the British Occupation of Egypt: Being a Personal Narrative of Events* (New York: Alfred Knopf, 1922, originally published 1907).
Bolten, Jonathan, *Personal Landscapes: British Poets in Egypt during the Second World War* (London: St Martin's Press, 1997).
Bowen, Roger, *'Many Histories Deep': The Personal Landscape Poets in Egypt 1940–45* (New Jersey: Associated University Presses, 1995).
Bowman, Humphrey, *Middle East Window* (London: Longmans, Green, 1942).
Brehony, Noel and Ayman El-Desouky (eds), *British–Egyptian Relations from Suez to the Present Day* (London: Saqi, 2007).
Caillard, Mabel, *A Lifetime in Egypt, 1876–1935* (London: Grant Richards, 1935).
Cannadine, David, *Ornamentalism: How the British Saw their Empire* (New York: Oxford University Press, 2001).
Cecil, Lord Edward, *The Leisure of an Egyptian Official* (London: Hodder and Stoughton, 1921).
Cecil, Hugh and Mirabel Cecil, *Imperial Marriage: An Edwardian War and Peace* (London: John Murray, 2002).
Churchill, Winston Spencer, *The River War: An Historical Account of the Reconquest of the Soudan* (London: Longmans, Green, 1899).
Coles Pasha, C.E., *Recollections and Reflections* (London: St Catherine Press, 1918).
Connell, John, *Wavell: Scholar and Soldier* (London: Collins, 1964).
Cooper, Artemis, *Cairo in the War 1939–1945* (London: Hamish Hamilton, 1989).
Cromer, Earl of, *Modern Egypt* (London: Macmillan, 1908), 2 vols.
Cuno, Kenneth M., *Modernizing Marriage: Family, Ideology, and Law in Nineteenth- and Early Twentieth-Century Egypt* (Syracuse: Syracuse University Press, 2015).
Darwin, John, *Britain, Egypt and the Middle East: Imperial Policy in the Aftermath of War* (London: Palgrave Macmillan, 1981).
Deighton, H.S., 'The Impact of the Egypt on Britain: A Study of Opinion', in P.M. Holt (ed.), *Political and Social Change in Modern Egypt* (London: Oxford University Press, 1968).
Douglas, Keith, *From Alamein to Zem Zem* (London: Editions Poetry, 1946).
Douglas, Keith, *Keith Douglas: The Complete Poems*, ed. Desmond Graham (London: Faber & Faber, 3rd edn, 1998).
Drummond Wolf, Sir Henry, *Rambling Recollections* (London: Macmillan, 1908).
Durrell, Lawrence, *Spirit of Place: Letters and Essays on Travel* (New York: E.P. Dutton, 1971).
Elgood, P.G., *Egypt and the Army* (Oxford: Oxford University Press, 1924).
Finch, Edith, *Wilfrid Scawen Blunt* (London: Jonathan Cape, 1938).
Fonder, Nathan Lambert, 'Pleasure, Leisure, or Vice? Public Morality in Imperial Cairo, 1882–1949' (PhD dissertation, Harvard University, 2013).
Forster, E.M., *Selected Letters of E.M. Forster*, ed. Mary Lago and P.N. Furbank (London: Belknap, 1983).
Forster, E.M., *Alexandria: A History and a Guide and Pharos and Pharillon*, ed. Miriam Allott, (London: André Deutsch, 2004).
Fraser, G.S., *A Stranger and Afraid: The Autobiography of an Intellectual* (Manchester: Carcanet New Press, 1983).
Fussell, Paul, *Abroad: British Literary Traveling between the Wars* (Oxford: Oxford University Press, 1980).
Gasper, Michael Ezekiel, *The Power of Representation: Publics, Peasants, and Islam in Egypt* (Stanford: Stanford University Press, 2009).
Gefu-Maidianou, Dimitra, *Alcohol, Gender, and Culture* (London: Routledge, 1992).
Ghali, Waguih, *Beer in the Snooker Hall* (New York: New Amsterdam, 1987; originally published 1964).
Goodrich, Caspar F., *Report of the British Naval and Military Operations in Egypt 1882, Office of Naval Intelligence* (Washington DC: Government Printing Office, 1882).

SELECT BIBLIOGRAPHY

Gordon, Lucy Duff, *Letters from Egypt* (London: R. Brimley Johnson, revised edn, 1902).
Graffey-Smith, Laurence, *Bright Levant* (London: John Murray, 1973).
Graham, Desmond, *Keith Douglas: A Biography* (London: Oxford University Press, 1974).
Graves, Robert, *Goodbye to All That* (London: Penguin, 2000, originally published 1929).
Haag, Michael, *Alexandria: City of Memory* (New Haven: Yale University Press, 2004).
Hall, Catherine (ed.), *Cultures of Empire: Colonizers in Britain and the Empire in the Nineteenth and Twentieth Centuries* (Manchester: Manchester University Press, 2000).
Hamouda, Sahar and Colin Clement (eds), *Victoria College: A History Revealed* (Cairo: American University in Cairo Press, 2002).
Hamamsy, Chafika Soliman, *Zamalek: The Changing Life of a Cairo Elite, 1850–1945* (Cairo: American University in Cairo Press, 2005).
Hanley, Will, 'Foreignness and Localness in Alexandria, 1880–1914' (Ph.D dissertation, Princeton University, 2007).
Hopwood, Derek, *Tales of Empire: The British in the Middle East 1880–1952* (London: I.B. Tauris, 1989).
Ilbert, Robert, *Alexandrie 1830–1930: histoire d'une communauté citadine* (Cairo: Institute Français d'Archéologie Orientale, 1996), 2 vols.
James, Lawrence, *Churchill and Empire: Portrait of an Imperialist* (London: Phoenix, 2014).
Johnston, Charles, *Mo and Other Originals* (London: Hamish Hamilton, 1971).
Kedourie, Elie, *The Chatham House Version and Other Middle Eastern Studies* (London: Weidenfeld and Nicolson, 1970).
Keown-Boyd, Henry, *The Lion and Sphinx: The Rise and Fall of the British in Egypt* (Durham: Memoir Club, 2002).
Kolinsky, Martin, *Britain's War in the Middle East* (New York: Palgrave, 1999).
Lambert, David and Alan Lester, *Colonial Lives across the British Empire: Imperial Careering in the Long Nineteenth Century* (Cambridge: Cambridge University Press, 2006).
Lampson, Sir Miles, *The Killearn Diaries 1934–1946: The Diplomatic and Personal Record of Lord Killearn (Sir Miles Lampson), High Commissioner and Ambassador, Egypt*, ed. Trefor E. Evans (London: Sidgwick and Jackson, 1972).
Lampson, Sir Miles, *Politics and Diplomacy in Egypt: The Diaries of Sir Miles Lampson 1935–1937*, ed. Malcolm Yapp (Oxford: Oxford University Press, 1997).
Landes, David S., *Bankers and Pashas: International Finance and Economic Imperialism in Egypt* (Cambridge, MA: Harvard University Press, 1958).
Lane, Edward William, *An Account of the Manners and Customs of the Modern Egyptians* (The Hague and London: East-West Publications, 1978).
Lawrence, T.E., *Seven Pillars of Wisdom* (London: Jonathan Cape, 1935).
Lawrence, T.E., *The Letters of T.E. Lawrence*, ed, David Garnett (London: Jonathan Cape, 1938).
Lassner, Phyllis, *Colonial Strangers: Women Writing the End of the British Empire* (London: Rutgers University Press, 2004).
Levine, Phillipa, *Gender and Empire* (Oxford: Oxford University Press, 2004).
Liddell, Robert, *Cavafy: A Critical Biography* (London: Duckworth, 1974).
Lively, Penelope, *Oleander, Jacaranda: A Childhood Perceived* (London: Viking, 1994).
Long, C.W.R., *British Pro-Consuls in Egypt, 1914–1929: The Challenge of Nationalism* (London: Routledge Curzon, 2004).
Longford, Elizabeth, *A Pilgrimage of Passion: The Life of Wilfrid Scawen Blunt* (London: I.B. Tauris, 2007).
Louis, Wm. Roger, *In the Name of God Go! Leo Amery and the British Empire in the Age of Churchill* (New York: Norton, 1992).
Louis, Wm. Roger, *Ends of British Imperialism: The Scramble for Empire, Suez, and Decolonization* (London: I.B. Tauris, 2006).
Mak, Lanver, *The British in Egypt: Community, Crime, and Crisis 1882–1922* (London: I.B. Tauris, 2012).
Manning, Olivia, *The Levant Trilogy* (London: Phoenix, 2003).

SELECT BIBLIOGRAPHY

Mansfield, Peter, *The British in Egypt* (New York: Holt, Rinehart, and Winston, 1971).
Martineau, Harriet, *Eastern Life Present and Past* (London: Edward Moxon, 1848).
Maurice, J.F., *Military History of the Campaign of 1882 in Egypt, Great Britain: War Office, Intelligence Branch* (London: J.B. Hayward & Son, n.d.).
Mellini, Peter, *Sir Eldon Gorst: The Overshadowed Proconsul* (Stanford: Hover Institution Press, 1977).
Mill, James H., *Cannabis Britannica: Empire, Trade, and Prohibition 1800–1929* (Oxford: Oxford University Press, 2003).
Milner, Alfred, *England in Egypt* (London: Edward Arnold, 3rd edn, 1893).
Mitchell, Timothy, *Colonising Egypt* (Berkeley: University of California Press, 1988).
Monroe, Elizabeth, *Britain's Moment in the Middle East 1914–1956* (London: Chatto & Windus, 1964).
Musa, Salama, *The Education of Salama Musa*, trans. L.O. Schuman (Leiden: E.J. Brill, 1961).
Nash, Geoffrey, *The Arab Writer in English: Arab Themes in a Metropolitan Language* (Brighton: Sussex Academic Press, 1998).
Nightingale, Florence, *Letters from Egypt: A Journey on the Nile 1849–50*, ed. Anthony Sattin, (London: Parkway Publishing, 2002).
Owen, Roger, *Lord Cromer: Victorian Imperialist, Edwardian Proconsul* (Oxford: Oxford University Press, 2004).
Peto, Gladys, *Egypt of the Sojourner* (London & Toronto: J.M. Dent & Sons, 1928).
Pollard, Lisa, *Nurturing the Nation: The Family Politics of Modernizing, Colonizing, and Liberating Egypt 1805–1923* (Berkeley & Los Angeles: University of California Press, 2005).
Rafaat, Samir, *Maadi 1904–1962: Society and History in a Cairo Suburb* (Cairo: Palm Press, 1994).
Reimer, Michael J., *Colonial Bridgehead: Government and Society in Alexandria, 1807–1882* (Boulder, CO: Westview Press, 1997).
Rodkey, F.S., 'The Attempts of Briggs and Company to Guide British Policy in the Levant 1821–1841', *Journal of Modern History* 5 (1933): 324–51.
Rogan, Eugene (ed.), *Outside In: On the Margins of the Middle East* (London: I.B. Tauris, 2002).
Russell, Mona L., *Creating the New Egyptian Woman: Consumerism, Education, and the National Identity* (New York: Palgrave, 2004).
Russell, Sir Thomas, *Egyptian Service 1902–1946* (London: John Murray, 1949).
Saad el-Din, Mursi and John Cromer, *Under Egypt's Spell: The Influence of Egypt on Writers in English from the 18th Century* (London: Bellew Publishing, 1991).
Said, Edward W., *Orientalism* (London: Routledge & Kegan Paul, 1978).
Said, Edward W., *Culture and Imperialism* (London: Vintage, 1993).
Said, Edward W., *Out of Place: A Memoir* (New York: Vintage, 2000).
Sayyad, Nezar al-, Irene A. Bierman and Nasser Rabbat (eds), *Making Cairo Medieval* (Lanham, MD: Lexington Books, 2005).
Sattin, Anthony, *Lifting the Veil: British Society in Egypt 1768–1956* (London: J.M. Dent, 1988).
Seth, Ronald, *Russell Pasha* (London: William Kimber, 1966).
Shaarawi, Huda, *Harem Years: The Memoirs of an Egyptian Feminist*, trans. Margot Badran (New York: City University of New York, 1986).
Spender, J.A., *The Changing East* (London: Cassell, 1926).
Starkey, Paul and Janet Starkey (eds), *Travellers in Egypt* (London: Tauris Parke Paperbacks, 2001).
Stockwell, Sarah (ed.), *The British Empire: Themes and Perspectives* (Oxford: Blackwell, 2008).
Storrs, Ronald, *Orientations* (London: Nicholson & Watson, 1937).
Strachey, Lytton, *Eminent Victorians* (London: Penguin Books, 1986, originally published 1918).
Thompson, Andrew S., *Imperial Britain: The Empire in British Politics c. 1880–1932* (Harlow: Longman, 2000).

SELECT BIBLIOGRAPHY

Thompson, Jason, *Sir Gardner Wilkinson and his Circle* (Austin: University of Texas Press, 1992).
Thompson, Jason, 'Osman Effendi: A Scottish Convert to Islam in Early Nineteenth Century Egypt', *Journal of World History* 5 (1994): 99–123.
Tignor, Robert L., *Modernization and British Colonial Rule in Egypt: 1882–1914* (Princeton: Princeton University Press, 1966).
Tignor, Robert L., *Capitalism and Nationalism at the End of Empire: State and Business in Egypt, Nigeria, and Kenya, 1945–1963* (Princeton: Princeton University Press, 1997).
Toye, Richard, *Churchill's Empire: The World that Made him and the World he Made* (London: Pan Books, 2011).
Van Nieuwkirk, Karen, 'Female Entertainers in Egypt: Drinking and Gender Roles', in Dimitra Gefou-Madianou (ed.), *Alcohol, Gender, and Culture* (London: Routledge, 1992).
Waterfield, Gordon, *Lucie Duff Gordon: In England, South Africa, and Egypt* (London: E.P. Dutton, 1937).
Waterfield, Gordon, *Morning Will Come* (London: John Murray, 1944).
Waterfield, Gordon, *Professional Diplomat: Sir Percy Loraine of Kirkharle* (London: John Murray, 1973).
Waugh, Evelyn, *Labels: A Mediterranean Journal* (New York: Penguin, 1985).
Wavell, Field Marshal Viscount, *Allenby in Egypt* (London: George G. Harrap, 1943).
Wissa, Hanna F., *Assiout: The Saga of an Egyptian Family* (Sussex: Book Guild, 1994).
Wright, Arnold and H.A. Cartwright (eds), *Twentieth Century: Impressions of Egypt: Its History, People, Commerce, Industries, and Resources* (London: Lloyd's Greater Britain Publishing Company, 1909).
Ziegler, Philip, *Omdurman* (London: Collins, 1973).

INDEX

'Abbas II, Khedive 196
'Abd al-Hamid, Sultan 71
'Abduh, Muhammad 31, 71
Abu al-Huda, Lulie 167–8
Addison, Herbert 108, 140–2, 205
al-'Adl, Muhammad 181
Ahmad, Muhammad (the Mahdi) 86
Alamein 160, 167
Alderson, G.B. 37, 104
Alexandria 8, 29–30, 34, 57–8, 62, 74–5, 96, 122–8, 152–3, 158–60, 178–81
Alexandria municipality 125–7
'Ali, Muhammad 13, 29–31, 34, 54–5, 60–1, 63–5, 68, 130
Allen, Geoffrey 102
Allenby, Edmund 14–16, 38, 153, 163–4, 185, 187–9, 199
Allenby, Lady 152–4
Ambron Villa 158
Amery, Leo 175
Amos, Maurice Sheldon 89, 99, 163, 186, 188–91
Anglo-Egyptian Agreement (1959) 42, 48
Anglo-Egyptian Treaty (1936) 16, 35, 43, 54–6, 164–5, 176–7, 192–3, 195–7, 200
Anglo-Egyptian Union 159, 168, 205–6
Anglo-French Entente (1904) 37, 120, 183
'Arabian Nights' (*Alf Layla wa Layla*) 61, 67–8, 73, 84

Association for the Advancement of Christianity in Egypt 99–100
Atiyah, Edward 105
Australians 116, 153, 161–2

Baker, Valentine 112
Baldwin, George 84
Baldwin, Stanley 195
Bank Misr 42
al-Banna, Hasan 46, 201
Barker, Alwyn 43–5, 47
Barker, Edward 30
Barker, Frederick 30
Barker, Henry 30, 34–7, 60, 104
Barker, Henry (Harry) 42–3
Barker, Henry Michael 17–18, 43, 45–8, 208
Barker, John 29–30
Barker, Oswald 36
Barker, Percy 36
Barker, Shelagh (Moore) 45
Barrell, John 5, 70
Battle of Rosetta (1807) 78
Bell, Gertrude 6
Bentham, Jeremy 64
Berlin Congress (1878) 70
Berque, Jacques 3–4, 140, 142
Blunt, Wilfrid Scawen 19, 34, 52–3, 65, 69–74, 76–8, 92, 95
Bowman, Humphrey 94–5, 100
Boyle, Harry 92
Braithwaite, Noel Duncan 162–3
Briggs, Samuel 30, 33, 57, 64–5

INDEX

British Chamber of Commerce 37–8, 40–1, 193
British Council 107–9, 158, 168–9, 215, 217, 219
British Union 47, 48–9, 61, 103, 126, 178, 189–90, 195, 197
Brunyate, William 37
Burj al-'Arab 130–1
Burton, James 54, 60, 62
Burton, Richard Francis 4–5
Byron, Lord 55, 70, 77

Caillard, Mabel 50, 92–3, 143, 152
Cairo 8, 13, 59–60, 151–4, 164–8, 181, 204–7, 215
Canal Zone 155, 218
Capitulations 25–8, 35–40, 48, 103, 114, 116, 193, 217
Carver, Percy 37
Cathedral of All Saints (Cairo) 102
Catherwood, Frederick 57
Caton-Thompson, Gertrude 130, 143
Cecil, Edward 86–8, 93–4, 109–10, 113, 140, 144, 163
Cecil, Violet 143, 150
Chamberlain, Austen 185, 191–2
Churchill, Winston 6, 14–18, 86, 109–10, 118, 141, 164, 170, 177–8, 182, 185–92, 198–200, 203
Church Missionary Society (CMS) 95, 97–9, 101, 103
Church of England 12, 83, 85, 94–102
Clare, (Sister) Margaret 109–10, 118
Clayton, Gilbert 163
coexistence 3–4, 28, 54, 138, 141–2, 217
Cohen, Eve 158
colonial vii, 6, 8–12
  histories 128–31
  identity 2–3, 7, 15, 17–18, 19, 40–2, 53–4, 63, 142–3, 146–7, 207
  intermarriage 26–7, 34, 67, 118–19
  justice system 112–14, 121–2
  lobby 17–18, 49–50, 64–5, 92–4, 145, 164, 178–9, 191–5
  officials 10–15, 87–92
  rule 15–18, 96–102, 126–9, 147–8
Colvin, Auckland 72–3

Commonwealth 142, 144, 236, 256, 265
Copts 97, 99–102
Cotton 26, 43, 90
Cromer, Lord 6–7, 9, 14, 18–19, 26, 37, 46–8, 50, 71–2, 85, 88, 90, 96–8, 100, 104, 111–13, 142, 178–9, 183, 187, 196
Curtis, Lionel 175

Davidson, Randall 95–7
Davies, Reginald 169
De Cosson, Anthony 129–31
Delany, Gerald 21–3, 25, 176–7, 182–205, 208, 216
demographics 9–10, 12–13, 39, 160
De Zogheb family 45, 47
Dinshawai 91, 95
discourse theory 3–7, 14, 19–20, 23–6, 38, 54, 56, 61, 64, 79–80, 129, 143, 159, 177, 180, 196, 207–8
Disraeli, Benjamin 32, 71
Douglas, Keith 159–60, 168–9
drugs 113–18
Dufferin, Lord 46, 53, 112
Dufferin Report (1883) 36
Dunlop, Douglas 94–5
Durrell, Lawrence 32, 103, 122, 124, 158–9

Eden, Anthony 39, 174, 177, 203, 215, 218
Egyptian Expeditionary Force 161–3
Egyptian Labour Corps 162–3
elites 10–11, 13, 30, 35–6, 39, 72–3, 89–91, 103–5, 112–13, 127, 147–8, 151, 178, 206–7
English School, the 109
European Debt Commission (1876) 41
Evans, Trevor 176

Faruq, King 60, 168–7, 196–8, 201
Fedden, Robin 141
Finney, Oswald 44, 124
First World War 40, 114–15, 130, 152, 160–4
French colony 11, 27, 35, 37, 45–6, 48, 65, 108, 120, 155

[227]

INDEX

Foreign Office 8, 11–12, 14, 41, 52, 73, 88, 107, 175, 177, 185, 193, 196, 202–3
Forster, E.M. 6, 122, 124, 128–31, 143, 158–9, 169, 179–82
Fu'ad, King 187
Furness, Robert 107, 179, 181, 186, 188–92
Fussell, Paul 154

Gallipoli 162–3
gardens 160
Germany 120, 197
Gezira Sporting Club 151, 165–6
Ghali, Butros 108, 120–2
Gladstone, William 13, 52–3, 71, 73
Gordon, Charles George 86
Gordon, Lucy Duff 65–9
Gorst, Eldon 15, 94, 183
governesses 146–8, 153
Granville, Lord 73
Graves, Robert 106–7
Greco-Roman Museum 124, 130–1

Halifax, Viscount 171
Hamamsy, Chafika 17, 90, 178, 207
Harari, Abdou Soliman 41
harim (harem) 35, 67, 143, 150–1, 153
Hassanein, Ahmad 163
Hay, Robert 54–7, 59, 61, 63–5
Haykal, Muhammad Husayn 21, 90, 107
Heath-Stubbs, John 215, 217
Henderson, Arthur 191, 195
hospitals 146–7
Hourani, Albert 3–4
Husayn, Taha 107

Ilbert, Robert 27, 125–6
imperialism vii–viii, 1–4, 6–7, 15–20, 85–95, 175–7
　conservative imperialism 71, 77, 179, 190, 194–5
　die-hards 18, 177–8, 185, 197, 203
　imperial duty 12, 14, 85–6, 88, 133, 142, 194
　liberal imperialism 24, 69–72, 177–9, 192, 195–6, 207–8
infitah 47–8, 215–16

internationalism 152, 175, 181, 185, 219
Isma'il, Khedive 31–4, 70–1
Isma'iliyya 10, 12, 24, 155
Italy 195, 197, 200

Japan 54
Jarvis, C.S. 140
Jennings-Bramly, Phyllis 204
Jennings-Bramly, Vivien 131, 143, 204–5
Jennings-Bramly, Wilfred 92, 130
Joint Note (1882) 73

Kamil, Mustafa 107, 120
Kedourie, Elie 178
Keown-Boyd, Alexander 88, 144, 197
Keown-Boyd, Henry 88, 144
Keown-Boyd, Joan 144, 198
Kerr, Archibald 190
Kitchener, Herbert 86, 88, 91, 111–12, 122, 125, 132, 163, 178–9, 183
Kolinsky, Martin 177, 183

Labour Party 18, 44, 102, 203–4
Lampson, Miles 12, 14, 16, 39, 102, 167–8, 176–8, 196–203
Landes, David 31–2
Lane, Edward William 4, 54–6, 60–3, 66, 84
Lane-Poole, Stanley 34, 62, 84
Lawrence, T.E. 163–4, 175, 193–4, 199
League of Nations 152
leisure 144, 201–14
Levant Company 25–7, 201
Levantine 8, 10, 26, 28–31, 39, 41, 44, 54, 104, 109–10, 123, 127–8, 132, 153, 181, 207, 220
Liberal Constitutional Party 186, 190–1
Lion, Guy Osborne 216
Lively, Penelope 134, 142, 168
Lloyd, Clifford 112–13
Lloyd, George Ambrose (Lord) 5, 39, 50, 108–10, 186–95
Lloyd George, David 140, 164, 177, 185
Loder, John de Vere 152–3, 163, 169

[228]

INDEX

Loraine, Percy 176
Louis, Wm. Roger 176–7
Lowe, Drury 76
lower classes 10–11, 17, 30, 39, 43, 124–5, 127, 175
Lyttleton, Oliver 202

Ma'adi 13, 142, 146
Mabro, Robert 122
MacDonald, Ramsay 187, 195
McMahon, Arthur Henry 37, 154, 163
Mahir, Ahmad 120, 160
Mahir, 'Ali 134, 184, 196–7, 200
Mahmud, Muhammad 87, 191
Malet, Edward 72–3
Maltese 8, 10, 30, 127
Manning, Olivia 106, 205
Mansell, Philip 28
Marlowe, John 176
marriage 74, 87
martial law (1914–22) 160
Martineau, Harriet 53, 65–7, 69
Mashal Brothers 41, 216
Mather, James 26–9
memory 7–9, 22–3, 48
Menasce, Jacques Levi de 42, 103–4
military bases 57, 164, 177, 190, 197
Milner, Alfred (Lord) 5, 14, 24, 90, 142, 183–7
Milner Mission 154, 164, 178, 182–5
Milner Report 176, 178, 186, 196
mixed courts 35, 37
Montgomery, Bernard 102, 197
Moss, Robert 37, 104, 125–6
Moyne, Lord 160
Mubarak, 'Ali 61
Mubarak, Husni 46
muhajjabat 150, 157–8
Munroe, Elizabeth 13
Murray, Archibald 163
Muslim Brotherhood 201

al-Nahhas, Mustafa 39, 46, 192, 196–7, 200–2
Napoleon III 33, 69
Nash'at, Hasan 119
al-Nasir, Jamal 'Abd 46, 178, 218

nationalism 2, 9, 46–51, 54–6, 128
  economic nationalism 35, 38, 43, 47
  radicalism 120–2
  revolt 7, 18, 181–2
Nightingale, Florence 4, 53–4, 143
Nubar Pasha 34, 100
al-Nuqrashi, Ahmad 121

Odair, Susan 111
Omdurman 52, 94, 122
Oppenheim, Henry 32
Orientalism 3, 62, 129, 158–9, 168

Palestine 163–4, 199
Palmerston, Lord 64–5, 70
Patterson, Reginald 186, 189
Peel, Edward 43
Peto, Gladys 148–50, 157
Port Said 10, 12, 155–6
professional associations 2, 10–12, 17–18, 32, 84–5
  artists 54–65
  business 14–15, 17, 39–42, 45, 49–50, 53–5, 83–5, 136–7, 193, 197
  journalists 18, 191–5
  nurses 14, 111–12
  officials 10–14, 88–92, 108–9
  poets 107, 159
  soldiers 13, 86–8, 160–1, 199
  teachers (men) 94–5, 108–9
  teachers (women) 14, 108–9
Protectorate (1914–22) 13, 37, 163, 185

racism 5, 8, 10, 16, 19–20, 24–6, 50, 53, 65, 85–9, 101, 105–7, 113, 129, 145–6, 198, 201–2
Rafaat, Hasan 197
Rafaat, Samir 205, 215
Raj, the 11–13, 33, 71, 73, 75, 112–13, 141
Rapp, Thomas 118–19, 142–3, 149–54, 206
Reid, Walter 176
Reimer, Michael 28
Reuters 64, 183, 196
Richardson, W. 162
Roman Egypt 128–31
Rommel, Erwin 199

[229]

INDEX

Russell, Dorothea 93, 204
Russell, Thomas 92–4, 116, 160, 197, 202

al-Sadat, Anwar 46, 216
Said, Edward 2–4, 11, 16, 20, 53, 61, 101, 103–5, 183
St Mark's Church (Alexandria) 133
Salisbury, Lord 70, 86
Salt, Henry 29, 55, 57, 60, 65
al-Sayyid, Ahmad Lutfi 14, 21, 90
schools 20, 102–10
Scott, James 84
Scott-Moncrief, Colin 93
Second World War 9, 16, 19, 42–3, 158, 160, 164, 198–205
segregation 12, 16, 20, 96, 140–1
sex trade 113–16
Shaftesbury, Earl 98
Sharif, Muhammad 94
Sharif, Omar 104
Shearer, Eric 201
Shelley, Percy Bysshe 70
Shepheard, Samuel 65
Sirri, Husayn 167, 200–1
Slatin, Rudolph C. 86–7
slavery 63, 151
Smith, Charles D. 177
Smouha, Joseph 41–2
Spencer, Bernard 107
Spender, J.A. 175, 183–5, 195
Sporting Club (Alexandria) 161
sports 10, 123–4, 150–1
Stack, Lee 120–2, 187–8, 190
sterling balances 44–5
Stoors, Ronald 94, 163
Suez 10–12, 155
Suez Canal 1–2, 13, 33, 35, 69, 96
Suez War (1956) 42, 46

Tal al-Kabir (1882) 44, 75
Taufiq, Khedive 34, 52, 72–4

Thomson, Donald 60
Thornton, Douglas 95–9
Thurburn, Robert 38–9, 64
tourism viii, 1, 4–5, 39, 63, 65, 68–9, 70, 80, 83, 97

Ultimatum (4 Feb. 1942) 19, 166–7, 201–2
Umm Kulthum 205
Unilateral Declaration (Feb. 1922) 18, 49, 56, 186, 188, 195
'Urabi, Ahmad 1, 34, 52, 72–6
'Uthman, Amin 119, 121, 160

Victoria, Queen 1, 74
Victoria College 20, 48, 102–3, 215, 217, 219
Victoria Trust 48
Vincent, Edgar 93

Wafd Party 59, 121–2, 182, 185, 189–92, 200–1
Warbrick, Richard 216–17
Waterfield, Gordon 176–7, 184–5, 187, 192
Waugh, Evelyn 118, 155
Wavell, Archibald (Archie) 196–8, 200, 203
Wavell, Archibald Percival 163–6, 188, 196–203
Westcar, Henry 54, 57–60
Whatley, Maria Louisa 97–8
Wilkinson, John Gardner 54, 61, 65
Willcocks, William 90, 140, 178
Wingate, Reginald 15, 86, 88, 163
Wolseley, Garnet 52, 74–5
Wright, Arnold 83–4

Yapp, Malcolm 88, 176
Young, John 151, 160

Zaghlul, Sa'd 14–15, 140, 182, 186–91

EU authorised representative for GPSR:
Easy Access System Europe, Mustamäe tee 50,
10621 Tallinn, Estonia
gpsr.requests@easproject.com

www.ingramcontent.com/pod-product-compliance
Lightning Source LLC
Chambersburg PA
CBHW030121240426
43673CB00041B/1352